Tap-Dancing in Treacle

a Nigerian Experience

For Myriam.

With best wishes,

Pam Cranny.

5/10/00.

This edition published December 1999
by Debut Publishing - info@debut.com.au

www.debut.com.au

Copies of this publication available from
PO Box 430 Ferny Hills Qld 4055
also
Pam Cranny is contactable on:
email: pcranny@ecn.net.au

ISBN 1 876329 24 6

This edition:
Cover design: Frankie @ Artrageous

For Peter

Acknowledgements

There are many people to thank and I do so with warmest gratitude.

I thank Peter for sharing this adventure, and our son Mark for insisting I collate my journals into a permanent record. Without such prompting, I may never have moulded them into book form. Extended family and friends were supportive even when I became mono-focused, and others have been generous in allowing me to use their stories. I was not able to contact everyone to seek permission and to these (especially Patrick), I owe a debt of thanks. Some names and locations are disguised to protect privacy, but in other respects, events occurred as stated.

I thank my publisher and friend, Paulette Gee. Her knowledge and enjoyment of writing kept me enthused and forever striving towards that final full stop.

I appreciate the help given by my son, Tim. With tact and skill, he persistently challenged his mother to produce her best, allowing her to retain her confidence as a writer and a view of herself as a successful parent. As for proofreaders Jo and Glen - what would I have done without you?

My memory of background information was refreshed by Nancy and Jim Gulley, while Maureen Akintewe consistently led me to a more enlightened view of Nigeria. Thank you, my friends.

Despite excellent assistance, there may still be errors and for these, I take full responsibility.

My final thanks go to Nigeria and to her people for providing me with one of the most stimulating experiences of my life.

NIGERIA

Sahara Desert

Niger

Chad

Lake Chad

Yusufari

Gashua

Kano   Damaturu   Maiduguri

Jos

Benin

R. NIGER   ABUJA

R. BENUE

Ibadan

Abeokuta   Benin
City   Enugu

Cameroon

Lagos   Sapele

Warri

Bight of Benin

Scale

0   100   200   300   400   500 km

Contents

Chapter 1
WELCOME TO NIGERIA

Perhaps this was what we'd been warned about.

It's like watching an act in mime, I thought, as I looked across the hotel carpark at the two men. I wished I could hear what they were saying. My husband Peter stood there, his head tilted and arms folded, stubbornness written all over him. His only movement was an occasional slow shake of his head and even from here I could see that he was unimpressed by the arguments of the dark-skinned young man in front of him. I wondered uneasily if we were over-reacting so once again I retraced in my mind the events since our arrival in Nigeria.

Last night Nigerian agents of the World Bank had delivered us from Lagos Airport to the city's Sheraton Hotel. The airport's reputation was firmly fixed in our minds before we arrived because we'd read that it was one of the most dangerous in the world. We'd been warned that predators would sense our inexperience and then the fun would begin. Corrupt officials would refuse us entry unless we bribed them, con men would use innovative ways to separate us from our money, and unless we had eyes in the back of our heads at least half our luggage would disappear. And all the while dishonest touts and adhesive beggars would clamour for our attention and our dollars.

From what we'd seen last night the warnings were justified, and there had been a few tense moments. Even when the World Bank agents took us in tow our problems weren't over. They struggled to maintain some semblance of order by barking at our tormentors to stand back and ordering us in terse, clipped English to speak to no one, to watch our luggage and to refuse all requests for money. Noise assailed our jetlagged brains and intrusive fingers were clicked in front of our faces demanding our attention.

Outside the building, we'd been swamped by a fresh batch of touts and beggars as we pushed towards the car, and our minders had told us curtly that we must hurry. Bundled into the vehicle, I was in the middle of a premature sigh of relief when a man in full military uniform banged on the car window and demanded that we open the door. Our driver had shouted back at him in English.

"Stand buck or yo'll be in BIG trobble!" He gunned the engine and with a shower of gravel, we speared through the throng of people and away.

It had been a relief to get away from the airport and as I had looked about the late-night activity of the streets, my jangling nerves had begun to settle. Once inside the hotel's foyer, I had felt almost light-headed with relief and I ranked getting out of the airport in one piece as a major accomplishment.

Before leaving us, the two World Bank agents had explained that no provision had been made for Peter to be driven to his appointment across town early the following day. Instead, he was to hire a car and driver at the desk in the hotel foyer, where the drivers were known to be honest and competent.

This morning as we'd eaten breakfast in our room, the phone had rung and Peter was told in a heavy Nigerian accent that there had been a change of plan. Sir was to be at the hotel entrance at precisely 8.30 am because a World Bank car was now available and he, the caller, was to drive him to 'de hoffice'.

Alarm bells were ringing in my head even before Peter replaced the receiver. My experience of having a personal driver at my disposal was zero so I couldn't explain why I was reacting so strongly. Perhaps I was remembering the sight in the hotel's car park the night before, as tired drivers stood around, waiting with endless patience for their employers. Yet here was ours nominating time and place and issuing instructions. Something was not right.

I paced the floor and lectured Peter on the theme of *Personal Security in Nigeria,* a topic that had been emphasised ad nauseam in the reams of literature sent to us by the World Bank before we left Australia. Peter's calm response to my warnings did nothing to reassure me that he was taking the matter seriously enough. With a wifely roll of the eyes, I accepted that if we were to survive Nigeria, it would be up to *me* to be vigilant.

At half-past eight we stepped through the hotel doors and were approached by a young Nigerian neatly dressed in slacks, shirt and tie.

"Mr Crunny? Dis way please, Sah," he said, and with a pleasant smile, he gestured towards a blue Peugeot in which two men sat. I was beginning to get the picture; I was invisible if Sir was around.

Peter made no move to get into the car. "Can I see your identification please?" he asked.

"I am sorry, Sah. I left 'ome in an 'urry and didn't bring it." A contrite expression spread across the man's face. "Please get in an' we kin go."

"No identification, no go," replied Peter. The combined might of the World Bank and myself had made an impression after all.

"Sah, we are stoppin' de traffic. Please get in an' we kin discuss de problem."

"No identification, no go."

"But if I go back wit'out yo', I will get in trobble." There was a hint of frustration in the man's voice as he lifted his shoulders in a slow shrug and extended his hands expressively. "Please, Sah, get in. We kin drive over to de carpark and discuss it more."

"You drive over. I'll walk, thanks."

So now I stood at the hotel entrance, out of earshot but watching every move. I could see our would-be chauffeur continuing to plead and his gestures grew more elaborate by the minute. My heart lurched in fright when one of the men got out of the car and moved around to stand behind Peter. I checked that hotel staff were nearby if I needed to call for help but, just then, with a dismissive wave of his hand, Peter turned on his heel and walked back towards me. The young man followed and as they came closer, I could hear his voice growing more agitated.

"Sah, I 'ave explained dat I forgot my identification. Why doan yo' believe me?" he asked. "If I go buck wit'out yo' I will lose my job. Please, Sah, come."

I had another pang of doubt. The poor fellow seemed genuinely upset. I caught the eye of a hotel employee and asked her advice. At my first words she dispatched a messenger and minutes later, hotel security men appeared and ushered us all inside.

As it turned out, we had every reason to be suspicious. It was a set up. Someone at the airport or perhaps in the hotel foyer had noted our name and the World Bank stickers on our luggage, and had decided that we were ripe for the picking. We were to be taken away and robbed of the large sum in US dollars that we, like all new arrivals, were carrying. What would have happened after that remains a mystery, but fresh in my memory was the report three months earlier of the hijacking here in Lagos of a vehicle carrying Australian diplomat, Rodney Cox. On that occasion, the robbers had panicked and Rodney had received multiple gunshot wounds and had been lucky to survive (*The Courier Mail*, December 24, 1992).

When the initial shock of our attempted kidnapping subsided, Peter and I discussed how family and friends were likely to react when they heard of our introduction to Nigeria. We suspected that we'd be in for some I-told-you-so's, but far from being intimidated, we felt smug at foiling this bit of skulduggery. As we relived the adventure and speculated about how the news would be received at home, we recalled the weeks leading up to our departure.

Peter, a forester, had taken early retirement from the Queensland Public Service, but it wasn't long before he began resurrecting an old ambition to work in a developing country. He decided that it wouldn't hurt to test the water and sent his curriculum vitae to several international agencies. A few weeks later he received a phone call that set our imaginations buzzing. The World Bank, located in Washington, wished to discuss a Nigerian forestry project and suggested he fly to Africa to look at the undertaking. He did so, and a month later he returned home full of enthusiasm. We decided to look more seriously at the idea.

If ever we were ready for an adventure, it was now. Peter was looking for a challenge and I needed a change from my stressful job as social worker in the Thoracic/Oncology Unit of a hospital. Our children were grown up and showing signs of pressing on happily with their own lives, and our three surviving parents, although elderly, were in good health.

When we finally broke the news that we were off to Nigeria for sixteen months, reactions varied. Our three sons and their partners approved wholeheartedly. Peter's parents' reaction was more guarded and they worried aloud about our safety. My mother was convinced that the racial unrest in South Africa would spill over into Nigeria and no number of geography lessons could reassure her of the unlikelihood of this happening. Friends were divided in their opinions. Some envied us this chance of a lifetime; others thought we should be locked up for our own safety.

A definite departure date proved elusive. As each nominated date approached it was rescheduled and we were told that we must wait until after the forthcoming Nigerian national election. We were puzzled about the extraordinary number of elections but we didn't worry, deciding it was a sign of rampant democracy. Then, quite suddenly, we were given the green light. Hours of research into what to take and what to leave went out the window, and we finished our packing to stand back to look in dismay at the usual excess of luggage.

On D-day, our family gathered at the Brisbane International Airport and as the chatter and laughter swirled around us, we waited for the call that meant we must say goodbye. Everyone was in high spirits to mark the start of this great adventure. Everyone, that is, except me. I would have liked, later, to boast of a brave heart and stiff upper lip but photographic evidence is stacked against me. Instead I must admit to swollen eyes and sodden handkerchiefs.

At the last possible moment we left our loved ones and moved through to the departure lounge. When called, I joined the queue that shuffled into steerage, the section so attractive to those paying for their own tickets. Peter remained behind and enjoyed a final cup of coffee before sauntering aboard our plane and settling into business class, as consultants are wont to do.

When I was seated, I surrendered completely to doubts. The good-natured jibes I'd heard in recent weeks came back to me sounding like inspired wisdom. We would be robbed of our last penny while malaria wracked our bodies. Rioters would trample us to an unrecognisable pulp in the first week. And, of course, the kids only *thought* they could survive without us. In no time they would need us desperately and we would be on the other side of the world. I sat huddled in my seat, alone, weeping surreptitiously.

When I had spent an hour in tearful remorse for encouraging this madness, I decided that I must compose myself. I watched the flight attendants as they advanced slowly down the aisle with their trolley and I remembered that champagne and misery rarely coexist. With a brave smile I accepted the neat little bottle and the plastic glass and found that my memory had served me well.

Now, as we stood in the office of the hotel's chief security officer listening to him describe our good fortune in avoiding the kidnappers' clutches, I felt elated. Obviously we were just too smart for the local villains. This was going to be a breeze.

I didn't realise that they hadn't finished with us yet.

Chapter 2
MORE FUN AND GAMES

So, to get across Lagos to the World Bank office, it was back to Plan A. We arranged for a hire car and driver to collect us at ten o'clock. The driver was delighted to have employment and reassured us that we'd find his car suitable. When he collected us at the hotel entrance, his pile of green scrap metal looked more like a geriatric frog than anything from the motoring world. With its engine idling, it shuddered spasmodically as if dreading the task ahead; when prodded into motion, it leaped away, croaking fumes into the already polluted air.

Our clothes clung to us in heat beyond anything I had ever experienced. Earlier, when I had first stepped out through the hotel's automatic doors, I had reeled as the air hit me in the face. Once in the car, though, there was so much to see and take in that we forgot the temperature and hardly noticed seat springs that burrowed into backs and buttocks.

Last night as we had travelled from the airport, this had seemed an exotic fairyland. Along the roadside, kerosene lamps had twinkled as groups of people chatted and played music in front of tiny stalls. Now, in the harsh light of the tropical sun, the same streets told a different story; the stalls were rickety, their offerings meagre and sun-damaged. Every inch of the wide streets throbbed with people and vehicles. One minute the cars and buses hurtled along in a frenzy then we'd come to a standstill, our driver clicking his tongue in frustration at being caught in another 'go slow'. Rattling, jerking buses travelled beside us and people hung from every opening. How did arms and legs stay attached?

The few functioning traffic lights were ignored. "It's better not to stop for de lights," our driver explained. "De hijackers can't get us so easily, den." I closed my eyes each time we approached an intersection.

I watched as young men worked hard at selling drinks, shirts, books, anything. In the searing heat they ran hundreds of metres beside moving vehicles as they negotiated sales. I remembered the maimed beggars at the airport and wondered if they once had been agile vendors like these, dashing between cars, full of confidence that their agility would preserve them. Whenever cars became ensnared in traffic, beggars descended in swarms. Our white skin seemed to act as a magnet but with a startled leap our frog-car would escape, leaving a string of disappointed faces lost in exhaust fumes.

Suddenly we came upon a fatal accident. Bloodstained survivors staggered to the kerb as the deceased lay dismembered in the middle of the road. Our driver swung around the gruesome obstacles without comment and we rejoined the confusion as every vehicle in Lagos tried to migrate from one side of the city to the other.

As I gazed about I realised that I would need to make huge adjustments if I were to survive this. Suddenly, I found myself seeing but not experiencing all that was happening around me. My emotions were switched off and my senses had become a video camera, recording sights and sounds to be processed later when I felt more settled. I was here for the long haul and there was no point in becoming so overwhelmed on the first day that I made hasty judgements about this country, its people and their culture.

All around I could see people living without things I took for granted but I also saw a great deal of laughter and energy. When friends met, a mini-celebration broke out. The stark contrast between dark skin and white teeth gave every smile vitality. Hands smacked together in high fives, jokes were exchanged and amusement was enjoyed with such boisterous body language that I wondered if indeed people could actually 'fall over laughing' as a favourite hyperbole of mine has it. There and then I labelled Nigerians as 'vivacious'.

Later in our first day, as we lunched in the hotel, I continued to soak up the atmosphere. This scene was easier on the conscience. The clothing of affluent Nigerians was wonderful. Most men wore long over-shirts and slim-legged pants but here and there, looking very formal, were those in flowing over-robes called, a helpful waiter told me, *agbada*. On each head was a *hula*, a pillbox hat made of the same material as the robes. Lilac, white, green, pink and gold, all were worn with aplomb. The women rivalled their menfolk in spectacle. They strolled gracefully in blouses, *boubas,* and wrap-around skirts of every colour, their heads topped with braids or wrapped in flamboyant headscarves. I caught my reflection in the restaurant's wall mirror and knew that those of us in Western clothes looked dowdy and under-dressed by comparison.

Our lunch arrived and I sat inspecting the obscure bits of meat that lurked in my bowl. I had ordered goat pepper soup but it must have been a strange goat indeed to have once owned all these body parts. I was to recall this skirmish with goat flesh a few months later when a Canadian acquaintance, a self-claimed connoisseur of Nigerian cuisine, expressed an appreciation of goat's head soup cooked in traditional manner, with the hide still attached. He said it enabled him to eat and floss at the same time.

But such revelations were off in the future. At the moment we still had the final leg of our journey ahead of us, a two-hour trip north to Ibadan, one of the oldest and largest cities in black Africa. Ibadan, situated in the centre of the Yoruba ethnic group's homeland, had an official population of 1.3 million, although most people spoke of it in terms of having closer to three million inhabitants.

We were to meet Paul, our Forestry Department driver, at half-past nine the following morning. Right on time we stepped from the elevator into the hotel foyer and immediately a tall, mournful-looking man of about thirty-five years of age stepped forward and introduced himself. As we shook hands, his expression remained unchanged, something new for us because we'd seen so much exuberance since arriving.

We set out on our journey but a few miles from the hotel, still in the thick of Lagos traffic, our car began to spray petrol from beneath the bonnet. Urgent calls and waves from passers-by alerted us to the risk of fire and Paul quickly turned off the engine. Several miles of traffic fell into line behind us and our horizon shrank to a sea of dark faces as helpers and onlookers, all shouting advice, surrounded us. Nigerians, I soon learned, enjoy shouting advice to everyone within earshot and beyond. As many people as could find space to lay a hand on the vehicle helped push it to a safer, off-road spot. Peter clambered out and joined in, much to Paul's alarm.

"Master! Enter de car! Enter de car!" he pleaded in vain, his face for once animated.

Meanwhile, I sat in the back of the car, trying to look slightly bored as if I spent part of every day in a car being pushed by two dozen Nigerians. Perhaps I imagined that if I looked the seasoned traveller, I'd somehow fend off the unspecified dangers that I could feel all around me. Meanwhile, the cartons of electrical appliances, highly visible in the back of the station wagon, shouted of our comparative wealth. I sat there wishing we'd arrived with toothbrush and one change of clothes. A face appeared at my window.

"Yo' should move on as quickly as possible, Madame. Dis is a very bud spot for de robberies!"

Madame swallowed her panic and thanked the gentleman for this snippet.

Within minutes a man appeared with precisely the engine part required to get us on the road again. He demanded an exorbitant price for the fuel pump, and when Paul mournfully assured us that we had no option, Peter paid up and we were soon back on the road. We were not to know then that within a week Paul would be dismissed from his job on suspicion of involvement in a scam. He had been the driver on three other occasions when, after fuel pump failure, someone had fortuitously appeared with the part in his hand, on sale for a huge amount. We took some convincing that Paul had tampered with the car, but when we were, I felt a rush of anger that he should take such a risk with our property and possibly even our lives.

We entered Ibadan and skirted around the edge of the city to reach the northern suburbs. When at last we arrived at the gates of the International Institute of Tropical Agriculture (IITA), we paused on the dividing line of two worlds. The city lay spread out behind us, its huge population fighting the same battle for survival as the people of Lagos. Everywhere were eroded streets lined with tumbledown mud shacks, rusting roofs, and hessian-covered stalls. Ahead of us, beyond security gates and guards, stretched a piece of heaven. The campus of IITA was to be our home only until a forestry house became available in the city but one look and I decided that I might prove difficult to dislodge from here.

Before we left Australia, I had heard about IITA because of its reputation as an oasis of comfort in the midst of deprivation. I had read that it is one of several institutes around the world dedicated to agricultural research and training, and funded by the Food and Agriculture Organisation, the World Bank and other well-heeled donors. Because IITA needed to attract and hold highly trained international professionals, a lot of money was poured into maintaining a high standard of living, and it showed.

"Oh, yes!" I couldn't help but voice my approval as I saw the tree-lined avenue, the acres of maintained lawns and flowering trees. Within the high security fence, a lush rainforest area stretched away to the left and on the right were well-maintained buildings fronting onto neat, sealed streets. From where we sat in our vehicle, I could read signposts inscribed 'Water Treatment Plant', 'Security Headquarters', and 'Medical Clinic'. My senses had taken a battering in the last forty-eight hours and I found this reassuring. The moral issue of inequality was tapping quietly at the back door of my mind but I needed some time to recover before acknowledging it. My main emotion just now was relief. For the first time in days, I felt myself relax.

Chapter 3
REUNIONS, REVOLVERS AND ROUGH JUSTICE

I smiled and shook my head in resignation as I heard a tap at the front door of our tiny unit. That would be Mrs Aziz, the lady responsible for cleaning our small unit. Any moment now I would hear the rattle of her keys and she would saunter in, a lady whose dark face gave no indication of her thoughts. I always gazed in awe at her tightly braided hair which emphasised the contours of her face and the deeply carved markings on her cheeks depicting her ethnic group. Once inside, she would grasp her broom, more a bundle of twigs, and give a few casual swishes before departing. A quarter of an hour later she would return for another friendly skirmish with domestic chores. Regular sorties would occur throughout the day but unlucky indeed the speck of dust that was more than temporarily inconvenienced. The routine was more effective in keeping me from a post-lunch nap than anything else.

Mrs Aziz was unusual in that she didn't encourage friendliness. She would enter, ignore my greeting and in one or two words directed at the ceiling, would summarise my current activity. Usually I overheard the words 'writin' letters' or maybe 'readin'.'

I struggled with a near-irresistible urge to bring some variety to our day by being upside down in a corner when she arrived, but I knew she would merely stroll by muttering 'standin' on head...'

But today, the knock at the door was repeated, this time more urgently and I hurried across the room, hoping that I was about to receive my first social caller. Standing there was a young man, his round, dark face beaming at me. He introduced himself as Samson, a forestry driver, then he produced a note in Peter's handwriting.

A week ago Peter had left with a large party of Nigerian and World Bank officials on a familiarisation tour due to last three weeks. I'd been invited to go, but had had to stay home because I was ill with 'Ibadan Belly', an unpleasant addition to the influenza I had picked up during our stopover in London. For days I had not cared about missing the tour; my sole interest was in staying close to bed and toilet, but today I was much improved and self-pity had set in. Not only was I missing all the excitement, but I was acutely aware that the only person on this continent who knew and cared about me was somewhere out there, unable to phone or be contacted. To make matters worse, he was probably enjoying himself thoroughly. I grabbed the note eagerly.

If I were feeling better, it read, Samson would call for me at 1pm the following day and take me south to Benin City to meet up with the touring party. I confirmed the details with the driver and he left. As I re-read the note, I felt tears rolling down my face and I admitted to myself how lonely I had been. Several times in the last week I had dreamed that I was a child again, and had chosen to go to boarding school, only to realise the extent of my foolishness too late, seconds after the metal gates clanked shut behind me. I would wake feeling sad, knowing that not since boarding school days had I felt so isolated.

But now, with Peter's note in my hand, I knew my solitude was about to end. I regained my composure, and to celebrate, I booked a call to home. It was my lucky day and I was connected immediately. Glen, our youngest son, reassured me that all was well and congratulated his parents on their savvy in avoiding the kidnap. As I chatted excitedly about the twin joys of receiving a note from his father and now hearing his voice, it occurred to me how differently my son and I were reacting. A handwritten note and a brief phone call - hardly enough to cause incandescent excitement in Australia, but major feats of communication here. The minute I hung up I began packing and by the time Samson called next day, I had been ready for twenty-four hours.

Samson found me a baffling passenger. For a start, I refused to sit in the seat of honour diagonally behind the driver but settled instead into the front seat beside him. He found this disconcerting.

"Madame, de big men sit in de back. So should yo'," he insisted, but I stayed put. I wanted the safety of the other seat belt. Besides, I was uncomfortable in the role of chauffeur-driven Grand Lady and felt worse if I sat in the back. With many sidelong glances, Samson accepted the inevitable but asked after my welfare with monotonous regularity.

It didn't occur to me to be so assertive, but I should have told Samson that my welfare would be best served if he took thirty kilometres per hour off our speed. I calculated that if we shot off the road, we would hurtle so far into the undergrowth that it would take a week to find us. The carcasses of cars and lorries littered the roadside. Most numerous were the charred remains of fuel tankers but such accidents, I gathered, were deemed *Acts of God* and had little to do with reckless driving. I tried to distract myself by looking about and soaking up the landscape that flickered by.

There were people everywhere. Most carried items on their heads, sauntering along gracefully under their loads. I was fascinated by people's ability to make huge bundles of firewood or bags of vegetables seem insignificant. Occasionally a man would help a woman lift a heavy load onto the coil of cloth upon her head then he would saunter off unencumbered, to attend to more masculine pursuits. Others, with total nonchalance, devoted this prime carrying spot to a single yam or perhaps a machete. On many women's backs, tiny black heads bobbed in the hot sun, as the next generation slept peacefully.

"Do Nigerian babies *ever* cry?" I asked Samson curiously, because I had yet to see one awake.

"Yes, Madame, dey cry at night," was Samson's wry response.

As we whizzed along, our high-speed progress was occasionally thwarted by bone-jarring speed bumps, put in place by roadside merchants to slow traffic to a crawl past their stalls. I looked closely at the items on sale; vegetables and prized 'bush meat' consisting of antelope, giant snails, snakes and grass cutters (rabbit sized, rodent-like animals). I was fascinated by what I saw, but not tempted. Within minutes we were hurtling along again.

Suddenly I cried out, "Samson, there's a man lying on the side of the road!"

The expression on Samson's face didn't change, nor did the speed of our car.

"Yes, Madame, but 'e is already dead."

I turned to look out the back window and watched as the figure became a speck on the horizon. For a while I could still see rigor-mortised arms outstretched in bizarre supplication, then they too became indistinguishable. Like us, the next car also sped past without altering speed.

"But...what could have happened to him? Who's going to stop?" I couldn't believe my eyes.

"I doan know what 'appened to 'im, Madame. I wasn't 'ere. Maybe 'e tried to run away and Security shot 'im."

I must try to stop asking silly questions, I reminded myself.

Later in the journey a police car overtook us travelling at tremendous speed. Ahead, two heavy vehicles blocked both lanes as they trundled up a hill in a slow-motion drag race and the police were still trapped behind them when we caught up. The vehicle in the passing lane was gaining ground and its driver seemed unwilling to surrender his advantage even in the interests of urgent police business. I was becoming acclimatised and wasn't even surprised when the policeman in the passenger seat produced a revolver and waved it menacingly out the window. The truck driver got the message. He pulled back into line behind his rival and allowed the police car to roar off.

At times, Samson and I had difficulty in understanding each other's English. English is Nigeria's official language but with his distinctive African accent and my Australian drawl, communication was something of a hit-and-miss affair. In time I was to appreciate how gifted Africans are with languages, managing English, the language of their own ethnic group and perhaps one or two others as well. At the moment, although I was improving, my ability to understand the Nigerian accent still had a long way to go.

We were hurtling along when Samson spoke, obviously asking a question, but I found it totally indecipherable. I asked him to repeat it and this time I understood the final few words "... yo' understand me, Madame?"

I didn't.

Repeated attempts did nothing to shed light on his meaning. Finally, with polite exasperation, Samson reworded his question. He slowed the car and turned his head to me as he spoke.

"I need to PISS. Yo' understand me, Madame?"

Some words are recognisable in any accent. With a straight face I assured him that he must feel free to attend to such matters whenever the urge took him.

By the time Peter and his group arrived back at the hotel from their day in the field, I had showered and had even cultivated an air of nonchalance about our extraordinary drive. We went for pre-dinner drinks and I met the team, including the World Bank African Project Manager, Helmut, and his young Australian off-sider, Ben. I soon discovered that my adventures ranked only in the middle of the field when the day's stories were related. I did, however, make a significant contribution to collective expatriate wisdom when I suggested that perhaps there is no such thing as paranoia in Nigeria. If you suspect that something untoward may be about to happen, it already has.

The next few days were full of discoveries. I went everywhere with the work group, seeing parts of the country unknown to most foreigners and listening as Nigerian companions described their country's political convulsions. For the first time I understood that our arrival hadn't been delayed by rampant democracy at all, but by a single election which was repeatedly postponed by a military government unwilling to hand over power.

One evening I listened wide-eyed as Ben and a female sociologist on the team told how, in a remote village, they had been interviewing a representative group of villagers when the Head Man had appeared in full regalia, his hands still dripping blood from a ceremony just completed. After Ben described the experience, he spoke to me in an aside.

"This was as close as I am ever likely to get to witnessing a voodoo ceremony. I had to remind myself that this was for real. I wasn't just looking at a picture from National Geographic; I was actually there - and I was trembling."

I seethed with disappointment that I had missed out on being there too.

A week later the southern leg of the tour ended and the touring party was to regroup in Abuja, the new capital of Nigeria. Abuja is a purpose-built city, diplomatically placed in the centre of the country to lessen internal jealousies. Peter and most of the group were to fly up and I was to follow by car with Pierre, a French-Canadian forestry consultant. Our driver this time was Dele, a wonderfully handsome young man who at first seemed hesitant to chat with us as we drove. When he did speak, the words came in quiet, clear English that Pierre and I readily understood.

It was a hot, ten-hour journey and at times I nearly nodded off to sleep but I was too worried about missing something interesting. Weariness was not an issue in the latter stages of the journey, though, because I was kept alert by a growing discomfort. The bladders of Dele and Pierre received consideration at regular intervals but always where no trees offered the female of the species even a modicum of privacy. At the roadside, chattily exchanging greetings with passers-by, the two men proceeded to 'ease themselves'. (Ah hah...so *that's* what Samson had been trying to tell me.) I hung on, too inhibited to claim equal consideration, all the while cursing male dominated cultures.

As we cruised along, Pierre and I encouraged Dele to give us insights into Nigerian culture and ways of handling life's problems. As he spoke, there at the roadside we saw a body encircled by a smouldering car tyre. We pressed Dele for a possible explanation.

"A rubber necklace," he said calmly, with a shrug that spoke volumes. "Maybe someone was treated badly an' took de law into 'is own 'ands." He went on to explain that there was little point in taking a complaint to the police. Even if it resulted in an arrest, in all probability money would change hands and the villain would walk free.

"Better to deal with de matter privately," our driver said. "It is what we call roff joss-tice."

Nigeria is one of the world's leading exporters of oil yet it was in the grip of a severe fuel shortage. Since our arrival we'd read in *The Guardian*, a newspaper that fearlessly attacked corruption and inefficiency at all levels, that the fault lay mainly with the country's refineries which were poorly maintained. Three out of four refineries were out of action, plunging the nation into a seemingly endless fuel crisis. The scarce supplies were being distributed around the country by huge petrol tankers but these seemed to be the focal point of many *Acts of God*, judging by the number of burned tankers littering the roadside. Any long-distance travel meant anxiety about where one would next be able to buy fuel. Of course it was always available on the black market, kept flourishing by tanker drivers who sold a portion of their cargo and pocketed the money, but dealing with them was risky. They often diluted the petrol with kerosene, causing serious engine damage and there was also a chance that the police might swoop then demand a large bribe to turn a blind eye.

Wages throughout Nigeria were low and it was common for workers to have extra ways of supplementing their income, not all of them legal. Dele told us that his wage was 750 Naira per month, about US$25, and the police, he guessed, would receive a similar amount. I tried to imagine existing, even in this economy, on ten times that amount and shuddered. I began to understand the financial pressures that led people into corruption.

Today, as we reached the halfway mark of Okene, the gauge was showing empty so Dele stopped at the end of a long queue of cars at a 'fool' station, as he pronounced it. For over an hour we inched forward and at last the car in front of us was being filled. Suddenly a police car arrived and the driver tried to edge in at an angle in front of us, demanding to be served next.

"I 'esitate to object. Dey are de police," said Dele and with that he leaped from the car and began remonstrating in anything but a hesitant manner. The ruckus drew the attention of the dozens of young men standing around the pumps and a chant went up, growing louder as they turned on the police, "Black Shirts, wait yo' turn! Black Shirts, wait yo' turn!"

Dele suddenly had a hundred or more supporters as he returned to the car and revved the engine defiantly and inched closer to the pump. A meeting of the cars' paintwork seemed inevitable. The pump attendant, seeing the police distracted with shouting threats at the mob, quietly slipped the nozzle into our car. When the officers saw this act of defiance they bellowed in rage but there was little they could do because they were trapped several metres away. Perhaps they realised that if they produced their revolvers there could easily be a riot and they might come off second best, for the crowd was spoiling for a fight. Dele hastily paid for the petrol, the crowd parted, and we roared off.

I didn't understand all the ramifications of displeasing the police until I noticed Dele's demeanour over the next half-hour. He drove like a fiend, both fists clenching the steering wheel and eyes forever flicking up to the rear-vision mirror. It was as if he expected the police to give chase and in some isolated spot, deal out a bit of their own rough justice.

We arrived at Abuja and I saw that although the city was still unfinished, it was already a place of contrasts. Endless amounts of money were being poured in to make it a worthy venue for politicians, the military elite, but on its outskirts were the inevitable poor. The only difference was that here their precarious shanties were built of new tin and scraps of fresh timber. Arriving in the centre of town, we booked into the Hilton, the best accommodation in town.

I had a wonderful five days, enjoying the surroundings and relaxing by the pool. I was almost as unaccustomed to this life of luxury as I was to being exposed to danger and squalor, and I spent a lot of time trying to make sense of the enormous contrasts.

One day I arranged for Dele to drive me around the city and I called briefly at a well-stocked supermarket. As I stepped from the shop and walked towards the car, I saw at my feet a crippled child, his disabilities more extreme than any I had seen before in my life. He dragged himself along in the red dirt, the skin on his little hands and knees as hard and cracked as old leather. One small hand reached up to me, beseeching a coin. I opened my purse but before I could hand him anything, I was surrounded by begging people, the young, the old and the lame, but none as severely disabled as the child at my feet. No one touched me but I felt assailed. For the first time since being here, I was completely overwhelmed. Robot like, I walked to the car and climbed in. The sheer magnitude of need made me numb and I made no move to halt Dele as he engaged the gears and we drove off. At the last moment, I turned and looked out the back window. The crowd had dispersed, all except the child who sat in the dust watching as our car drove away.

The episode affected me deeply. I returned to the luxury of the hotel and sat with my thoughts, going back over the incident, and my reaction. How easy I found it to tip and be generous to those who served me, yet when surrounded by many who needed assistance, I had helped no one. I was overcome with remorse and dissatisfaction with myself. I decided to return the next morning to make amends, but opportunities are not always repeated. I stood a long time at the supermarket entrance, but no one came.

In a graphic illustration of the inequalities in our world, my evenings were spent dining with the team; long, pleasant dinners where I enjoyed not only the shop talk but the general conversation and company, especially that of the two female consultants. I had had only limited opportunities to socialise with other women during the past month and these gatherings recharged my batteries. I particularly enjoyed meeting Janice Olawoye, a woman near my own age. A white American sociologist, Janice had married a Nigerian she'd met at university in the USA where he'd been training to become an agricultural economist. Their decision to marry had been taken amid the concerns of both families. I was in awe of the strength and confidence of anyone who, at such a young age, could make such an important life decision. Now, after twenty-five years of successful marriage, Janice offered me predigested information that I found fascinating. I enjoyed hearing about Nigerian family life from one who had an intimate knowledge of two very different cultures.

As I followed the ebb and flow of the conversation, I learned more of the background to Peter's project. With the impressive title of Chief Technical Advisor and Project Manager of the Tropical Forests Action Programme, one of Peter's responsibilities was to oversee the development of a management plan for what remained of Nigeria's forests. Nigeria is Africa's most populous nation, with an estimated one hundred million people (belonging to almost three hundred different ethnic groups) occupying an area only slightly larger than New South Wales. Because of population pressures and environmental problems, the National Forestry Action Plan placed its major emphasis on conservation and social forestry, for example the establishment of shelter belts, community woodlots and the sustainable harvesting of non-timber forest products.

Each evening when the team gathered, the general discussion strayed onto Nigerian history. I listened to stories about the English colonisation of Nigeria, of the granting of independence in 1960 and the country's attempts at democracy. Since independence, each democratically elected government had fallen to a military coup, and once in power members of the military hierarchy ensured their own wealth while largely ignoring the plight of their fellow Nigerians.

The tour had been fascinating, but now it was over. Most of our companions headed for Abuja Airport to fly to Lagos, where they would catch international flights back to Washington. Janice, who lived in Ibadan, was also flying down to Lagos, while Peter and I set out for home with Dele at the wheel. I was looking forward to returning to IITA to make new friends and to settling down to less excitement.

A long day of travelling behind us, we paused at IITA's security gates and identified ourselves. Suddenly I remembered that our first bundle of mail from home should be waiting for us. The thought almost took my breath away.

Chapter 4
PEOPLE AND PARASITES

I saw the parcel, fat and inviting in its DHL Courier Service wrapping, the moment we came through the door.

"Now, Girl, first things first." There was a weariness in Peter's voice after ten hours of travelling that suggested a shower and a beer would go down nicely. His use of my nickname added pathos to the words. "Let's get a bit organised before we start an orgy of letter-reading…"

The rest of his sentence was lost in the sound of snipping as the kitchen scissors were brought to bear on the polythene bag. If this constituted an orgy, I was about to have me one. Recognising defeat when it stared him in the face, Peter sighed and lowered himself onto the couch beside me while I sorted through our treasures.

Thirteen letters, an audiotape and a video cassette, plus an assortment of newspaper clippings and photos lay spread before us. I put everything in chronological order and began reading aloud. At first my voice kept fading because I was forgetting to breathe. I forced myself to calm down until each word was being savoured, sipped like a fine red wine. As I continued, I realised how fortunate we were, how loved and blessed. At that moment I wouldn't have swapped places with anyone in the world.

The next day, feeling more settled than at any time since arriving in Nigeria, we attacked the rest of our boxes and suitcases. When everything was in place and the hi-fi and television connected, we stood back and admired our little home with as much satisfaction as first-time homemakers.

Our domain consisted of a tiny kitchenette, generous lounge room, bedroom and a small bathroom. We chose not to remember that our rent was the equivalent of a four-star hotel in Australia. Instead we compared our lifestyle with the problems we'd be enduring if we were living outside IITA gates. Any doubts were put to rest by the hum of the giant air conditioner as it toiled day and night. Each time there was a power failure it switched to IITA power, reminding us with a gentle cough that beyond the perimeter fence, blackouts could last for weeks.

For the first time since I had entered hospital with labour pains twenty-nine years ago, I was experiencing the sensation of having no major responsibilities. Before coming, I had considered doing my masters degree by correspondence with an Australian university, but common sense prevailed when I realised the limitations of Nigeria's mail service. No, for sixteen months, I'd luxuriate in the role of support person.

I unwrapped the gift of a tapestry canvas given to me by daughter-in-law Michelle before I left. I smoothed out the untouched square and looked at the outlines of an Australian landscape, and the bundle of colourful threads still neatly coiled. To make a success of this, I'd need patience and enough sense to ask for help when necessary. *A bit like this Nigerian experience*, I thought. Both were first-ever experiences for me. In the coming months I would be working on two tapestries, one of them invisible but equally as real. I threaded a needle and began, gingerly.

Early in my stay at IITA my senses were alive to the novelty of everything around me. Each morning my eyes sprang open before daylight as unaccustomed sounds woke me with a start. I could hear eerie wails in the distance. Voices approached, using a language I didn't know. Bats squeaked in the still air and there was no hum of traffic to lend normality. I recalled the time in my childhood when I had overheard my parents discussing the Mau Mau uprising in far off Africa and I had lain in bed, letting my imagination run riot. The dark was full of invisible terrorists creeping towards the

"Big House" where I lay listening to bloodthirsty plots being hatched in a whispered, unfamiliar language.

Now, forty years later, I ignored the geographical distance between East and West Africa and amused myself by trying to recreate that delicious, spine-tingling terror. But adulthood had tamed my imagination. The eerie wailing was the Moslem Call to Prayer at a far-off mosque and the approaching voices didn't sound sinister, just loud and cheerful. These were workers from outside the gates, arriving for the day. Their laughter-punctuated chatter seemed to reach a crescendo as it passed our unit. I was learning that Nigerians, vivacious even at this hour, didn't fret unduly about noise or its effect upon other people's comfort.

I lay there wishing I could understand the Yoruba language, because Ibadan was in the heart of Yoruba territory. If I were not allowed sleep, it would be nice, at least, to know what was so funny.

Thoroughly awake now, I'd get up as daylight arrived and set out to explore my surroundings before the stifling heat chained me to the air conditioner for the day. I had been told it was safe to stroll alone around IITA and I relished the freedom. I began by circumnavigating International House, a large, hotel-type building which formed the physical and social hub of IITA. We had been told that the institute did not offer accommodation to the general public and this caused considerable gnashing of teeth amongst visiting expatriates. Those who couldn't prove some link with IITA's function had to seek accommodation elsewhere. Now, as I walked around behind International House, I saw the trappings of Western indulgence; outdoor bar, swimming pool, barbecue area, tennis courts, manicured lawns. I intended enjoying them to the full.

Moving on, I strolled along tree-lined streets, which lay in semicircular rows with International House as the centre. Here and there I saw vacant houses and I paused in front of each. Most were similar in design, large, cool and stylish - but not for the likes of us. I struggled with my covetousness by remembering that Peter's project was not strongly connected to IITA. We were allowed stay in a dormitory unit as a courtesy to the World Bank because it was a major contributor to IITA coffers. Unfortunately, that didn't put IITA under an obligation to offer us one of the empty houses, as Bill Powell, Deputy Director General and He-Who-Held-The-Authority had told us. I instructed myself to stop looking wistfully at vacant houses.

Once I was familiar with the residential area, I switched to walking the nine-hole golf course, soaking up the beauty of the place. At this hour the air had a delicate, unfamiliar perfume. Particular trees and shrubs were still strangers to me but I found myself thinking of spices. The last of a light, drifting mist added to the magic. The surface of several small water holes rippled as water birds set about their breakfast. Sometimes a tiny antelope darted across a fairway, giving the guinea fowl another excuse to scuttle around at a frenzied pace. If I were early enough, the grass still twinkled with hundreds of fireflies. I found it breathtakingly beautiful.

Near the end of my zigzag journey up and down fairways that stretched between avenues of grand old trees, I'd arrive at the edge of a small lake. Its clear water held a mirror to huge trees and to one or two clouds that had come on ahead to forewarn of the wet season. Two large geese, white as snow, waddled with well-fed hauteur beside the water's edge. They were undisputed royalty in this little Kingdom and they honked loudly just to remind everyone. As I passed I showed due respect because I'd been warned that if they took a set against me, walking in this area could prove a challenge. Disrespectful golfers soon discovered that playing the hazards of the fourth hole took on a whole new meaning.

After circling the lake, I turned towards home. Now, to my left across two fairways, I could see the back of a house that seemed so at home in this setting it must have grown there. Its unfenced back yard melted gently onto the verges of the golf course, offering those who lived there an unimpeded view to the lake. My resolution not to be envious slipped and I imagined myself sitting on that back porch, eating my wheaties as I watched the mist rise from the water.

A hundred metres from home my path took me past the Cappa Bar, a multipurpose building which also served as the Golf Clubhouse. It was the domain of Levi, a diminutive gentleman who took great pride in the efficient running of the premises. The walls of Cappa Bar's lounge were lined with an assortment of books donated by departing residents and the variety was as diverse as the tastes of the donors, ranging from the writings of Karl Marx to Mills and Boon. I had stumbled upon this treasure trove by accident and was invited to make use of the informal lending library. I became a regular visitor, strolling down mid-afternoon to make my selection while the rest of the world worked.

Sometimes I would linger, buying a cool drink and taking up a comfortable chair under one of the overhead fans on the Cappa Bar's patio. By looking up, I could see the entire length of the ninth hole. Its tee was perched above me on a steep little hill and down on the same level where I sat, away to my right, lay the "brown", an oiled sand version of a putting green. At the foot of the hill, between tee and brown, was a small dam, irresistible to golf balls. As I sat I'd watch mother ducks and their babies enjoying one last peaceful swim before the afternoon's golfers arrived. Soon, small white balls would be whistling around their heads, but they seemed to accept it all with good grace.

One afternoon I sauntered down to Cappa Bar and was deeply engrossed in selecting books when the door opened and in filed a group of women. Many wore stunning Asian or African traditional dress while the Europeans looked smart in neat Western attire.

A lady approached me and introduced herself as Agnes Uryio, a Tanzanian. With a friendly smile she thwarted my escape and guided me to one of the chairs forming a large circle around the room. A meeting of the Women's Group was about to commence, I was told, and I was most welcome. My protests that I was not suitably dressed were ignored and I was doomed to sit gazing in horror from the knobbly knees that protruded from my shorts to the finery that sat in a graceful arrangement around me. I castigated myself for stepping outside our unit in house clothes.

But my self-consciousness gave way to interest when each

person in turn was invited to introduce herself and to speak briefly about her reactions to living in Africa. The format of the meeting had been prearranged for the benefit of a visiting research officer who wanted information about expatriates' reactions to living in West Africa. It provided me with a wonderful opportunity to learn more about the other women. I forgave Agnes for capturing me and settled down to enjoy the afternoon.

Later, over a cup of tea, I stood with a group as they discussed the rising crime rate in Ibadan. In quaint Nigerian terminology, things were being 'carried' at an alarming rate. IITA, too, was feeling the effects. Only this week a 4WD vehicle had disappeared from outside one of the houses. As we stood clicking our tongues, Alice, a handsome Nigerian woman took up a position beside me and joined the lament. Her generous frame was made more imposing by her flowing robes as her ample bosom inflated with indignation. She clasped my arm in a vice-like grip as she spoke.

"I 'ave 'eard about de 4WD. If dey do dat, what is to stop dem entering our 'ouses and carryin' us?" I looked from Alice to my own generous proportions. It crossed my mind that they wouldn't carry us far. Taking my cue from others, I closed my eyes, pursed my lips and shook my head disapprovingly.

We drifted outside, finishing off any topics that had so far escaped, before we dispersed. Jeanette Kang whom I had met after the meeting, turned to me and with a warm smile, invited me to drop in one day for a cup of coffee. To provide her address, she turned and pointed down the first fairway - to the house above the lake, the house I loved. I laughed in delight, but left it until a later date to explain my reaction.

A woman with dark hair and alert brown eyes that hinted of Italy included me in her goodbyes as she left. During the meeting, I had been surprised when her accent betrayed a southern USA connection. She had introduced herself as Nancy Gulley, a teacher trained in remedial education. She and husband Jim had been in Nigeria a long time, working as missionaries, but in recent years the expense of putting three sons through university led Jim, also trained in Agricultural Science, to take a job at IITA. I liked Nancy immediately for her sense of humour and no-nonsense air, but then anyone whose family consists of three sons was off to a good start with me.

As I headed home I realised how much I had enjoyed the afternoon. I am a gregarious creature at heart so the timing of today's visit to the library, unlovely knees and all, was most fortunate. I returned to our little unit well pleased with life.

The situation with Mrs Aziz was getting ridiculous. Here we were, two mature women, playing the roles of Maid and Mistress of the Household and it had to stop. Next time she appeared, I planted myself in front of her and waved a photograph under her nose.

"Mrs Aziz, I would like to show you my family."

She stopped in her tracks, her face expressionless. Without taking her eyes from my face, she took the photo and only when she was sure that I had not taken leave of my senses, did she lower her eyes. She studied it for a long moment then her face broke into the first smile of our acquaintance.

"Yo' family!" She prodded each in turn as I identified them for her. "Dis one like yo', Madame, dis one like Sah." Round and round the finger went. "Son, son, son. Wife, wife, girlfren!" She handed it back reluctantly. "I am so happy yo' show me."

From that moment on we were firm friends. We exchanged details about our families on a regular basis, but Mrs Aziz's appetite for news outstripped our four-weekly mail delivery by courier service so I began doling out fresh news in economical instalments so as not to disappoint her. Her interest in my welfare was kindled and dust, having rested peacefully for weeks, was sent flying.

One day Mrs Aziz arrived for work and propped herself against a wall. Her hair was in its usual tight braids above her round face, but from the hairline down she glistened with perspiration. Her gnarled feet, dressed in the inevitable "slippers" - thongs to Australians - had merely shuffled in, noisily signalling that all was not well. She looked a picture of misery.

She pointed to her brow and various other trouble spots.

"I have a hake 'ere and 'ere, and my belly is twistin'," she informed me. "I jes want to CUT!" and she drew an ominous finger across her throat.

I had just had my first look at malaria.

Peter had flown to Abuja on business so when I saw a poster at International House inviting one and all to "An Evening in Latin America", I decided to go as a change from evenings alone at home. I smothered myself in mosquito repellent and strolled up in the twilight. I settled down by the pool, with drink in hand, for an enjoyable evening of people-watching.

Lively Latin-American music filled the air and a handsome, dusky-skinned couple did the samba beside the pool in a demonstration of rhythm and grace. The dancers hailed originally from Colombia and this evening's theme had been their suggestion. I looked around the gathering crowd, identifying other people I had met or knew by reputation.

Nearby, I noted a young man wandering from group to group in lost-sheep manner. I judged him to be a visitor, perhaps here for a few days on some agricultural project. Whenever he spoke he held one side of his mouth clamped into a straight line while the other side formed a large "O" out of which he puffed words. I mentally placed a candle on his left shoulder and tried to guess what words would result in the candle being extinguished but my project was interrupted when a lively group approached and settled in to share my table. They introduced themselves in a variety of accents, all using IITA's verbal-shorthand, designed to give concise information to like-minded professionals. My hand was wrung in friendly fashion: "Good evening. Indira, cassava research," and "Hello. David, pilot." It was nice to have company.

Later I stood in front of the food that was spread on a long table, admiring its presentation and aroma. *Tostones* made from fried green plantains, grilled chicken steeped in spices and covered with avocado and cheese; the selection was exotic and wide-ranging and as South American as possible under the circumstances. As I stood there, the candle blower joined me and when I smiled hello, he extended a hand.

"Colin. Bananas," he puffed. A startled pause followed until I realised he was referring to his occupation rather than his mental state. A disjointed conversation limped along as I struggled in vain to look anywhere but at his mouth and the imaginary candle on his shoulder. Thankfully, he soon tired of me and wandered off to find someone more interested in diseases of tropical fruit than in his oral arrangement.

By the time Peter arrived home from his trip to the north, the car that was to be for our personal use had arrived. Peter's office was the other side of Ibadan, at the headquarters of FORMECU (Forestry Management and Coordination Unit) and each day at eight o'clock a driver arrived to take him to work. Unless I needed the car, it and driver would remain at FORMECU for the day until five o'clock, when Peter would be brought home. In our first weeks in Nigeria we had had a succession of drivers but now Patrick Iyasele was appointed to the position permanently. Peter brought him back to the unit to meet me.

"Girl, this is Patrick," said Peter. During the introductions, Patrick glanced only fleetingly at my face but he must have wondered at Sir's distorted impression of life stages. He nodded briefly and looked away. I knew we'd be in each others' company a great deal in the coming months so I hoped that his initial lack of friendliness was due to shyness rather than to a dislike of his assignment. After the irrepressible Samson and the handsome Dele, I looked at Patrick with interest. He was of average height and well built. His face was round, made to look more so by his hair which was so closely cropped that the peppercorn pattern of its growth formed mere dots on his scalp. His complexion was a dark, rusty tan rather than the near-black of many of his countrymen. I judged his age to be mid-to-late thirties although I invariably underestimated the age of Africans.

From the start, Patrick called me 'Marm', although he slid quickly across the 'a' making it sound more like 'Mmm'. Until now I had always been called 'Madame' ('M'darm') as were all married women so Patrick's choice was a surprise.

Now, as the men stood discussing the following day's schedule, I noticed that if Patrick's lips were moving, so were his hands. He spoke in rapid, heavily accented English that we found difficult to understand but his digits worked overtime, offering vital clues as to the meaning of his words. Fingers dancing at the end of an extended, upward facing palm meant that whatever he was asking required a simple yes or no answer, a helpful starting point. A hand facing downwards, the fingers fluttering lightly in front of his face usually accompanied a lengthy explanation of something we needed to be told. We soon learned that Patrick didn't always ask for clarification if he couldn't understand us. At such times he would use a protracted 'Ho Kaaay...' which often meant 'I haven't a clue what you're talking about.' But sometimes 'Ho Kaaay...' could be interpreted as 'You probably don't mean that, so I'll pretend I didn't hear it.' We soon realised that we disregarded Ho Kaaays at our peril.

One Friday afternoon Peter announced that his secretary, Beatrice, was bringing her family the following day to 'greet' me. I prepared food for afternoon tea and made sure we had some 'minerals' (soft drinks). Wise in the ways of children during social visits, I put my mind to organising some entertainment and by the time they arrived I had a variety of items ready. I hoped that tennis balls, an inflatable globe, photos, a few Australian magazines (pictures of near-naked bodies removed) and some electronic gadgets would keep them entertained.

Beatrice's chubby face beamed with pleasure as Ayo, her husband, introduced the family. The children looked delightful. Sade, a ten year old, was all cuteness with her hair twisted into topknots all over her head, each one tied with a tiny red or white ribbon to match the white blouse, red skirt and lacy white socks she wore. The two boys, younger than their sister, were like miniature businessmen in long-sleeved shirts, slacks and gleaming black shoes. One by one they bowed respectfully and took their place on the lounge. The two older children were away at boarding school, we were informed.

Beatrice and I had chatted many times at the FORMECU office

but today, each time I tried to draw her into conversation, she'd turn to Ayo. He'd reply on her behalf even when I had asked about her work or family matters. Likewise, the children were silent as their father made their replies. It dawned on me that I was witnessing a strong Nigerian custom. Beatrice sat, smiling but mute; the children perched quietly, hands in laps, ankles crossed. *Oh dear*, I thought. *This is going to be a long afternoon.*

Finally we exhausted the pleasantries, and I was beginning to wilt when Ayo stood and turned to Beatrice. "I will go now, Madame, and let you 'ave a nice talk with Pum." He admonished the children to behave and left. Peter soon excused himself to attend to outstanding paperwork, leaving the women and children to their own devices.

Beatrice was transformed before my eyes. She initiated conversation, discussing politics, Nigerian customs and fashions in an animated way. When she spoke of family life, she described a struggle, against hopeless odds, to give the children a decent education in a country where the education system had all but collapsed. She explained that teachers in government schools had not been paid for months and although they came to school, they refused to teach. If parents wanted their children to learn, they must send money to pay for classes that began at the end of school hours. By this time the children were tired and the teachers resentful. Beatrice's round face looked uncharacteristically sad as she listed her fears for her beautiful children's future.

With Dad out of the way the children also came to life. Surreptitious pokes and prods were exchanged and they struggled to suppress giggles or squeals. The toys I had assembled were second best to the flush toilet, which was unquestionably the highlight of the visit. One by one the children were stricken with weak bladders requiring repeated visits the bathroom and much button pushing. It was time to produce a diversion. Out on the grass the tennis balls became sibling-seeking missiles rather than catching objects. The children, while polite and respectful to adults, were reassuringly normal when at play. Beatrice pretended not to notice the more boisterous aspects of the boys' wrestling or Sade's less-than-ladylike tumbles on the soft grass.

Much later, Ayo returned and was welcomed with smiles from his family, but his arrival marked the end of spontaneity. Back to folded hands and crossed ankles. I unearthed a dictaphone and when Ayo instructed the children to sing they did so, chirping obligingly in unselfconscious tunelessness. Even their father's presence couldn't prevent an attack of giggles when they heard themselves. We produced our *piece de resistance*, Peter's new toy, the video camera. Soon cameraman, artistic director and subjects were engrossed in unsophisticated enjoyment of the technological age.

Eventually, just when I had begun to wonder how I'd feed five extra mouths on half a kilogram of mince, Ayo rose and signalled the end of the visit. At a word from their father the children knelt before us in thanks then the men walked ahead out to the car. As Beatrice and I strolled behind, I complimented her on her stylish outfit. She offered to introduce me to her tailor and I accepted immediately. I urgently needed clothes more suited to the climate so right away we settled upon a suitable date.

A week passed. We had decided to join the group who met each Friday evening to play tennis up at International House, but as we dressed to go, Peter suddenly complained of feeling exhausted. We changed our plans and he took himself off to bed, stirring an hour later with a burning fever. He was sure that he was developing a severe bout of influenza but I became alarmed and hurried up to the tennis courts to ask advice. Nancy was there with her husband Jim and after brief introductions, we discussed Peter's symptoms. The Gulleys both felt sure that Peter had come down with malaria.

"Just treat it as malaria tonight by increasing the prophylactic drugs and ring the doctor in the morning," Jim said calmly.

I found his unruffled approach reassuring and headed home but once there I became concerned all over again because Peter's temperature seemed higher than before. Late as it was, I rang Tom Akintewe, IITA's senior doctor and he directed me through the process of administering the drugs I had on hand, and told me to bring Peter to the clinic the following morning. To my relief, the increased chloroquin soon took effect and during the night the patient reported that although he still felt woeful, there had been a definite improvement.

A blood test proved the diagnosis correct so the same treatment was to be continued, with bed rest. Peter is an uncomplaining type and I misinterpreted his stoicism as evidence that Mrs Aziz had been exaggerating her symptoms. Five days later a follow-up pathology test ended with a smiling technician informing Peter that 'de parasites 'ave fled.' Another Rite of Passage completed.

One evening soon after, when I was in the middle of telling Peter an amusing incident from my day, it was my turn. Suddenly I was overcome with weariness. Fifteen minutes later my joints ached wickedly, my head pounded and my teeth chattered. I felt as if I had run full speed into a brick wall. Like a wilting heroine in a melodramatic jungle movie, I wiped perspiration from my brow. Why hadn't someone told me that malaria was so horrid? I swallowed the first batch of tablets, set the alarm to wake me for the next dose and lowered myself gingerly onto the bed. *I'm much sicker than Peter was*, I told myself piteously.

Presuming that Tom would only repeat the directions he'd given me regarding Peter's illness, I dosed myself accordingly. Weeks of intermittent misery followed. Just when I thought I was returning to health, I would succumb once more. I was full of self-righteous indignation. Hadn't I taken all the recommended precautions, even to commencing the prophylactics before leaving Australia?

When my aching head would allow, I turned to needlework to relieve the tedium. On the horizon of the Australian landscape I stitched deep purple shadows on a mountain range, and I used more sombre shades still, to colour a corner of my Nigerian tapestry.

One morning I was so ill that I knew I must get help, so Peter took me down to the IITA clinic before he left for work. A doctor examined me thoroughly and in asking about my recent health, she directing every question to Peter. Malaria makes one 'liverish' and as they discussed me in the third person I wondered irritably why a medical officer serving an international community would retain this custom. Meanwhile the patient's spouse was responding positively to the role of spokesperson. Dear as this custom obviously was to the Nigerian doctor and to my protective husband, it was not for me and with a slight repositioning of my chair, I placed myself so that they had to crane their necks around me to speak. It worked. Doctor discovered that it was possible to speak directly to me and that I even understood her instruction to go down the corridor for a blood test.

A couple of hours later I received a phone call telling me that although I was suffering from a strain of malaria resistant to the usual treatment, I did not have any of the other nasty bugs that doctor had considered possible. With a simple change of medication, all would be well.

Resolving not to diagnose my own illnesses in future, I began the new course of treatment and took myself off to bed. Within two hours I could feel the pain in my limbs draining away as the parasites fled. I wished them good riddance.

Chapter 5
INNOCENCE PERSONIFIED

When the malaria finally left us, we found to our surprise that we felt marvellously well, but perhaps it was merely the sensation of being well again. Whatever the cause, it was with an extra sense of *joie de vivre* that we took to the tennis courts the following Friday evening and relaxed afterwards with friends, sipping beer and eating *suya* (delicious, peppery strips of meat threaded onto skewers and cooked barbecue style).

The number of people who gathered at the courts on Friday nights fluctuated, but usually a core of regulars came and the casual atmosphere proved an ideal setting for friendships to develop. As we got to know the Gulleys, we saw how well matched they were. Jim, rock solid, calm and quietly spoken, provided the perfect foil for the outgoing, sometimes volatile Nancy. They initiated a lot of activity, both social and altruistic and somehow things always seemed to be more fun when they were around.

Another of our regular tennis partners was Rahim Wakili, an Afghani-New Yorker who was the manager of a large humanitarian project in this part of Nigeria. Rahim and his family lived in a compound with other expatriates in an Ibadan suburb not far from IITA. There they endured a myriad of inconveniences to do with poor security, unreliable electricity and water supplies, and worries about their children's education. While Rahim struggled with the frustrations of his job, his teenage daughters fretted for the life that New York offered. The Wakilis visited IITA regularly as social members and although they wished to live on campus, they too had been told that their project was not sufficiently linked to the institute's function to warrant the offer of a house.

Each Friday evening, Rahim would amuse us with yet another anecdote from his week.

"I am really pissed off this week!" he'd declare, his dark, handsome face glum and his tone indicating that last week's pissed-offedness was insignificant compared to this. He would warm to his subject as we waited for the latest episode.

Only yesterday, he told us one evening, he'd been driving to work when he found himself directly behind another of his agency's vehicles, one of a large fleet supplied for the purpose of assisting needy children. The vehicles all carried a distinctive logo and Rahim knew that adverse publicity could damage his agency's support so he'd always insisted that staff be scrupulously honest in the use of its property.

Now, as he tailgated the utility truck, he was looking into the mournful eyes of a trussed bullock. His annoyance at such blatant misuse of an official vehicle was only slightly offset by amazement that anyone could get such a large beast into such a small space. Certainly the animal's lolling tongue and sad eyes spoke volumes about its thoughts on the matter. As the vehicle turned in at the local markets, Rahim recorded the registration number for further action.

He tracked down the vehicle but his interrogation of staff was met with wide-eyed innocence. No matter what tactic Rahim used he got no closer to finding the driver of the vehicle. Even in the face of evidence left behind by the indignant beast, his staff insisted that Sah must be mistaken. De vehicles were for official use, not for transportin' animals!

As we laughed, Rahim confided that he had returned to his office and sat pondering about how long he would need to bang his head on his desk before his frustration eased.

"I think," he concluded, with the air of one making a profound discovery, "that if I were asked to give Africa an enema, I'd insert the tube at Lagos and push it up as far as Ibadan!"

While we laughed, Jim merely smiled quietly. He and Nancy had lived in Nigeria for many years and he used a different yardstick to measure progress. He had an impressive store of tolerance and had long since learned to roll with the punches of life in Africa.

In forestry circles, the lofty status occupied by Peter and his Nigerian counterpart Mr O'Kenyi was acknowledged by the bestowing of a very special key. Only they were to cross the portal of the executive washroom, humble though it was. The honour did not seem to be diminished by the fact that Ibadan's water supply was unreliable and most of the time the toilet couldn't be used. Being a practical man, Peter dispatched Patrick to buy a large plastic container and next morning they sallied forth with it brimful of IITA water. It was duly secreted behind the locked door, ready for the next emergency.

Next morning the container was gone. No one had any explanation and no one seemed to think there was any point in pursuing the issue. Peter gave up, deciding that in matters to do with bodily functions, self-control was the way to go. But even on those occasions when absolute necessity coincided with running water, Peter had problems. He hadn't yet learned to accept with aplomb, Nigerian's fondness for offering congratulatory greetings to senior officers at what seemed inopportune moments. He continued to find it disconcerting, on his way back from the toilet, to be greeted with cries of, "Well done, Sah!"

Although admitting defeat over the water container there were other toilet-related matters that puzzled Peter. What facilities did everyone else use? Water closets, he knew were status symbols, not to be provided willy nilly - as it were - yet he couldn't see any outhouses either. Andrew, a personable young forester on Peter's team laughed heartily at Peter's question.

"If yo' want to tilt at windmills, Sah, I would suggest yo' pick a more serious one. Let's jes say dat Nigerians doan worry much about toilets!"

When we tried to satisfy our curiosity about other aspects of Nigerian life by quizzing Patrick, the exercise wasn't always successful. Patrick obviously judged certain matters to be the business of Nigeria and Nigerians alone. Asked about these, he'd give the stubble on his head a thoughtful massage then launch into an unintelligible torrent of words that left us flummoxed. The usually eloquent hands offered no assistance, and requests for clarification merely unleashed more of the same until we indicated surrender. I sometimes even heard a quiet chuckle of satisfaction as he turned off the barrage of words. There were times when we had to accept that, in a few meanings of the term, we weren't in the race.

Peter needed to go to Lagos for meetings and I decided to accompany him because it was time we made arrangements for our personal banking. Peter's salary was paid into a Washington Credit Union and when we needed money he was to send a prearranged coded message to initiate a transfer of funds. Ibadan, a city of perhaps three million people, did not have a bank that the World Bank considered secure enough for this purpose. Several expatriates had lost large sums of money when clever scams diverted money en route from overseas to a Lagos account. We had been advised to deal in minimum amounts and to withdraw funds as soon as possible after their arrival. That meant carrying US dollars back to Ibadan and keeping money in the house, but this was considered less of a financial risk than leaving it in the Lagos bank.

Patrick swung the car southwards and almost immediately we were embroiled in the first go-slow of the day. As we waited to move on we were treated to impromptu street theatre. A truck had overturned, leaving its load of squawking chickens scattered around in cane baskets. A noisy crowd had gathered with people shouting, waving arms and offering huge amounts of free advice. We could see that it was as much as Patrick could do to restrain himself from joining in the pandemonium. But there in the midst of what looked like chaos, progress was being made. We could see young men collecting ropes, poles and rocks and as we moved off Patrick told us with something like regret, that the truck and chickens would be right way up before we next passed this way.

We fell into procession behind a truck laden with cattle, West African beasts that bore little resemblance to the breeds I was familiar with at home. These were long, tall and narrow, constructed with abrupt angles and sharp edges, so unappealing that not even a tetse fly could love them. Viewed from end on, admittedly a less-than-flattering angle for most living things, I was reminded of upright razor blades on legs. Imagining portions of these fellows on a plate was enough to convert one to vegetarianism. I thought wistfully of small, round, tender-looking Herefords.

The driver of the truck ahead must have had a keen entrepreneurial streak because across the top of the cattle pen stretched several stout planks. On these sat men and women; paying passengers Patrick informed us. A metre below them swayed the needle-sharp horns of the cattle. As the truck lurched and swayed, the people bounced around on the planks with total disregard for comfort or safety.

We overtook the truck and as we gathered speed on the highway Peter reminded Patrick that while driving for us, there would be no speeding.

"Ho Kaaay..." replied Patrick.

"Ho Kaaay nothing!" said Peter, recognising the fob-off. He repeated the instruction and this time Patrick accepted with resignation, this interference with a driver's God-given rights. In Nigeria there is a certain status in getting one's employer from A to B in the shortest possible time. The rueful shake of Patrick's head may have implied that life with Sah and Marm was not going to be easy.

In past weeks, we'd also tried to wean our driver off the habit of horn blowing.

"But de people woan know I'm cummin!" he'd protested when we broached the subject after he'd stalked a pedestrian then almost sent her into orbit with a protracted horn-blast.

"You're a bushranger, Patrick!" had been Peter's frustrated but totally meaningless reproof to a non-Australian. Not surprisingly, it had little effect. In the end Patrick wore us down and we heard him chuckle and celebrate our surrender with the mischievous 'Yi,

Yi, Yi!' that we were hearing more often these days. I did, however, draw the line at horn-blowing within the grounds of IITA, thereby marking out the territory of an endless battle of wills between us.

Now in Lagos, we went to our bank and began the complicated arrangements for getting money from across the Atlantic. We stood at the counter and thought we were making reasonable progress when the banking official unexpectedly shouted in our faces, "Innocent! Innocent!"

I jumped in fright and was about to insist that we hadn't accused him of anything when a young man appeared at his shoulder.

"Yo' called, Sah?"

As Innocent was dispatched to collect some forms, I silently added to the list of first names that had already taken my fancy. I now had Sunday, Monday, Friday, Chastity, Charity and Innocent.

Before we left Australia, the Department of Foreign Affairs advised us to visit the Australian High Commission in Lagos and register our presence. We now set out to do so, plugging across town and running the gauntlet of street sellers, beggars, wild drivers and go-slows. It felt as if half the world's population was here with the specific intention of creating chaos, as pedestrians and cars jousted for supremacy. One-and-a-half hours later we had covered the short distance and were at the security gates of the Australian High Commission, waiting clearance to enter.

I was looking forward to meeting other Aussies. Once inside we waited, then waited some more. I became convinced that somewhere in a back room our fellow countrymen were deciding by drawing straws in a best of twenty-five series, which one must attend to us.

Suddenly a stream of uniquely Australian swearwords erupted from a nearby room, then a guilty face topped by a head of fair, curly hair appeared around the doorway and smiled at us engagingly.

"Sorry, folks. Its just that I get so bloody frustrated when I can't even contact the British High Commission across the road."

We assured him that we understood but he stepped into the

waiting area, obviously feeling the need to explain further.

"Everything here's a bloody mess. The phones are always out, so that means no faxes, and of course email's just a fantasy." He sighed wistfully, then continued. "Anything we've ever posted has never been seen again. Once we even employed a messenger to physically deliver stuff to and from the Brits across the road, but he went and got run over." The man disappeared, shaking his head in self-pity at the inconvenience of it all.

Eventually the drawer of thirteen short straws loped in. He dropped his long, thin frame onto a chair and introduced himself as Tony Irons. When he spoke his drawl was rasping and querulous. I listened as my mind's eye pictured a coil of barbed wire being dragged across a sheet of tin. As his distinctive voice scoured our ears, he lifted his feet to the coffee table between us, rolled up his trouser legs and began scratching the impressive number of mosquito bites on his hairy shanks. He fixed Peter with an inquisitive look.

"Why would you come to Nigeria if you didn't have to? I hate the place." He interrupted his scratching briefly to concentrate on examining us. "And they told you to visit us? I'm amazed you even bothered. Nothing is worth spending time out in that!" and he wagged his head in the general direction of the street outside. We deflated further as he went on to offer advice that we could well believe:

"If this election business turns nasty, stick with the World Bank crowd. They can give you more protection than we can." We watched and listened as long as we could bear it, then thanking him for his time, we beat a hasty retreat, both hoping never to hear that voice again.

It was important to be off the streets before dark, so we returned to the Sheraton and walked past the scene of the earlier hijack attempt. We were old hands now and hardly gave it a thought.

Later, refreshed after a shower and rejoicing in the wonders of air-conditioning, we went downstairs to the lounge and sipped a drink while we conducted a post-mortem on the day. Our reactions mellowed with hindsight as we relived our meeting with

Mr. Irons. Although we regretted how poorly he represented our country, we had to concede that the incident had not been without humour.

We drifted into the hotel's Pili Pili restuarant where the staff looked splendid in uniforms that satisfied western fashion while respecting the traditions of African dress. After welcoming us warmly, the waiter offered us the menu. We took all of thirty seconds to make our selections, for leaping out at us were the words 'imported beef'.

When the food arrived we fell into a reverent silence as we savoured every mouthful. The background was a gentle blur of soft music and indistinguishable murmurs of conversation. I offered a brief prayer of thanks; may I always have the good grace to count my blessings. Then, no louder than the surrounding sounds, a fragment of conversation reached me as clearly as if spoken in my ear.

"I fly into Brisbane, stay a week, then go on up to Cairns and the Barrier Reef."

I felt a constriction in my chest, a physical pain. I took a second to compose myself, then turned and gazed at the fortunate soul who so soon would be in my Queensland, close to my family. The suddenness and intensity of my yearning shocked me and for some time I had to struggle to retain my composure. I turned and looked across the table at Peter. He had told me that he was beginning to realise the enormity of the task he had undertaken and the extent of the difficulties that stood in his way. I realised that the last thing he needed now was the extra burden of an unhappy companion. *That's enough*, I chided myself.

Later that evening, as a panacea, we rang home and wrapped ourselves in news and reassurances that as usual, all was well. Feeling much better, I congratulated myself on having weathered my first bout of homesickness.

As we drove back to Ibadan next day Patrick entertained us with stories of armed hold-ups on this road.

"De main problem is de police. Dey go off duty, take off de black shirts, an' use de same guns and road blocks to become robbers."

As he spoke, I recalled the many barricades I'd seen, where heavy planks bristling with long nails stretched across the road. Our semi-diplomatic number plates usually meant that police allowed us through, but locals were stopped and ordered to contribute a small donation for the right to proceed. Mostly, a blind eye was turned to this practice of salary enhancement but the arrangement had come unstuck a few months ago when the police stopped an army officer at a roadblock. Their cheekiness incensed him and he refused to cooperate, so they shot him dead. This displeased the ruling Army junta and they punished the entire police force by cancelling their normal duties and confining them to barracks, but the police were not so easily thwarted. Immediately, armed robberies and carjacking reached epidemic proportions, this time targeting diplomatic and semi-diplomatic cars. This of course was considered an outrage, and such political pressure was applied to the military government that they had no choice but to return to the status quo. Once more diplomatic staff and the likes of ourselves were waved through while struggling Nigerians had to pay up or face the consequences.

"Life," said Patrick, shaking his head ruefully, "is not issy!" We had to agree with him. For most Nigerians, life certainly wasn't easy.

As we arrived back at IITA that evening, I cancelled with Patrick our next day's plans for a shopping trip. I had promised Nancy Gulley that I'd take over her weekly visit to a nearby orphanage while she was on annual leave and tomorrow she was to show me the ropes. Even as I agreed with Patrick that life wasn't easy, I already had the feeling that tomorrow's excursion would show me the extent of that understatement.

Chapter 6
I MEET THE KIDS

Nancy was relieved that she had found two women who could visit the Child Care Facility while she and the majority of IITA residents were away on leave. I'd never met Cielo, the Colombian lady who was to share the task with me but I was relieved to hear from Nancy that she was familiar with the delicate politics that existed between the facility and the Women's Group.

"Cielo," said Nancy with a crooked smile that hinted at both admiration and exasperation, "is a bit of a doer."

What that meant exactly I didn't at first know, but I learned more as Nancy spoke. She went on to describe an incident where she and Cielo had become involved in helping a child.

Last year Cielo had visited the Home and found a child in acute distress although staff were denying that there was a problem. A boy, who was deaf and mute, had also had a leg amputated some months earlier when he'd been left on a railway track. (In our sixteen months in Nigeria, we saw two trains in working order, a sight that had Patrick enraptured, so this child's luck was completely out.)

At the Home, Cielo had found him lying outdoors, his remaining leg bent at an extraordinary angle. There he lay, his leg obviously broken, not allowed inside because of his understandably poor personal hygiene. Cielo scooped the child up and took him to a Catholic hospital, but he couldn't be admitted without pre-payment of fees. Cielo left the child in the care of her driver while she returned to IITA to enlist Nancy's help, then together they drove back to the hospital to tackle the admission procedure.

Hospital staff recognised the boy - they'd nursed him following his 'accident' on the railway line. His name, they said, was Deaf and Dumb Unknown. It didn't remain so much longer. As Nancy and Cielo went through the administrative tangle of having him admitted, they held their own little naming ceremony.

'Joseph' was Cielo's favourite name and Nancy decided to contribute by involving the State Governor. His name was borrowed and as the hospital forms were completed, Joseph Ishola came into being.

The two women took turns to visit Joseph in hospital and Nancy persevered until she extracted an undertaking from Government sources that after discharge, he would be admitted to a training programme for the deaf.

Unfortunately, while Nancy and Cielo were on annual leave, Joseph was discharged to a work-training programme that didn't cater for his type of disability. Although the director of the facility visited Nancy regularly to complain about Joseph's unsuitability for his programme, there was nothing she could do to get him transferred to a more suitable establishment, and his fate remains unknown.

Now, with the other women away, Cielo and I were to visit the children on different days each week, so I was glad of today's chance to go with Nancy to meet the children and staff at the children's home. Hopefully I would get to understand what was expected of me.

We set out mid-morning and as we stopped at the security gates Nancy exchanged cheery greetings with the guards and opened the boot of her car for a routine inspection. This formality was aimed at reducing the number of items being 'carried' from IITA, but everyone knew that thieves didn't find it too difficult to entice particular guards to turn a blind eye when required, provided the right inducement was offered.

Nancy pulled out into the traffic and I noted that this was my first experience outside IITA without a professional driver. I was curious to see how an expatriate would cope with oncoming traffic that routinely used the wrong side of the road to avoid deep potholes, burnt-out car-bodies or mounds of garbage. I soon found that the gladiatorial challenge held no fears for Nancy. She had been forged into a worthy combatant over the years and now put her local knowledge and natural assertiveness to good use.

While we threaded our way through the congestion Nancy told me about the institution called The Juvenile Remand Home and Child Care Facility, and the special interest that the Women's Group had in the children we were visiting today. I had to distinguish which words were directed at me and which were meant for fellow road-users who assumed they had right of way even when visiting our side of the road.

"The rainy season is very hard on the kids. Don't toot at *me*, thank you, I'm on the correct side of the road."

The fierce look directed at the trespasser softening again as Nancy's thoughts switched back to the children. "Most of the kids slip back in weight and general health between July and September. Hey, don't just cut in like that!"

A firm thump to the steering wheel emphasised her territorial rights. "Before we all go on leave, we try to make sure that the nurse at the Home has a supply of chloroquin to cover malaria attacks as well as enough medication for the epilepsy sufferers. Excuse me, Madame, but this is a *road*, meant for *cars*."

The institution housed two separate groups of children, Nancy explained. The Remand Home normally held fourteen or fifteen youths whose average age was about fourteen years. They had been charged with a crime, usually theft, although at times the institution held adolescents charged with more serious offences. In theory they were to be held for a few weeks until their cases came to trial, but in practice it took extraordinary means, usually money, to bring a case to trial. Failing such lubrication of the justice system, a child might languish there for a year or more, under the care of the warden.

"You'll get to know him well," said Nancy, and I detected an ominous note in her voice.

The Child Care Facility was run by a matron who was

subordinate to the Remand Home warden. This section housed about sixteen or eighteen younger children, most with physical or intellectual disabilities, the abandoned waifs of the region. I recalled Jim's comment one evening at tennis when someone had condemned any parent who would abandon a handicapped child.

"Remember, though, that just getting money for the next meal is an endless struggle for some. There is no social security to fall back on. It must be hard to have to choose between caring for one child with disabilities or feeding the others."

I soon discovered that healthy and well-nourished children were brought to the Home occasionally, after becoming lost or abandoned for unknown reasons. Parents who knew about the Centre soon reclaimed the fortunate ones but the identity of others remained a mystery. Some were too young to give helpful details so there they remained, small, grieving tots, gradually giving up hope of ever being reunited with their families. Nancy warned me that I would see despair in some the children I was to meet today.

"The healthy, attractive children are usually adopted out after a while," she said. "We wonder about the motives of some of the adoptive parents but generally it is seen as a blessing for the child to be gone from the Home."

She went on to explain that children as young as two years of age were admitted and if not adopted, spent their childhood there. Some simply did not survive, the emotional and physical neglect too much to endure. Expatriates were allowed visit the younger group but were discouraged from having contact with those on remand except for the two or three who were seconded to help with the care of the smaller ones.

Our car turned off the road and headed up a long driveway lined with river oaks. To our left were scraggly crops of corn and cassava. A group of teenage boys hoed listlessly between the rows as a few men armed with sticks, stood in the shade of a tree guarding them. Nancy pointed out the closest building, a long, low construction fresh with paint, as the home of the younger children. A child drew water from a well nearby and carried it to a covered breezeway that divided the length of the building. This was the children's eating area, with heavy wooden tables and long stools filling the space.

Nancy pointed to the left end of the elongated building and explained that the children slept in one big room there. Further to the left was the latrine, I was told. It crossed my mind to wonder at the government providing this many facilities for those who must surely be on the bottom rung of the ladder in a land not known for its benevolence. A freshly painted building, a well, tables and stools and a latrine; these were conveniences that tens of millions of West Africans were denied.

Nancy tut-tutted when she saw that the children were dressed in near-rags. Inside, she explained, were cartons of children's clothes that had come from America through the generosity of a friend of Bill Powell's, Nina West. Nina was a lawyer in Los Angeles who encouraged other members of the legal fraternity to contribute also, so the quality of the items was impressive. Bill Powell provided free delivery of the clothing and Jim and Nancy ensured that the items reached the children here and at the Motherless Babies Home. Now Nancy was finding that staff at the Remand Home were unwilling to dress the children in the nice clothes even though she had promised there would be more when these wore out. She thumped the steering wheel with feeling.

"We are trying to break down the attit-tood that these kids are just not worth the bother. All we can do," and she sighed in a dispirited way, "is go on showing that we value each child. Maybe something of it will rub off eventually."

We drove to the back of the building and I saw another dwelling standing at right angles to the first. It was unpainted and looked a dismal place. This was where the youths on remand were held. As I got out of the car I was introduced to the matron in charge of the little ones' area, Bose, ('Beau-sie') a lady in her thirties. Her easy, friendly manner as she welcomed us warmly, suited her pleasant face and neat appearance. She was new here and I could understand Nancy's hope that she might gradually improve the plight of the children. We were especially welcome, Bose said, because they had no food and the children had not eaten for almost twenty-four hours.

Nancy turned her attention to the band of children gathering around her. They made a sombre welcoming party as they stood, subdued and patient, waiting to greet their friend. She spoke to each child, bending down to provide hugs when thin arms reached out to her.

"Well hallo there, little Sunday. And Kimi...Oh my goodness, look at y'all. And Bosiyo...why, hallo."

Meanwhile the children inspected me gravely and put me on probation, then they turned to the car and were given items to carry. One by one they lifted small loads onto their heads and traipsed inside, a strange little parade, as noiseless as ants.

As the children waited quietly for their food, their sadness seeped into my head and my heart. Expressionless faces told of their depression and as I looked about me, I wondered how long a child can survive in an environment where no emotional and few physical needs are met. I was reminded of candles spluttering in an oxygen-starved room. Taking refuge in activity, I busied myself with the task of washing leathery little hands before serving the meal.

At first glance I had judged the majority of the children to be four or five years old, but as the morning progressed, I realised that I'd underestimated their ages. Malnutrition had stunted the growth of some and many of the children were intellectually disabled, although others looked back at me with wise old eyes. I picked up what I thought was a three-year-old and was told that this was Little Bose, who was eight. I crouched down and spoke to a baby sitting on the concrete floor but later when he opened his mouth to receive food, I saw a full set of teeth. As Matron Bose walked past, she smilingly told me his name was Friday because that was the day when he was brought to them.

I caught the eye of a boy who hadn't come out to the car to meet us when we arrived. His body was badly distorted, with a swollen belly bulging above thin, misshapen legs. When he walked, he locked his knees together for support before shuffling with unsteady steps on splayed feet. He was the size of a two-year-old but his eyes met mine with the intelligent, worldly-wise look of an older child. When I knelt on the floor beside him I was treated with a cool indifference that implied that if I thought he was going to break out in a rash of gratitude just because I visited him, I had another think coming. This was one child who might be down, but he wasn't out. His name was Gbade and from that first day, he could wrap me around his little finger.

IITA women had found that they must stay until the food was eaten if it was to reach them at all. Staff were untrained and poorly paid and at home their own children were probably undernourished too. If donated food was left unattended it often did not reach these particular children. I asked myself to what levels I'd sink if my own family was wracked with malnutrition and I couldn't answer with certainty.

The older children selected to help feed the little ones went about their duties in silence. Nancy chatted to the oldest boy, Taju, and he replied in monosyllables. She explained later that he was not awaiting trial but had been a resident of the Child Care Facility for many years. Now a teenager he had been shifted to live with the youths in the other building. A girl called Mahdi, about eleven or twelve, had also been sent down from the remand section and she moved silently about helping the younger children. I watched as she fed Rose, a child severely disabled with epilepsy and cerebral palsy, and her actions were so gentle and patient that I wondered at her being in this place. She did not respond to Nancy or myself in any way and it was plain that more than a language barrier separated us. Her face bore markings, not the harsh, carved grooves I was accustomed to seeing, but fine tattoos which dotted her cheeks in a decorative pattern below each eye. Her delicate features were unreadable and I wondered what thoughts and emotions were hidden behind that gaze.

Some of the children had mutilated feet, scarred and twisted. I watched as a child called Ibimie hobbled about and I recalled something about the treatment of epilepsy in isolated areas. I was right. Nancy confirmed later that this child, an epileptic, had been made to stand in glowing coals to drive demons from her body.

She had been rescued from that suffering, but the price had been to come here, far from family and everything she knew.

Bose led us into the dormitory area to meet a newcomer. We entered a dark, cheerless room where a youth of about fourteen was washing the floor. As we stepped carefully onto the damp concrete, the dank smell hit my nostrils. There were no beds but around the walls were bundles of rags and rolled cane mats. Foam squares were stacked in piles and the ones I could see were stained and torn. Bose led us to a corner of the room where a small figure lay on a bundle of rags. He was called Unknown, she said, because they had no information about him.

I bent down and met the gaze of a child dying of malnutrition. His face was familiar because I had seen its likeness on television reports beamed from Somalia and Ethiopia during famines, but today there was no television screen to cushion the impact. I touched his hand and the little claw closed over my finger. I had no words or even thoughts, just a sense of being with this child, near, but not of his world. The moment was beyond emotion and I remained there for some minutes, I think, before I became aware of Nancy and Bose speaking. I disengaged my hand and stood, but a long time passed before I could join the conversation. As we walked from the room, I heard Nancy arranging to deliver a special milk formula for the child as Bose had nothing suitable to give him.

After packing up Nancy and I sat for a while talking to the children. Gbade dismissed overtures of friendship with a disdainful turn of a small shoulder. Despite the language barrier most of the children responded to the attention and several showed enough assertiveness to request time with each of us. Others, more severely damaged, remained lost in their own worlds, but I hoped it was a more comfortable place with food in their stomachs.

Eventually we said *odabo*, goodbye, got into the car and headed out the gate. I had had time to collect my thoughts and my questions tumbled out with Nancy answering them one by one.

The government provided food for the children but the quantity was diminishing and delivery was becoming more erratic as inflation eroded the purchasing power of the Home's budget. Today's experience of finding that the children had not eaten for a long time was happening more frequently.

The reason the Child Care Facility was painted was that IITA people had done a lot of lobbying to obtain the improvements. The well was dug with money from a Presbyterian Congregation in USA; the youth group of the Methodist Church in Sterling, Virginia, had funded the painting of the home; and the British Embassy had paid for the construction of the latrine. Electricians from IITA had come out to repair unsafe lights and offered to install more, but staff feared that extra lights could attract robbers who would interpret the glow as a sign that people with money lived there. The Women's Group supplied money for milk, bournvita and sugar for the children, as well as attending to any emergencies that arose. Bose had become concerned and confided to Nancy that there was a risk in providing further improvements. It was possible that envious government officials would decide to relocate the children to another site and use this one for a 'worthier' purpose, namely a government office.

The Women's Group had purchased the sheets of foam for the children when they had been found sleeping on the concrete floor, but the mattresses had not been cared for and rapidly deteriorated into health hazards. One child, prompted by hunger or some other aberration, kept pulling pieces from his mattress and eating them. Staff had responded with severe punishment but it didn't stop him.

Physical punishment was the order of the day in both buildings. Nancy and her colleagues often arrived to find the children with bruises and abrasions that did not always tally with the given explanation of epileptic seizures.

"But the mood isn't always like it was today," Nancy assured me, answering my unspoken question as to how she could remain philosophical. "As well as their hunger, something must have happened this morning the make them so subdued. Wait until Bosiyo treats you to his sense of humour and you see Kimi's beautiful smile. You'll get hooked on those kids, believe me."

As Nancy probably well knew, I already was. One last question. Why was the gentle, sad Mahdi in the Remand section?

"Mahdi is the only child of a senior wife. When the second wife produced a son, the first lost her position of favour. The only way she could be reinstated was by getting rid of the male child. Mahdi obeyed her mother's instruction and dropped him down a well. She is waiting to face trial for murder."

Chapter 7
GATHERING STORMS

The wet season was approaching and the conversation amongst IITA's expatriates increasingly focused on holiday plans. Fieldwork was limited during the months from June to August because of daily rain and because many places on earth were enjoying a better climate at this time, it suited international staff to stagger their annual leave over this period. One Friday, Peter and I joined those sitting around after a game of tennis. Travel seemed to be on everyone's mind.

"Have y'considered what you'll be doin' wit' yourselves f'the holidays?"

"Well, we hafta visit with folks in California the first week, but then we'll move to Florida for a vacation on our own. Leastways we'll be outta here come June 30. And what about y'all?"

"Perhaps a few days in the Greek Islands on our way back from Switzerland."

The accents were Irish, American, Swiss and the conversation touched nonchalantly on destinations that were straight from travel brochures. For Peter and I, the idea of an exotic destination had once meant choosing Surfers Paradise over Caloundra, so this was heady stuff. *These people aren't boasting,* I reminded myself, *They're merely referring to journeys home, visits to rellies, or trips to their local beach.*

I was beginning to feel at home in the IITA community, so early the following week I decided to follow up on the invitation I had received from Jeanette Kang when we'd met at the Women's Group meeting. She had suggested I call in for a cup of coffee, so after a quick phone call I walked down to the house above the lake. She was a handsome woman in her mid-fifties, who spoke and moved with the calm poise that I had noticed in other Indonesian women. When I was inside, Jeanette introduced me to her husband who was about to return to work. I was struggling with his first name so Doctor Kang quickly came to my rescue.

"It is totally unpronounceable to non-Indonesians, so please do what everyone else does. Just call me by my initials, BT," he said, as he left the house.

The house was all I'd imagined it would be; open, cool and comfortable. I explained to Jeanette why I had reacted with amusement when I had heard where she lived. As I described my walking track and confessed to daydreaming about the view they must have of the lake with its early morning mist, she led me across the lounge room to the side porch. There, in just the right location, was their breakfast table. While we stood looking out, the largest of the geese appeared at the water's edge and honked a distant greeting before waddling on its way.

Jeanette admitted to loving this house and garden. She explained that IITA accommodation was allocated on a points system, based on scientific or administrative seniority, plus size of family. Doctor BT Kang, a soil fertility scientist, (currently specialising in alley farming) had been involved in many significant research projects over his twenty-three years here, and held a senior position on staff. He and Jeanette had raised their family of three on IITA, hence the happy accumulation of points that led them to this house. *No wonder Bill Powell was not developing ulcers worrying about the Crannys who had arrived two months ago*, I thought.

As I described our unsuccessful attempts to persuade the Deputy Director General to rent us a house (on the basis that we'd move out if it were required by anyone else), Jeanette's brow furrowed with thought for a moment, but she did not comment, and we moved onto another subject.

In the next hour we chatted in lively fashion about our histories, families and plans for the future. When we said our farewells it was obvious that we both had enjoyed our morning and we decided to share more cups of coffee overlooking the cool garden that stretched towards the lake.

Peter and I had rejoiced in the feast of mail arriving from home via the courier service and now it was our turn to respond. I had promised to send home a few pages of journal each month but there had been so much to tell that it had grown into a regular missive of twenty pages. Now we wrote many letters and spent time preparing photos and videos because we were keen to show everyone why we were so fascinated by the place. At last our parcel was ready and on Monday morning I asked Patrick to drive me across town to the DHL office.

I emerged from the building and told an amused but not unsympathetic driver of my experience inside the building, at the hands of a four-year-old.

As I was waiting to be served a small boy scrutinised me carefully from my fair hair to the toes that protruded from my open sandals. Finally I was declared, loudly, to be 'whart' and strange-looking. The boy's mother showed equal amounts of embarrassment and amusement while trying to hush him but, predictably, this had the reverse effect. Soon the child took to somersaulting around the room, interrupting his tumbles only to glance upon my pallidness, grab his throat and pretend to gag using horrendous sound effects. My feet, apparently, were my worst feature. The boy would pause, inspect them carefully, then using a small finger, he'd prod my big toe. When I responded by wiggling it, he'd submit to another paroxysm of revulsion. The reputation of small boys everywhere was in reliable hands.

We proceeded to Bodija Markets and as I looked about, I realised how different it was to be here rather than merely seeing it on television. Enjoying being part of the scene, I listened to voices babbling in another language, to unfamiliar music, even the disconcerting hiss used by stallholders to attract my attention. Bells rang, horns tooted and the sound of laughter and arguments swam all around me, saturating me with atmosphere. The air was full of interesting smells as roasting corn and plantain sizzled on home-made grills over sawn-off drums. Everywhere I turned something new caught my eye. One moment my path would be blocked as a woman staggered around in laughter at a friend's amusing story, the next moment I was distressed as a frightened child ran from me, crying in fear at this white apparition.

"Hisss…here, *Oyinbo* (white person). Madame, please buy somethin'. Please, Madame, I beg."

"No thank you, no thank you, no thank you." It became my mantra as I declined the opportunity to buy a million things.

As well as being our driver, Patrick was fast becoming self-appointed bodyguard, interpreter and general assistant. If at a market I selected a carving and opened negotiations with what I thought to be just the right degree of disinterest, Patrick always interrupted, exclaiming in disbelief at the vendor's reply.

"What? Nor, nor, nor! Dat is too motch," and he'd throw up his hands in disgust and stride off. When I resumed negotiations, Patrick would return and similar skirmishes would follow, with me being given only minor parts to play. Suddenly he'd turn to me nonchalantly.

"It's hokay. Yo' kin pay 'im now, Marm."

I told him crossly that I would never develop bargaining skills if he kept interfering but he just chuckled, scrubbed his head and continued his unrepentant ways.

As we made our way through the cobweb of streets that had evolved into Bodija Market I looked at the food stacked everywhere. Large cardboard trays of eggs were stacked into small mountains, an endless variety of vegetables lay spread on the ground, and dried fish hung from poles. Vendors arranged crudely carved pieces of meat on open trays, swishing aside the flies so potential buyers could admire cuts to their full advantage. I had naively presumed that this abundance meant that no one went hungry in Nigeria, but I was finding that this wasn't the case. Now I looked at all the produce and wondered how it was that this profusion of food could coexist with widespread hunger. Surely in a hot climate, with little refrigeration, the forces of supply and demand would result in this abundance of perishable food being cleared daily at affordable prices? Shaking his head, Patrick told me that stallholders would let things spoil rather than sell at a loss.

I found this difficult to understand so I took my question to a fellow IITA resident, Maureen Akintewe, a Scot married to IITA's Nigerian doctor. She had lived in Nigeria for many years and had considerable knowledge of how things worked in Yorubaland. She was able to give me background information and a perspective that I would otherwise have missed. Pricing decisions, she told me, were not made unilaterally on the part of a stallholder. The market women's associations were quite powerful, particularly here in the south. One of their functions was to determine a fair price for any given commodity, taking into account prevailing market conditions. This, I now realised, explained the fierce exchanges that I sometimes heard between female stallholders while I shopped. I couldn't understand what they were saying, but I had guessed that nearby stallholders were checking any tendency of a colleague to undersell her peers. So Patrick's observation about them not selling at below-cost prices was correct because stallholders knew they had to be tough and united to survive. They were also astute and kept wastage to a minimum. What was left over after a long day's trading was the family's food for the day or was cooked and sold the next day as pre-cooked fare. Selling off produce at the end of the day's trading would not have worked here, Maureen told me. Customers would simply wait to get the cheaper prices, and soon the stallholder would be out of business.

I urgently needed more cotton clothes to cope with this climate, so I took the advice of Beatrice, Peter's secretary, and bought material at the markets. On a prearranged day, I gathered up the fabric and a dress to be copied, and called for her at FORMECU. Beatrice gave Patrick directions and he drove to a nearby suburb, then accompanied us as we walked through a maze of stalls, boxes, puddles, children and goats until we finally came to the tailor's workshop. We wobbled our way across a plank that acted as a bridge over a gaping drain and arrived at the tailor's premises. On his door was a large sign:

"JESUS IS LORD OF THIS HOUSE".

In keeping with the message, loud singing was coming from a back room:

"Praise de Lord, praise de Lord. All de pepples, praise de Lord."

Hopefully the Lord appreciated the sentiments because the tune left something to be desired. A young man appeared, doing an admirable job of singing and using a toothpick at the same time. A raised eyebrow inquired as to our business and with a flourish Beatrice spread the dress to be copied in front of him and asked the amount of material needed to make such a dress for Madame.

The Lord was deprived of praises momentarily while the tailor considered the question. Meanwhile Beatrice explained to me in a loud stage whisper that we would cut off any excess material before we left. That way, she added, I wouldn't be 'sheeted' out of my remnant.

"Nigeria," she informed me, "is full of sheets. When dey see yo' whart skin, dey say to demselves, " 'ere is someone I can sheet.' "

I wanted to ask what the Lord of the House would think of such goings-on but I concentrated instead on looking nonchalant as the tailor circumnavigated me, eyeing my proportions with a practised eye. An estimate was given, surplus material removed and a price agreed. We departed after setting a date for the collection of my new dress.

On the day arranged I walked into the tailor's shop to find the toothpick hard at work.

"I am sorry, Madame. Yo' will 'ave to come buck next week. De dress is not ready."

I was not impressed and before I left, I extracted a promise that it would certainly be ready the following week.

This time Beatrice insisted on coming too and we must have looked a formidable envoy as the three of us stomped across the plank and into the shop. Our friend came from the back room, switched the toothpick to a holding position and began a casual apology.

"Sorry, Madame, " he said, deliberately looking past Beatrice at me, the softer target. "I 'ave not finished. Come buck next..."

The remainder of his sentence was lost in the chorus of outrage from Beatrice and Patrick.

"Dis is too motch! Madame 'as come two times and yo' 'ave let 'er down. She is disappointed an' angry. It is jus' too motch!"

They continued their tirade, creating the level of hullabaloo I had come to expect of Nigerian confrontations. The tailor looked at each of us in turn with little sign of remorse. My facial expressions couldn't keep pace with the flurry of emotions being attributed to me so I put on a stern frown that hopefully covered them all while hiding my growing urge to laugh. Suddenly Beatrice delivered her trump card.

"We are goin' to sit 'ere until yo' *do* finish it!"

Following her lead I sat defiantly on a nearby chair. With a resigned shrug of one shoulder, the tailor disappeared and soon we were enduring songs better left to Mahalia Jackson. Eventually the garment arrived and we filed out, passing the next customer in the doorway. As we crossed the bridge Beatrice explained, "We 'ad to do dat at some stage, Pum. It may as well 'ave been dis week as next."

Just then we heard shouting from the shop, "Yo' said dat last week. I am jest goin' to sit 'ere until yo' finish it!"

What chance would I have had on my own?

Peter was not having things all his own way at the office. Unreliable power meant that Beatrice's computer and photocopier were of little use. Most of the staff found it impossible to work in the stifling heat, in inner rooms with no lights or air conditioners, so each time the power failed, they'd head outdoors to find cool places to sit until it was time to go home. Telephone communication with the rest of Nigeria was impossible and fuel shortages prevented urgently needed information being hand-delivered from outlying forestry areas. The team had worked at frenzied pace to prepare for a vitally important national workshop, which now looked like being cancelled because of transport problems.

One afternoon after shopping I called at the office to wait until Peter had finished for the day. The power came on suddenly and he asked me to help with typing while Beatrice quickly attended to some urgent photocopying. She reappeared and announced ruefully that the office was out of photocopying paper. It was all too much and Peter let the Almighty know of his frustration.

"God, I'd like to *shoot* somebody but I don't quite know who!" he thundered.

A head appeared around the corner of his office and we saw Andrew's dark eyes twinkling above a mock-serious expression. "Perhaps dat's fortunate, Sah..." and he hurried off down the corridor, chuckling.

Nigeria doesn't have summer and winter, just *harmattan* (dust haze) and the rainy season. Our arrival had coincided with the final stages of *harmattan* so we were to experience the rains before we felt the full effect of the dust that sweeps down each year from the Sahara. Already finished with Chad, one of Africa's driest nations, the rains lingered briefly in northern Nigeria, then pushed southwards, lengthening their stay at each place as they came. By the time they reached Ibadan in June, the season would last three months. The air was already growing oppressive in readiness.

One night I woke to discover that they had arrived. I remained awake enjoying the silver threads of lightning and the rumbled response of thunder that toured the sky before fading away. The morning sky was clear, marked only with little clouds, dots of white on a blue-grey background, but by afternoon they had thickened into storms that filled potholes and created slippery red mud underfoot.

The market places made few concessions to the changed conditions. People went about their business, carefully stepping between the puddles, sure of foot even on the glass-like surface of mud.

As we drove to the three supermarkets that I needed to visit each week to complete my list of Western-type groceries, I wondered about the garbage strewn along the roadside. Before the rainy season the smell of burning garbage often wafted across the roadways but now the rains had come and I waited to see if they caused their own odoriferous problems.

We discovered by accident that IITA had its own church services, including a Catholic Sunday Mass. Until now Patrick had arrived each week to drive us to Mass at Ibadan University and although he beamed at the opportunity to earn extra money, we felt uneasy about increasing his already long working hours. The IITA venue was more convenient but the following Sunday as we walked across to the Conference Centre, Peter and I agreed that we would miss the freshness and spontaneity of the congregation at the University.

We were pleasantly surprised to find that the Nigerian influence was not entirely lost at the IITA gathering because most of the congregation consisted of visitors from outside the gates, with staff providing a smattering of other nationalities. The priest and ourselves were the only Caucasians present and Peter and I looked with interest at the tall American clergyman from the nearby Jesuit community. We had heard of his charismatic personality and looked forward to his homily.

It was Pentecost and as the priest began to speak, he identified symbols that reminded him of the Holy Spirit. He held up a glove. In itself, he said, this is a lifeless object but just as a hand fills and enlivens a glove, so too does the Holy Spirit change the character of our lives. Then he gave a jaunty, optimistic thumbs up sign and asked if someone in the congregation could tell him what it meant. Silence. He waited patiently then repeated the gesture and the question. Another brief silence, then a Nigerian voice came from the back of the room.

"Farder, in Nigeria, dat means 'Up you!' "

Our burst of laughter brought down the priest too. Then, regaining a fragile composure, he struggled valiantly to salvage what he could of his theme but it had been dealt a mortal blow. Neither Peter nor I was much good for the remainder of Mass; a mere exchange of glances was enough to send us off into another attack of shoulder-shaking laughter which we were powerless to suppress. Eventually I turned to the rest of the congregation in helpless apology but saw only puzzled faces. The priest had asked a simple question and received a simple answer. What's so funny, their looks seemed to ask.

The following Sunday an Afro-American priest arrived and we sat transfixed as he spoke fiercely about the plight of the poor who had been tyrannised long enough by 'African despots'. His ancestral links lent passion and credibility to his words as he challenged us to give prayerful thought to our responsibility in tolerating or resisting oppression. There was no laughter that day and we walked home, deep in thought.

The date approached for the long-awaited national election, the one that had played havoc with our departure from Australia, and dark clouds and ominous rumblings were evident on more than the meteorological front. The political climate was also charged with suspense. Since Independence, Nigeria had experienced only brief periods of civilian rule and the most recent of these, between 1979 and 1983 had ended with yet another coup and all promises of democratic elections since then had proved empty.

Until lately there had been a sense of optimism that this time the election would actually happen but now a conviction was growing that all was not well. Against the tide, Peter's young colleagues Simon and Andrew clung to the hope that a president would be elected who had widespread support. Perhaps such a man would find solutions to Nigeria's serious economic and social problems.

Beatrice and Ayo were more cynical. They believed that the military had no intention of handing over genuine power or, if they did, that the new president would be no more honourable than the present one. They decided not to bother voting.

"De politicians are too corrupt. Already dey are buying votes. De results will be meaningless," Beatrice informed me, her round, cherubic face unusually glum.

Certainly, things were taking a strange turn. The fuel shortage was serious and cars queued two and three abreast for miles waiting for the 'fool' stations to receive their quota. The streets in these areas became hopelessly congested while the rest of the city was free of the usual heavy traffic. The previous week Peter had worked from home and Patrick had queued for forty-eight hours to obtain petrol so our car still functioned and Peter was able to get to the office when absolutely necessary. He had taken the precaution during times of plenty of having Patrick fill a couple of fuel containers. These were stashed in a locked concrete storage room at IITA and were to be kept for utmost emergencies. I curtailed my outings in our car, travelling with those IITA friends who were brave enough to take vehicles outside the gates. IITA cars remained mobile because, for the time being at least, IITA could provide each employee with a small weekly ration of fuel from its own reserves. I followed the example of friends and purchased extra food in case we had to withstand a siege.

International calls to IITA came via satellite so I could speak to the World Bank in Washington but not to Peter at his office. Ben rang to check on our welfare. The pre-election tension in Nigeria was, he told us, headline news in America and he advised us to remain at IITA and not accept the forestry house now awaiting us in the city. Oh, well, if we must.

Andrew was convinced that the fuel shortage and the near-continuous blackout were deliberately planned by the military government to incite riots. Civil unrest would justify the government sending in troops to maintain order and provide the perfect excuse to cancel the election.

The riots didn't eventuate but a strange sense of foreboding filled the air. Patrick was concerned.

"Anythin' could 'appen. Pepple are very angry," he said, in response to my question about the mood on the streets. As a precaution we sent him off to buy emergency supplies for himself and he took home a large bag of *gari* (a flour-like derivative of the staple crop cassava) and extra kerosene for cooking. The cost of food in the marketplace began to rise and everyone felt that things could only get worse.

Presidential Election Day, June 12, 1993, came and went and still the uneasy peace held. Days passed, then one afternoon those of us who were outdoors at IITA heard an excited roar coming from the city. We learned a rumour had filtered through that Chief Moshood Abiola, of the Social Democratic Party, had received widespread support and soon would be declared President. Before the election, a major fear had been that ethnic loyalties would prevent any candidate getting sufficiently widespread support to be considered a national leader. If the story of Abiola's victory was true, it was a remarkable result and indicated his unique qualifications for success. As a Yoruba, he was assured of support in the south west of Nigeria, but, unusually for a Yoruba, he also was a Muslim and this fact was sufficient to override prejudices in the northern states where the Islam faith predominated. To the people of Ibadan, his rumoured success was wonderful news. International scrutineers were declaring this a free and fair election and hopes soared.

Days passed without the results being officially announced and once more the tension mounted. At the office Andrew was like a caged lion as a new story circulated. The military was not impressed with the results, rumour had it, for Abiola was an unexpected winner and not 'their' man, and everyone knew that when the military was displeased, something had to give.

On June 26 1993 President Babingida addressed the nation and declared that the results of Nigeria's first democratic election in ten years were to be annulled in the national interest. Not enough people had turned out to vote, Babingida said, therefore the result was not a true representation of the nation's wishes.

Our Nigerian friends reacted with disbelief. Andrew was devastated and his mood alternated between anger and profound despair. The streets filled with people, students from universities around the nation began marching, searching for ways to force change. Frustration caused by the fuel shortage fed anger at the Military Government. Thousands of people demonstrated and every vehicle capable of moving was bedecked with green branches, the symbol of protest.

Peter had been working from home but before the annulment he had sent word to Patrick to come for him on the morning of the 27th as he needed to be at the office that day. When we heard the announcement, we thought that Patrick would assess the streets as unsafe, but to our surprise he arrived as scheduled. He looked stunned, but insisted that things were not too bad out there in the streets.

"Its hokay," he assured Peter. "Dey wone touch us," but his voice lacked conviction and Peter left not knowing what he'd find.

During the day I went to International House with my carton of money to pay the rent. As I chatted with desk staff I was alarmed to hear of the growing number of protests in the streets so it was a great relief to see Peter and Patrick walk in that afternoon. They looked jaded but I insisted they fill me in on their adventures immediately.

In the early afternoon everyone at the office had decided it would be prudent to head home as tension was mounting. Before leaving, Patrick had placed branches on the car to make it less conspicuous, hiding the 'CC' numberplates, which looked too official for Patrick's comfort. The vehicle suitably bedecked, they set out but had not gone far when they came across a barricade of burning tyres. They stopped some distance off and while they discussed what to do, Peter took the opportunity to roll the video camera. For once Patrick showed unease and suggested he put it out of sight.

The students had commandeered the city's buses and tens of thousands of people were walking home along the streets, but their mood was good-natured in spite of the inconvenience. Everyone seemed united in the wish to rid the country of this Military Government. Suddenly several truckloads of soldiers arrived and forced their way through the crowd, waving guns at the students who were armed with sticks. The protesters evaporated into the bushes at the sides of the road so the troops removed the barricades and drove through, proceeding slowly up the road, their guns at the ready. Patrick, keeping a few cars between himself and the troop carriers managed to slip through before the protesters reappeared. Slow but consistent progress followed until the troops turned off and their paths diverged.

The journey home continued, with many stops and detours. At one crowded barricade Peter reined in the excitable Patrick who wanted to turn and search for another route. Peter was tired of detours that landed them further from home than ever so he told Patrick to stay put. Asked to interpret the shouts and chants of the mob, Patrick reported that the protesting students had run out of fuel for burning the tyres on the road. Suddenly about fifty demonstrators surrounded the car, banging it with their fists and demanding money and petrol from the tank to continue the fight for democracy. Peter remained inside but Patrick jumped out and joined the melee. For minutes it appeared that everyone was shouting and no one was listening but suddenly Patrick returned to the car and started the engine. A portion of the barricade was removed, the crowd parted and he drove through.

Now, in our lounge room, I was full of admiration for our driver and I asked him what he had said to the protesters. Patrick had the grace to look sheepish.

"I jes said Sah is an American an' America is on de side of democracy, so why tekk it out on 'im?"

The students had seen on CNN television that the United States of America were strong international supporters of Nigerian democracy so Patrick's argument carried the day. I told Patrick I thought him very brave and I commended Sir for showing considerable intelligence by sitting tight-lipped in the car. Later we were to play a joke on family by sending home a video of the brief shots Peter had obtained, fleshed out with excerpts from *Out of Africa* where lions charged and *Maasai* warriors shook spears defiantly. But such hijinks were far from our minds today.

Civil unrest and near-riots continued for a few days but things eventually settled sufficiently for Peter and his colleagues to proceed with an important bush trip east through Benin City to Enugu. This was new territory for me so I decided to accompany them, although I suspected I was again coming down with malaria. My resolution not to diagnose my own illnesses had worn off so I dosed myself up and set out with throbbing head, aching joints and 'twistin' belly' as Mrs Aziz would say. Somehow Patrick had obtained sufficient fuel to fill both tanks of the FORMECU Land Cruiser plus a few jerry cans so we concealed the fuel cans in cartons and set out on the four-day excursion.

Before we cleared Ibadan we were stopped by demonstrators and were told, quite politely in English, that if we proceeded through the barricade ahead, the vehicle would be 'spoiled'. Patrick found an alternative route out of town. In Benin City the riot police were out in force, brandishing shields, tear-gas cylinders and guns and as we watched them making arrests, I shuddered for the young men we saw being led away. As we made our way through streets strewn with debris, we were pulled over by police and Peter was asked if he had any complaints to make against demonstrators. He prudently reported that all was well.

After a seven-hour journey we reached Enugu and settled into a comfortable hotel. My condition worsened and next day I could not join the touring party on its field trip. During the day I turned on the television to hear on CNN that in Nigeria, Lagos had exploded into violence and dozens were dead in the streets. We later learned that the number killed was seventy-four.

Feeling slightly better I ventured out with the team the following day and was impressed by their dedication. Inspections of troublesome erosion sites completed, they decided to work late investigating the worth of non-timber forest products in the region. Selflessly they sampled the local palm wine, which can have an alcohol content of up to seventy percent. I manned the video camera to ensure that their professional assessment, which grew more effusive as sampling proceeded, was recorded for posterity. I also kept a watchful eye on the drivers to ensure that they were not recruited into the impromptu research team. Full of anti-malarial drugs, I also abstained, grateful of an excuse to avoid the evil-looking brew that bubbled out of bottles and jars.

During the journey back to Ibadan Peter developed malaria

too, and we jolted along in feverish silence, longing for the journey to end so that we could be miserable in the comfort of our little unit. But first we had to run the gauntlet of more demonstrators. In Benin City we were stopped at a blockade by a crowd of several hundred people and because there was no alternative route Patrick was all for ramming through the obstacles in our heavy vehicle but Peter was unwilling to do so. We sat there in a stalemate, the focus of attention of hundreds of demonstrators. Suddenly a large bus approached from the opposite direction and as one, the protesters rushed to block its path, reinforcing the debris that littered that side of the road and forming a human wall around the bus. As the demonstrators banged their fists on the bus and others shouted at the passengers, we were momentarily forgotten in the noise and chaos. Peter and Patrick exchanged looks and with a whoop of excitement Patrick took the vehicle through the most fragile part of the barricade and we were off. Seeing what had happened, the crowd tried to catch us but we were gone, their shouts and Patrick's "Yi, Yi, Yi!"'s echoing in our aching heads.

Home at last, we felt too ill to be more than mildly interested to learn that Ibadan too had suffered several bloody riots during our absence, although not on the same scale as Lagos. Our appetites for excitement were quite satiated for the time being. We visited the doctor then took ourselves off quietly to our sick-beds.

The election remained annulled, and Abiola, the one said to have won the election, fled the country when rumours circulated about his imminent arrest. Nigerians realised that once again their attempt at democracy had been thwarted. The press reminded the people of the nation's suffering during the Biafran war back in 1967-70, and Nigeria pulled back from the brink of civil war.

Chapter 8
VISITORS & VISAS

Almost two weeks passed before Peter and I felt the exuberance that we had come to expect as the aftermath of malaria. Now, feeling wonderful, I walked out to the car one morning, to be greeted by Patrick's concerned enquiry.

"Mornin', Marm. 'Ows de body?"

Nigerians enquiring into the state of my health had often asked me this question and unless I was still feeling particularly unwell, I always struggled to resist saying: 'Actually, it could do with a bit off here and here...'

With my return to health, I longed for a decent steak and I let wishful thinking overrule wisdom. I bought two respectable looking T-bones from the supermarket and that night we settled ourselves in front of the carefully prepared meal, full of happy anticipation. I bit down and my jaws rebounded as if from indestructible rubber. My eyes swung to Peter's face and I saw my own shock reflected there. Through full mouths, we vowed to persevere and we gnawed on, giving our all, encouraging the other when efforts flagged. But, alas, no further injury could be inflicted upon the unfortunate beast. Peter's shoulders slumped from exhaustion as we stared defeat in the face. We kept starvation at bay by consuming extra vegetables. There just had to be steak available that was better than this.

We sought guidance and incredible pieces of advice flooded in. Pound the meat before frying. We ate thin rubber. Wrap each steak in papaw leaves for an hour before grilling. We were left with an unattractive, slippery mess. Soak the meat in milk overnight before cooking. No way. Each suggestion sounded more repulsive that the last. Then, Indira, a Sri Lankan friend, provided a grain of hope, "I'll send Mr Titoloye to see you. He sells reasonable meat, pork and prawns, but remember to shout at him if he tries to charge too much," she advised.

I awaited his arrival with mixed feelings, at last hopeful that we might get decent meat but worried that I would come off second best in the financial dealings, for I am not a good shouter.

A few days later I opened our front door and knew instantly that I was gazing at Mr Titoloye himself. Standing there was a wizened little man dressed in voluminous robes. Perched on top of his small head was a bright green cap, a hula of the same fabric as his *agbada* and slim-legged pants. Suddenly I found myself paraphrasing somebody, perhaps Twain or Dickens: here was the smallest man I had ever seen, wearing the largest robes I had ever seen.

His sweeping bow caused such a flurry of green satin that he almost disappeared, then the perky little face re-emerged well below my own. The ritual of greeting over, I was then treated with friendly condescension as the apparition swept past me into our lounge room, announcing that he knew he was expected because de other Madame had told him so. Now, if we could get down to business, he would take my order but first I must open my account with him by handing over N1000.

I knew instinctively that this was the time to start shouting but the words didn't come. The best I could manage was to clear my throat and pretend to be a fastidious shopper.

"Are the prawns fresh?" My voice sounded high-pitched, not the intimidating boom I had hoped for.

"Nearly alive, Madame," was the breezy reply. "Dey 'ave no 'eads but de 'ands are still hon. Now," and a small finger waved authoritatively under my nose to ensure I was listening closely, "all de Madames at IITA 'ave accounts wit me. We must write dis down." Uninvited, he pulled out a chair and seated himself at the table.

"See, I 'ave written dat yo' pay me N1000 today. Each time

yo' buy, I deduct de purchases. Now, yo' want prawns? Please bring me yo' kitchen scales, Madame. Dat way, yo' doan sheet me an' I doan sheet yo'." The finger wagged furiously at the very thought.

As I scurried to obey, I saw that Peter's jaw had finally lifted from the floor, and he was now barely containing his mirth so I frowned menacingly at him, knowing it was imperative for my self-esteem that I retain authority over *someone*.

Before handing over the money I decided to take a stand. I relieved the vendor of his sheet of paper and made the necessary entries in the Debit and Credit columns. The little face folded into a picture of polite frustration at my interference but when he regained possession of the sheet and looked over my entries, he grudgingly admitted that they did indeed reflect the facts. A few arrows, however, from here to here and from there to there, would make things much easier to understand. With a triumphant flourish, he held under my nose a document that now looked more like construction plans for a satellite than a pork and prawn account.

"Yo' fillet steak, Madame. Do yo' want it clean?" Peter's guffaw from the corner did nothing for my equilibrium. I really must demonstrate some authority.

"Mr Titoloye, I will not buy *any* food that isn't clean. If your meat isn't clean, please take it away." My tone said clearly: Don't mess with *this* housewife.

I was rewarded with a pained expression. "All I meant, Madame, is do yo' want your fillet steak free of bone an' gristle?" I wondered at the quality of any fillet steak that provided this option, but I was a broken woman. I replied that yes, please, I would prefer it clean, if that was OK with him.

He left at last and I tolerated, with sour amusement, Peter's laughter at my expense. Much of the remainder of the day was spent wishing I had used Indira's suggestion and shouted long and loud. My mood did not improve when, that evening, I cooked the fillet steak with utmost care, only to find it came from a near-relative of the beast that had enjoyed the last laugh over us only days earlier. Next evening, we tackled the prawns. They were wonderful. Ah, come back Mr Titoloye. All is forgiven.

I wondered why some people were enthusiastic about having their photos taken while others recoiled whenever a camera or video appeared. We knew of the legal restrictions on photographing official buildings so we carefully avoided filming government property but we were disconcerted to hear that recently, an IITA staff member, while carrying a permit to film certain sites off campus, had been arrested and taken to a police station. A policeman offered, for a considerable sum, to help him sort out the problem of his arrest, but the prisoner had refused to co-operate. Eventually the frustrated police released him without having supplemented their income, but by then the photographer had spent half a day in jail. I preferred that something similar did not happen to us.

There were no restrictions on filming on IITA of course, so I invited Patrick to bring his family for a visit the following Sunday and we would take a family portrait of them. He was delighted at the idea.

On Sunday when Patrick emerged from the car, we saw him for the first time in traditional dress. He wore a long over-shirt and matching pants in a rich burgundy colour. We were solemnly introduced to Mercy, his wife, and two daughters Gladys and Margaret, aged ten and eight years respectively and Christina, aged six, a young relative living with them. Mercy looked magnificent in a multicoloured wrap-around skirt and a gold embroidered blouse that showed up her honey-brown skin to perfection. The skirt was bright with swirls of red and gold and a bright red headscarf finished the outfit. The children wore Western style dresses, shoes and socks. I received a jolt when I saw that the girls' heads were closely shaved because I recalled Beatrice's daughter's delightful topknots. Then I remembered that in the poorer suburbs heads are kept close-cropped to help with hygiene.

Our welcome to the children was received with wide-eyed seriousness. Obviously, they were nervous about this whole exercise. I forgot that all conversation must go through the male and several times I addressed Mercy directly. Each time, she turned her head to Patrick and looked enquiringly at him.

"Mercy is having trouble understanding my accent, Patrick," I said apologetically but he denied this immediately. Then the penny dropped and I remembered the cultural influences. *This is just great*, I thought sardonically. *I can talk to Patrick every day of the week.*

The children were extremely shy and no smiles lit their tense young faces as they sat rigidly to attention. They bowed their thanks when given food and soft drinks, but didn't speak a word. When we moved outside to the attractive gardens, we had them pose in a range of different combinations for the camera. We soon gathered that informal poses were off the agenda. This was a serious business and even smiles might detract from the final result. Use of the video camera produced particularly severe bouts of moribund behaviour, somewhat detracting from the whole point of the exercise, I thought. Later, when Peter connected the camera to the television, the children's jaws hung open in amazement at seeing themselves on the screen. They exchanged shocked glances then the first hint of smiles appeared, but never the relaxed, uninhibited behaviour we had enjoyed with Beatrice's children.

Today, as well as having the Iyasele family visit us, we had arranged for a tour of the city. I was nervous about filming but Patrick assured us it would be OK and after his handling of the rioting students, I had to believe him.

The seven of us piled into the car and drove to Patrick's home to drop off the family. I was about to say goodbye when I overheard Patrick and Mercy speaking in Yoruba, then Patrick addressed me with a return to the shyness I hadn't seen for many weeks.

"Marm, would yo' mind entering a dirty 'ouse?" His fingers fluttered in front of him anxiously as he waited for my response. I guessed that his words probably meant something like 'How do you feel about entering a house that is humbler than what you are used to?' I was chuffed to be asked and soon we were following him towards a three-storey concrete-brick building. As we walked along, we were greeted with smiles and nods from dozens of bystanders outside the building and here and there Patrick beckoned forward friends to introduce them, but we were not approached by anyone else. Dozens of poorly dressed children scampered around in a game of chasey on the compacted red dirt of the street. I was surprised to note that Patrick left the car unlocked, the first time I had seen him do this. Obviously he felt secure here on his own patch.

Patrick answered our questions as we wound our way up a series of staircases. I estimated that each floor of the building covered about the same area as a large suburban house in Australia, but here, each level housed five families. At last Patrick drew aside a curtain and we entered a large room crammed with a lounge suite, a neatly made double bed, a fridge, a dining table and chairs. Perched high on a shelf was a black and white television set. When we sat down, Mercy and the children brought us minerals then disappeared, not to be seen again this visit.

I was relieved that we weren't offered anything to eat because it is a fact of life that our Western stomachs couldn't cope with food prepared and stored in the local manner. The bottles of carbonated drink provided the ideal answer to our host's responsibilities. As we accepted the drinks, the front-door curtain was brushed aside and a young man stepped inside the room and introduced himself only as 'Patrick's brother'. Obviously, we'd arrived during his ablutions because his only garment was a towel draped around his waist. He made no reference to his unusual attire and throughout our visit he conducted a friendly, relaxed conversation with utmost poise. Patrick stood quietly by, leaving the talking to the younger man who, we learned, worked in a bank in Lagos and came home on weekends.

"Yo' are welcome," he said, then his face formed into a mischievous smile. "Not *all* wharts would 've come," and keeping a precautionary hand on the towel, he sprang up and strutted around the room in a contemptuous swagger, swishing his elbows. Patrick clapped his hands in mirth and nearly fell over laughing.

The young man lowered himself back onto the chair. "Patrick's friends will be jealous," he continued, piling on the flattery. "We like meetin' whart pepple." He inspected us closely, then running fingers across the steel-wool hair that covered his own head, he added unexpectedly, "Yo' all 'ave such nice 'air."

My unruly mop of hair was not coping well with African conditions, but I took the opportunity to throw an arch look at Peter as his hand went instinctively to his near-bald pate.

"*Do* we?" he asked incredulously, and amidst the general laughter it was agreed that perhaps the compliment had been a bit too general. I caught my husband's eye. *Serves you right for enjoying my suffering at the hands of Mr Titoloye*, my look signalled.

The Women's Group had a final meeting and break-up luncheon before going into recess for the holiday period. This was Nancy's final meeting as chairperson. She had been an impressive president, keeping the meetings focused and effective and showing diplomacy when traditional rivalries flared between women of different nationalities and religious groupings. No doubt this required considerable self-control on Nancy's part because, from what I knew of her already, she had little patience with such 'narn-sense'.

A week ago I had been puzzled by a curt dismissal when I'd made a prearranged phone call to Zareena, a member of the Women's Group, to finalise plans for accompanying her to the children's home. The purpose of the planned visit was to give me more experience in handling orphanage visits before everyone left on annual leave. But Zareena now indicated that I was not welcome to accompany her. I asked a friend what could have caused the sudden change of attitude. My sin, I was told, was to be seen talking in a friendly manner to someone she disliked, a woman whose religious beliefs were opposed to her own. Zareena took a dim view of me fraternising with her enemy and as a consequence, our joint visit to see the children was off.

A few days later there was a knock at my front door and there stood Zareena, petite of frame and demure of manner. As usual, she wore traditional costume, swathed in layers of floating pinks and lilacs, with a soft wrap draped flatteringly over her dark hair.

As she accepted my invitation to come in, I caught the soft fragrance of the perfume she always wore, one that called to mind not squabbles, but trees and flowers and open fields on beautiful days.

She took a seat and told me in a subdued voice that Nancy had heard of our telephone conversation and had called to remind her that personal hostilities were to be left out of all Women's Group matters. To her credit Zareena had accepted Nancy's censure and had come to apologise.

Later, I told Nancy of the visit. "Well, now, I couldn't be more pleased," Nancy drawled happily. "I *told* her to get her butt around there and say sorry." Somehow I couldn't imagine even Nancy using exactly those words with Zareena, but whatever the expression used, it proved effective.

Zareena, her adversary and I were to form an uneasy triangle for the remainder of my Nigerian stay. Many times I had to insist upon a change of subject whenever the 'enemy' was mentioned, making it clear to whichever was my companion, that I was not prepared to discuss their dispute.

The following week I was about to depart for the children's home on my first solo visit, when Mrs Raj, a visitor to IITA from India, phoned and asked if she could come too. She was staying at IITA for a few months with her son and although she enjoyed visiting the children, she did not have a vehicle at her disposal. Patrick and I loaded the food I had prepared then we called at the Raj house to collect our passenger.

As we drove up the driveway of the Remand Centre, as everyone called the complex, we overtook Taju who was returning from the street, carrying an empty cardboard box. The children greeted us quietly and as we began to take the food inside, Mrs Raj suggested that our purses would be safe in the car because the driver would be there to mind them. But Patrick had no intention of staying in the car.

I realised that Nigerian men didn't usually get involved in the hands-on care of their children. Now, as a toddler wrapped tiny arms around Patrick's knees, he hesitated, then bending down, he scooped the little girl up into his arms. From that moment on, Patrick was an equal partner in my work with the children. He washed hands, wiped faces, fed open mouths and chatted away to them in Yoruba throughout our visits. His presence also meant I could communicate with the children, making a tremendous difference in my relationships with them.

Bose told me that the baby we had seen in the dormitory last week, had died only hours earlier. For a moment I relived the sensation of that tiny hand clasping my finger. Taju disappeared into the dormitory and the significance of his cardboard box hit me. The little body was to be disposed of in a cardboard box marked 'Paper Rolls'. I pushed away a host of complicated emotions to deal with them later. I wished Nancy were there. Along with her affection for the kids was a realistic attitude that would have helped me cope with the cheapness of life I saw all around me.

As we were about to feed the children, I heard a commotion nearby and a tall, thin man appeared, dragging a protesting child by the scruff of the neck. I could not understand the words of the man or the unfortunate teenager but I could see that somehow I was involved in the discussion. Stopping in front of me, the man replaced the angry expression on his face with a simpering smile while keeping a firm hold on the trembling boy. He introduced himself as the warden in charge, and apologised for the youth, a new arrival, who was refusing to go to the well because it meant passing near me, a white person.

"Go on, greet her!" the man shouted and unceremoniously shoved him forward. The terrified boy prostrated himself on the ground in front of me and remained there, perhaps waiting for some terrible white magic to smite him.

I asked Patrick to tell him that I would not harm him in any way. On hearing this, the child scrambled to his feet, his eyes still enormous, and after one more glance at me, he took to his heels in the direction of the well.

The warden loitered a few minutes, addressing me in jovial manner before returning to the Remand Section. When he next appeared, he was holding the arm of a different child, beating him with a thick stick. As the child cried out, Mrs Raj, who was standing nearby, turned and remonstrated with the warden, telling him sharply to stop or he would kill the child. The man said something to Bose but ceased the beating and disappeared into the building. My main concern was what would happen after we left. It had been stressed to members of our Women's Group that no 'meddling' would be tolerated. Later I asked Patrick about the incident and he confirmed my fears.

"He said dat 'e would just wait until yo' leave den de boy will get what 'e deserves," he replied.

One of the most difficult things I had to accept about Nigeria was the level of physical punishment that was acceptable. In environments such as this institution, where little affection and few legal restraints stayed the hands of untrained 'carers', punishment was often extreme. I admired Mrs Raj's courage but I feared the consequences.

As the morning wore on, we saw that it was indeed a bad day. Little Friday, the two-year-old I had mistaken for an infant last week, was deteriorating. When he was lifted from the sheet of cardboard on the floor and placed on a stool, he showed no interest in the food but leaned forward and lay his small head on the table-top and stared into the distance with glazed eyes. His chest rattled with every breath and he did not respond to anything Patrick said to him. I knew that unless we did something, Taju would soon be searching for another cardboard box.

I offered the use of the car to take him to medical assistance but with a worried frown and a furtive glance towards the upper building, Bose refused my offer, saying she preferred to wait until tomorrow. If Friday were still refusing food, she would take him then. I knew that it wouldn't happen. Nature was going to be allowed take its course. I could see that Bose was intimidated by the warden, but I was too unfamiliar with the politics of the place to know how best to support her without ruffling his feathers. Meanwhile, the child's need was urgent. Most of the IITA women had left a few days earlier, so I decided to locate Cielo, the lady with whom I was sharing the orphanage visits, as soon as I got back to IITA, and ask her advice.

Her response was immediate. "Let's go. Be outside your unit in ten minutes and we'll take the child to hospital and pay expenses. We'll think of something to say to the warden," she said, living up to Nancy's description of her as a 'doer'.

When we arrived at the home, I explained our reappearance as tactfully as possible to Bose, adding that we feared tomorrow would be too late. This time, she only hesitated for a moment, then gathered up the child and came with us to the Catholic hospital where Cielo and Nancy had taken Joseph, the amputee.

I looked around the hospital. Considering the general chaos that was being experienced throughout Nigeria, I was impressed. I could hardly believe the sheer number of people milling about and I couldn't distinguish between in-patients, outpatients and visitors. Wards were sparsely furnished but clean and nurses in neat uniforms moved about between the people. Although services were stretched to the limit, we eventually reached the head of our particular queue and a tired young doctor examined Friday who had rested listlessly in Bose's arms all the while. Without expending any of his remaining energy on pleasantries, the doctor diagnosed a severe lung infection and wrote a prescription. I joined yet another queue leading to the hospital pharmacy. By the time we delivered Bose and Friday back to the Home, it was late afternoon.

I had noticed that unless we insisted otherwise, food was offered to the children for a short time only, then removed. The strong children could wolf down enough food in that time, but any child who was too listless to eat quickly or who had difficulty swallowing, often got no more than a few mouthfuls. Cielo and I decided that one of us would visit each day until little Friday was well, to spend time encouraging him to eat and to ensure that the staff remembered his medication. Next day was Cielo's turn and she rang afterwards to report that she could already see an improvement in him. Although he still was not eating, his breathing was quieter and more regular. Bit by bit our efforts were rewarded. Next the little battler began to eat small amounts and by the end of the week I heard a delighted chuckle from Patrick.

"Yi, yi, yi! Dat little Friday, he squeaked at me when I tried to put de milk away. He is goin' to be hokay, Marm," he said with a laugh.

And so he was. One day Patrick announced excitedly that he had received a smile. Next visit, with a bit of coaching, he and Patrick were exchanging hi fives. He was turning into a handsome child. Then, a few weeks later we arrived one day to be told that Friday was no longer there.

"I think 'e will be well cared for by de doctor and his wife who adopted 'im, Madame," was Bose's explanation.

I couldn't help but feel sad that Patrick, Cielo and I had not said goodbye to him, but it was a timely reminder that we were only bit players in the drama of these children's lives. All things considered, I was pleased to go home and tell Cielo of Friday's new chance in life.

That evening I selected threads of green and white to work bright, hopeful colours into my tapestry.

Before leaving Australia I had purchased birthday gifts for family members and left others in charge of presenting them at the appropriate time. Now I felt flat at having no one to buy for. I decided to remedy the situation.

"Patrick, when do Mercy and the children have their birthdays?" I asked. To his credit, he was able to provide the information and I was pleased to hear that Mercy's birthday was only three weeks away.

"Let's buy her a birthday gift," I said. "You can be thinking about what we should get her."

"Ahh. I know what she'd like, Marm. She would like some whart material for a dress, material from Guinea." It was settled. Patrick was to ask around for the best place to buy and when the day came, we set out for markets at New Bodija. We arrived early in the day after dropping Peter at work and walked up and down the alleyways between the open-fronted stalls crammed with everything one could imagine. As I stepped into the entrance of one, Patrick drew my attention to women as they stood in a close circle at the back of the tiny shop.

"Jes a minute, Marm, dey are prayin'." Only then I noticed their posture and back-pedalled. Eventually they turned to us and soon had us half-buried in bolts of material. I stepped outside the little shop so that he could make the final selection himself, but suddenly he rejoined me, his hands massaging not only his head, but face too.

"It's too motch money, Marm," he said in worried fashion. "We need five metres an' dat comes to N300. Dat's too motch for yo' to pay." I decided that $12 was not outrageous for an entire outfit.

"Its OK, Patrick. Go and get it." He disappeared into the shop, only to re-emerge a minute later.

"But, Marm...it is *N300!*" I banished him back into the shop.

This time when he emerged, his eyes were sparkling with excitement. "Yi, yi, yi! I will ask Sah if I can take it 'ome at lunchtime. She will be *so* 'appy."

My protests that it was to be kept until her birthday didn't even register.

That evening when Peter came home, he was laughing. "What on earth is Patrick so excited about? I could hardly understand a word he said. All I got was that he just *had* to take the car home at lunch time to see Mercy."

I had enjoyed the exercise as much as Patrick had done.

When we were preparing to come to Nigeria, we'd been granted visas for three months and told that people staying longer had to apply from within Nigeria for an extension. In good time we gave our application to Femi, a clerk in the Lagos office of the World Bank, whose responsibility it was to follow the matter through. We reminded him that all the relevant documents had been hand-delivered to him as requested, when we first arrived in the country. He assured us that he would attend to the matter.

Days and weeks passed and in spite of our increasingly frantic reminders, no renewed visas appeared and finally our existing ones expired. Meanwhile, political tension was mounting again as it became obvious that President Babingida had no intention of honouring promises he'd made during the last outbreak of rioting.

Ben, the young assistant to the World Bank's African Project Manager, rang from Washington to warn us that we might have to leave the country at short notice if things worsened, so we felt particularly vulnerable at not having visas. Phone contact within Nigeria (beyond IITA gates) was a fluky affair. I tried for days to be connected to the Lagos office of the World Bank and when I finally succeeded in speaking to Femi, he said he had sent our papers to Abuja, but now they were required back in Lagos and this was causing the delay. He filibustered when I asked why he had sent the documents to Abuja, but he promised to follow up the matter immediately and if I would ring him back after two o'clock, he would update me on the state of affairs.

I could have written the script before I made the call. Amazingly, I got through to Lagos but there all progress ended. "Yo' will 'ave to ring back another day, Madame. Femi is not on seat. No, Madame, 'e is not expected back agin dis afternoon. Dat is why you 'ave to ring back another day."

The situation could not be left unresolved so I persevered over the following week, but even when I managed to be connected, I got nowhere. Femi was not on seat; Femi was in a meeting; Femi was away ill today. Femi was going to be strangled when I got hold of him.

We were in Nigeria without visas and I did not like the feeling one bit.

Chapter 9

PASSPORTS, PAPERS AND PULLING SWIFTIES

Above the sound of my gnashing teeth, I overheard Peter arranging for Patrick to drive Simon and Ajayi, a FORMECU colleague, to Lagos the following day. I decided to go with them, to see if the personal approach would prove more effective than phone calls had been in obtaining either residency permits or extensions of our visas.

Mid-morning next day, Patrick delivered me at the gates of the World Bank compound. Inside the building I paused in front of the elevator that, in theory, should whisk me to the fourth floor. I poked my head warily through its open doors and saw vital organs hanging from the control panel. No sign declared that the lift was out of order and I knew that if I offered a small incentive to one of the young men standing nearby, he'd probably connect a few wires and have us on our way, but I wasn't tempted. Deciding that the exercise would do me good, I turned towards the stairs.

As I puffed my way up the stairs, battling the heat and the humidity, I had an inspirational moment. It was time to apply one of my own counselling tenets - if something isn't working, stop doing it. I paused at the entrance to the fourth floor and as my gasps subsided, I resolved never to deal with Femi again. I turned and retraced my steps to the level below, intending to see the Manager of the World Bank in Nigeria. I approached his receptionist's desk and when she heard my name, her eyes grew wide in recognition and she launched into her own agenda.

"Mrs *Crunny*! We been tryin' to contact yo'. Are yo' hokay?"

Then her brow furrowed into a stern frown. "If we don't reach yo' by phone *every* week, yo' must ring us or send word somehow. With all de riots goin' on, we must have regular contact with yo'".

I told her that although I appreciated her concern, I had a problem and until that was sorted out all other matters were mere trifles. I asked her assistance in getting to see the manager as soon as possible. I was midstream with my request when a tall, fair-headed man emerged from a nearby office and we pounced. When we had been introduced, I explained my visa dilemma. He was tsk tsk-ing before I even finished.

"This is preposterous. Someone is holding out for a bribe. We'll get to the bottom of it immediately," he said and instructed his secretary to introduce me to a senior staff member, Gordon 'Uzor. As we trudged downstairs, I felt a glimmer of hope that I might be getting somewhere at last. I was shown into the office of a pleasant looking man whose appearance and accent made me think immediately of West Indian cricketers.

Gordon was charming and time proved him to be a wonderful support during the remainder of our stay in Nigeria. Now, over tea and biscuits, he listened to my sorry saga. When I finished speaking, he pressed the intercom on his desk and asked that Sunday Osobo join us. A dapper little man came in, his whole manner suggesting competence. At Gordon's request, I again outlined the problem, this time with commendable brevity.

Sunday eyed me coolly and with a mild edge to his voice said, "Yo' first mistake was to send de papers to Abuja, Madame. Yo' *should* have just handed them to Femi..."

Aghhh! It was too much. As punishment for doubting me, he was subjected to the unabridged version and as he listened, his brow fell into creases. I could almost hear the whirr of cogs behind his shrewd expression. He and Gordon exchanged grim smiles and slow nods as they listened.

"Sunday, collect all the documentation from Femi's desk and take Mrs Cranny to the Department of Immigration to sort this out, please," Gordon said. "When you get the Crannys' passports, they are *not* to be out of your sight. If the Immigration Department wish to photocopy pages, go with them. I repeat, the passports are *not* to be out of your sight."

As we reached the door I heard his intercom click. "Please tell Femi to come here. *Immediately.*"

As the World Bank driver wrestled our vehicle across the city to the Immigration Department, I tried to discuss tactics with Sunday and to remind him that Certificates of Residency, rather than extended visas, would be the ideal solution for us. I also mentioned that I had photocopies of twelve of the fourteen documents that had gone astray, should they be necessary. Sunday didn't seem particularly interested and asked no questions about the remaining two documents. He gave the clear impression that all would be well if I simply left everything to him.

"But...but..."

"Don't worry, Madame. Photocopies won't be necessary. Everyt'ing will be hokay," he said soothingly.

I wished I shared his confidence. I had heard Gordon telling him to take photocopies of everything on our file, yet he had ignored the instruction. I was beginning to wonder if he were the right man for this job.

I was surprised when our driver stopped in a depressed area, at the security gates of an enclosure containing one-storey 'temporary' structures in poor condition. The windows of most buildings were broken or had glass that had been painted, then a large portion of the paint scratched off, presumably to let in more light. We got out of the car and I followed Sunday as he meandered in the general direction of the buildings that stood on three sides of a large, dusty courtyard. There were people everywhere and Sunday seemed intent on greeting them all. I traipsed behind, not being introduced but welcomed by friendly nods and smiles from all and sundry.

As we neared the entrance to the closest building, Sunday stopped again and with great deference, greeted a huge woman who was bursting out of a shabby khaki uniform. The two engaged in a ritual of hand-slapping pleasantries, responding at length to each other's exhaustive inquiries into the state of their health and that of their families. Eventually the lady told Sunday that although the boss was not on seat at the moment, he probably would be back soon.

She swept me inside to a waiting area and invited me to sit, but every chair that was blessed with a seat in its frame already had a bottom firmly ensconced. This was no obstacle to the large lady who tapped a young man on the shoulder and told him, loudly, that he was wanted outside. With a cheerful smile, she offered me the empty chair and went out to join Sunday in the shade of a tree.

Near me, an Immigration Department employee juggled a fistful of passports as he sat entering details in a dog-eared foolscap pad on his lap. Suddenly the documents slipped from his grasp and showered around the room, disappearing under chairs and between boxes that were stacked nearby. He gathered up the little books but as he settled again to his task, he became discontented with his rickety chair. A passport wedged beneath the shortest leg worked wonders. He resumed work and as I glanced down at an open passport, I wondered if the *Oyinbo* pictured there had any idea of the perils facing his precious document. I breathed a prayer of thanks for Gordon and his injunction to Sunday that our passports not leave his sight.

From where I sat I could hear the booming voice of Large Lady declaring how much assistance she had given the World Bank over the years and now she needed an air-conditioner. Surely the World Bank had one that needed writing-off? Sunday didn't know of any but he *did* have a personal friend in the electrical business, who offered wonderful bargains in certain circumstances. Large Lady appeared satisfied with this news.

She came inside and fell into conversation with a colleague while Sunday disappeared to places unknown. Suddenly she realised that he was missing.

"Where dat World Bank mun?" she bellowed.

The question was delivered with the cadence and volume of a machine gun and caught me so unawares that I leaped into the air in fright. The woman hoisted herself from her chair and lumbered off in the direction of the yard, a formidable sight. My nerves stopped jangling in time for me to look out and witness the recapture of Sunday. The two spoke briefly and I saw him slip a roll of money into her hand. When they came back inside, Large Lady disappeared through a door beside my chair, then reappeared almost immediately to invite Sunday and me into the small office.

She had been the only one through that door since I had arrived and as I glanced around the office, Sherlock Holmes-style, I noticed that the only other opening was a window with security bars. *Ergo*, I surmised that the gentleman who sat gazing at us from behind the desk had been 'on seat' all the while.

We sat down and I was introduced to the official who looked at me with interest but addressed all questions and comments to Sunday. To my chagrin, Sunday put little effort into pleading our case and made no reference to my exhaustive and frustrating efforts. The only words to come from my knight in shining armour was a timid request for an extension of the visas and a letter of authority to enable us to proceed with an application for residency permits. Then he sat in silence. The official said nothing as he leafed through our passports. Occasionally he glanced up at me with curiosity, then continued his perusal.

"Dey bin lots o'places," he said at last, with more envy than accuracy. Sunday held his peace while I sat silently rehearsing the words I'd use when I took over the negotiations, for it was looking likely that I'd have to do it myself after all. The man shut my passport and said the words I'd been dreading.

"Many documents are needed if I am to issue de extension. Nothing can 'appen until I 'ave dem all." I glanced at Sunday, but he just sat there with an infuriatingly blank look on his face. I turned back to the official, drawing breath to explain the situation but from the corner of my eye, I noticed Sunday's hand making urgent 'keep quiet' signals below desk level. My mouth snapped shut as I realised in a blinding flash that the good Sunday was actually working to a strategy. His deference, his infuriating silences, the little payments here and there and especially his wish for my silence - all were part of a master plan. The lecture we had just received from the man behind the desk was merely a face-saving exercise. Overwhelmed with admiration, I sat back and left Sunday to it.

Sunday was told, quite firmly, that the Crannys could have a three weeks extension to their visas, no more, and during that time they must collect all documents (originals, not photocopies, thank you) and then apply for a residency permit. My faith in Sunday didn't waver but I thought he overdid the warm thanks when we took leave of our stern friend. Sunday led the way out and asked me to resume my wait in the outer room. He disappeared again, but occasionally I caught sight of him going in and out of doors, slipping folded notes of currency to junior staff and chatting in a friendly way to all and sundry.

Once in the car, I asked if I owed him money for what I euphemistically called 'out of pocket expenses' but he reminded me coolly that we had already paid a fee to cover the cost of two visa renewals and that amount automatically included 'dash'. I knew that dash is not considered a tip, nor is it seen as a bribe. It has, instead, connotations of a gift freely given. By sheer coincidence, it is always freely given immediately before or after a satisfactory transaction. Fine lines abound in Nigeria.

"Everyt'ing is hokay, Madame," Sunday again assured me and, of course, he was right. Had I been using the same crystal ball I would have seen that within days I would be invited to return to Lagos to collect our passports, both now sporting beautiful, two-year residency permit stamps. And all without so much as another whisper about original documents or even photocopies.

As we clawed our way out of Lagos that afternoon amidst the usual congestion, there was a crash and the tinkling of broken glass as the car immediately in front of us rammed into the rear of the 4WD in front of it. The startled driver leaped from his 4WD and after a horrified look at the rear of his vehicle, he strode back, arms flailing, to the other car. A heated discussion was well underway when he reached through the open window and grabbed the keys from the ignition of the opposition's car. He ran back to his own vehicle, climbed in and within seconds, was revving the heavy motor. Pedestrians scurried in all directions as he took the 4WD up onto the footpath, over a treacherous drain and away. The last we saw of the other driver, he was galloping in futile pursuit, shouting loudly at the damaged backside of the 4WD as it disappeared around a corner with his keys. The abandoned vehicle had to be pushed forward to let us escape, then Patrick returned to our car and we continued on our way. He was highly amused by the incident. I think he would have been disappointed if Lagos hadn't produced its usual quota of entertainment.

"Ah, dis Lagos. Wot a bud place," he said, chuckling, obviously glad he lived elsewhere.

As we headed out of the city, Simon pointed to the burnt-out shell of what had been, until last week, the headquarters of the Department of Defence and repeated a story that I'd already heard elsewhere.

Nigeria has a tradition of 'accidental' fires which occur in Government buildings immediately before the overthrow of a regime, and sensitive documents that would prove embarrassing if they fell into the hands of the next coup-masters are always destroyed in the fire. As Simon told the story, I looked at the building with interest because only this week *The Guardian* had featured a photograph of President Babingida and his entourage as they inspected the damage. The camera had caught the military leader at an inopportune moment, laughing. Cartoonists had a field day, one depicting a bystander muttering as the amused President and his friends walked by: 'Anyone would think they were going to a house warming!'

The cartoon had made me realise how often I laughed aloud here. Undoubtedly I was influenced by the uninhibited expression of mirth that I saw around me, for laughter and humour seemed to be enjoyed more openly here than anywhere else I'd been. Added to that were the occasions when the humour was unintentional, presumably amusing to me only because of different cultural perceptions. *The Guardian* had a habit of stating the obvious in the most serious of tones, and although the topic was often far from humorous, the effect was. I recall being disarmed when, full of dismay, I was reading about the tragic death of an entire

Zambian soccer team in a plane crash as they flew to Senegal recently to play in a World Cup match. The newspaper described the incident in full then concluded with the words, 'The match has been cancelled.'

Now, driving through Lagos, we could see that all over the city, Nigerians were turning their potent humour against Babingida's rule. On street corners statues of military figures in poses of strength and courage were now objects of mirth, as they stood in conquering poses wearing tee-shirts and gaudy board shorts. Soldiers patrolled the city, angrily tearing off the offending garments but the 'civvies' were replaced almost before the soldiers were out of sight.

We drove on and with the city only a few kilometres behind us, we came upon a more sombre sight. The body of a young man lay on the road. I asked my companions why no one, ourselves included, ever reported such things. Simon told me that to do so would invite big trouble because the police would try to implicate us in the death in the hope of getting a substantial bribe to drop charges. Simon, Patrick and Ajayi speculated as to the cause of this young man's end. Perhaps he was shot; maybe he had been pushed from a moving vehicle; maybe he simply fell asleep as he sat perched atop a laden truck. The spectacle particularly upset Ajayi who had turned for a closer look at the young man's body as we drove past. Now he put his head in his hands and said in a distressed voice, "Dat poor boy will jes lie dere, an' his fam'ly will be sayin' 'Where is our sonn?' and de dogs will comm...Oh, Nigeria, Nigeria!"

We continued on in silence, lost in our own thoughts. Later in the journey Simon drew me into conversation about families, religion and the role of women in our different countries. Soon everyone in the car was involved in the lively debate. Simon agreed that Nigerian men had a narrow view of women and that the nation was the poorer for not encouraging females into higher education. Describing the role of women, he told me that men were often harsh in their treatment of their wives.

"For example," he explained, "if I am using de table and my

wife wants to set it for de evening meal, she must kneel at my feet and ask permission. If dat displeases me, I 'ave de right to put m'foot to her."

The men laughed aloud when they saw my face. I hesitated about putting the obvious question but decided to ask it anyway.

"And do you?"

Amidst renewed laughter, Simon answered slyly, "Ah, I didden say I *did* it, Madame. Only dat I 'ave de right, if I choose."

I turned to Patrick in disbelief and asked him to deny that this custom existed. My reaction continued to amuse them, and Patrick's reply did nothing to convince me that I was being given the full picture. "An' after de meal, my wife an' children must thank me for providin' de food."

The whole topic fascinated me. "Patrick, what if Mercy *didn't* kneel to you? What if one night she said, 'Your turn to wash up tonight Patrick, because I am very tired.' What would you do?" I asked.

Patrick's laughter echoed around the car. "Nor, nor, nor. She wouldn't say dat, Marm."

"But what if she did?"

The scene defied his imagination apparently, and this time I was sure he wasn't pulling my leg. All he could do was shake his head. "But she wouldn't *do* dat. It jes couldn't 'appen," he repeated.

It occurred to me that Andrew and Simon might enjoy reading the English newspaper that we bought each weekend. *The Times* was two weeks old and cost the equivalent of AU$8 by the time it reached Ibadan, but it gave us $80 worth of enjoyment. Andrew took to meeting Peter at the car each Monday morning.

"I doan suppose yo' 'ave finished de pepper yet, Sah?" he would ask, with the eagerness of a child awaiting a comic book.

Peter came to enjoy his discussions with his young colleague who would drop into his office at lunchtime with a list of questions arising from articles in *The Times*.

"What is de role of Government Whip in the Westminster

system, Sah?" asked Andrew, keen to learn as much as possible about the workings of democracy.

The Nigerian press was raging against the downward spiral of the Nigerian educational system, declaring that the ongoing feud between the government and teachers was creating an entire generation of illiterates. Andrew was downcast when *The Guardian* exposed a scam involving the sale of fake education certificates. Parents knew that jobs were scarce and that it would be impossible for their children to find employment without qualifications so they were resorting to paying teachers to provide bogus documents. Andrew was depressed that parents and teachers, instead of joining forces to insist on a solution, were creating yet another problem.

"What is *wrong* with dis country?" he asked in despair. "Can't pepple *see* what dey are doin' to de children?"

By coincidence, an article appeared in *The Times* that week, about the arrest in London of people suspected of falsifying A Level certificates and selling them to parents. As I read, I imagined that the article might provide Andrew with some consolation, however bittersweet, when he saw that Western countries, too, were struggling with this form of corruption. Then I read on. 'Police are questioning two Nigerians in relation to the matter....." Poor Andrew.

One day an invitation arrived, with a note enclosed, from Janice Olawoye. It was soon to be her husband's fiftieth birthday and a big celebration was planned. Janice urged us to come. "It will be," she wrote, "an interesting part of your Nigerian experience."

The official ceremony was to commence at '10am prompt' but when we arrived a few minutes early, the huge tent was still being furnished, so we returned to the car to await developments. When we finally made our way to the entrance, half an hour later, we were still the first to arrive. An usher claimed us and offered us the front row. We didn't want to be approached later and invited to sit lower down (we had read somewhere where that *can* happen), so we settled in the second row. It was a fortunate decision, because when the guest of honour and Janice processed in, they settled immediately in front of us, on the seats first offered to us. Janice, the only other white person at the gathering of about five hundred people, turned and welcomed us warmly. She and her husband were dressed in rich, traditional robes of the same white embossed satin material, trimmed with gold braid. Around her blonde hair Janice wore a large, shimmering headscarf in gold material that flattered her fair complexion. The focus of all eyes, the Reverend Doctor OO and Doctor (Mrs) Olawoye made a striking couple.

Janice's Nigerian husband had gained tertiary qualifications in Agricultural Economics and Natural Resource Economics in Ibadan and the USA. After many years in this profession, he trained and was ordained as a pastor, and formed the Faith Bible Ministry in 1988.

Today's ceremony was a new experience for us because we had never before attended a ceremony where revivalist-type exuberance predominated. It began when a slightly built man, with animated face and boundless energy exhorted us all to "Prayer-ze de Lorrrd!" which the five hundred strong congregation did with gusto. I was impressed with the energy and enthusiasm around me but I was not about to abandon my own inhibited style. All video cameras were drawn to the guest of honour but they inadvertently captured for posterity, the restrained participation of the *Oyinbos* in the second row.

Swaying, foot-tapping choirs sang, feisty females preached and the Reverend Doctor Olawoye launched the book he had written recently, *Strength for the Battle,* in which he exhorts his flock to remain vigilant against the wiles of the devil:

In 1984, we had a twenty-one day revival at the church. A woman was brought to us who was seventeen months pregnant. She was under the attack of a satanic woman in her house. This woman threatened that the pregnant woman would not deliver unless she would do so through her mouth.[1]

Later, as I read such segments of the work, I longed for an opportunity to sit with Janice and discuss certain ideas presented in the book. I knew that her Western upbringing would help her understand my confusion if the words were to be taken literally. Unfortunately everyone but me lived busy lives, and such an opportunity never arose.

The Kangs were the first of our IITA friends to return from holidays and one day as we were catching up on news, Jeanette told me that BT was to take twelve months sabbatical leave, starting in September. I was disappointed and said so, because this meant that we would only have their company for a few more weeks as we would be back in Australia before they returned to Africa. Jeanette did not hear my words because she was still speaking.

"...and we wondered if you and Peter would be interested in minding our house for us while we are away?"

I gasped, flew to cloud nine, then came back to earth with a bump. I remembered how often we had approached IITA's Deputy Director General for permission to rent one of the empty houses and how often we had been knocked back. An image of Bill Powell appeared before me, a thin, unrelenting smile upon his lips. I groaned in despair.

Jeanette didn't share my concern. "This is different. This house has been allocated to us, so they'll listen to our request. Besides," and her eyes twinkled mischievously, "Bill's on holidays for the next month and it'll all be over before he even knows what's happening. We'll pull a swiftie," she said, using an expression of mine that had amused her when she'd first heard it.

Memos flew backwards and forwards between Kangs and Housing, then Housing and Crannys. Then, one beautiful day, it was all settled. IITA's Acting Deputy Director General informed us that we could have Kang's house in their absence, but we'd have to pay more rent than they did because we were not IITA staff. He nominated an amount that was about half what we were currently paying for the tiny unit so we concealed our glee and accepted. Jeanette and BT generously invited us to use whatever of their possessions we required. Pots, pans, crockery, cutlery, even the cartons of beer in the pantry, were at our disposal. I lay awake in the small hours, unable to believe our luck and visualising us at breakfast time, looking out across that wonderful garden, down to my geese on the lake.

Jeanette and BT employed two men; a full-time gardener, David, who had been with them for twenty years and a steward named Reuben, who had worked for them for twenty-four years on a part-time basis, in addition to his full-time employment at IITA. Part-time jobs were vitally important to Nigerians and if we didn't intend employing the men, Jeanette and BT planned to provide them with some form of extra income to avoid hardship. Reuben, who came three times a week, had first worked for the Kangs as a teenager. Now he was married with seven children. He and his family lived in a nearby village but David, an elderly man, was single and lived in the 'boy's quarters' adjoining the house. Kang's offer of this house was a wonderful gift and we were keen to fit in with the established routine, even though I didn't relish the thought of having staff.

Gritting my teeth, I decided to approach the matter as yet another part of 'the Nigerian experience' but in the small hours I'd wake and tremble when my imagination ran riot and painted one or both the men as replicas of Mr Titoloye.

Kangs were due to fly out in four week's time on the evening of September 14 and BT's advice was for us to move in as soon as possible afterwards. Bill was due back any day and he would be less inclined to reverse the decision if we were in residence. As we chatted, Jeanette described David's and Reuben's reactions when they were told that another couple would be moving in. Reuben had accepted the news with calm interest but David was cast from more volatile material. On hearing the news, he had drawn himself up his full 4'11".

"I do not approve!" he declared.

BT was experienced in the handling of David and asked where, then, did he intend living during the Crannys' stay in the house? David decided to give the matter more thought and, having done so, informed the Kangs that he would stay in residence after all. The Crannys, it seemed, were allowed to come.

"He is a strange little man," Jeanette warned me.

Oh dear, not another one, I thought. I could see ten months of trouble ahead.

She continued, "You'll often see and hear David talking to himself while he works in the garden. He'll be praying aloud. It's probably best not to engage him in conversation. Just greet him briefly, then leave it at that."

We arranged a time to meet Reuben and David, but before that could happen, the political scene deteriorated and it looked as if our plans were all in vain. As requested, we had kept in regular contact with the World Bank in Lagos, by phone when possible, otherwise by courier. Riots were a daily occurrence now and the press was full of talk about possible military action against the protesters so we were told by our World Bank minders to pack essential items and move to Lagos immediately. The reasoning was that we could be airlifted out of Nigeria at short notice from Lagos whereas, if we stayed in Ibadan, we may not be able to get down there in a hurry if evacuation became necessary. If this crisis passed, as the others had, we could return to Ibadan in two weeks' time. We packed, said a few halfhearted goodbyes because we were confident we'd be back, organised for Patrick to buy himself extra grain and kerosene, locked up our apartment and headed for Lagos.

The Lagos unit provided an interesting view over one of the city's lagoons, and in the distance we could see a major arterial road, strangely empty. As we looked around our temporary home, we noted that between the lounge room and the corridor to the bedrooms was a heavy-duty steel door, the last line of defence if intruders succeeded in breaking down the front door. Outside, the city was eerily quiet because a general strike was in progress and fuel was almost unprocurable.

An Englishman, John Harrison, another World Bank employee, lived with his wife Kay in an identical building across the compound's quadrangle. Good company, they made our brief stay in Lagos a great deal more enjoyable than we had anticipated. Kay took me with her when she visited a home for motherless babies where she was a regular volunteer, and she put on a morning tea for me to meet some of her friends. I arrived early and was delighted to see that cucumber sandwiches were on the menu. I had always wondered if such things actually existed. As we waited for the others to arrive, Kay assured me that there was one guest in particular that she was sure I would enjoy meeting.

Patty was an Australian, the wife of a business executive in Lagos and she was an excellent foster mother to teenage girls who would otherwise be on the streets. She earned the confidence and respect of the often-difficult girls by being 'a straight shooter', Kay told me. I was to find out what our hostess meant the moment I said 'G'day' to Patty.

"Stone the bloody crows, another Aussie! What brought you to this gawd-forsaken place, Luv?" and she laughed in delight and grabbed me in a bear-hug. I couldn't have nominated a more stereotypical Australian had I tried.

Patty kept everyone entertained with her colourful language and infectious laughter and as Kay served the dainty food, I could see that far from being shocked by Patty's earthy manner, she enjoyed her company. When I was offered a cucumber sandwich, however, I nibbled it in a manner most refined, just in case the image of Or-stralians abroad needed bolstering.

We were told the secret evacuation plans that would be used if serious trouble erupted. The airport was not the place to be if a coup was underway so we were told that if the worst happened, we were to make our way to a particular lagoon and there be lifted out by means of a seaplane. It all sounded rather exciting, but I hoped things settled down quickly so we could get back to Ibadan and do some serious house shifting.

By looking out the window or by watching CNN, we were getting a better idea of the state of affairs than by watching state-sponsored local television stations. Few vehicles other than those belonging to the military were using the roads and stony-faced soldiers sat in Army tanks on street corners. According to CNN, people were being forced into submission by hunger because banks were closed and wages and savings, if any, could not be accessed.

The local press denied that there was any money to give the people even if the banks did open. Indeed, one newspaper article solemnly informed us, 'the banks were full of empty vaults.' I would have liked to visit the food markets to see for myself if the usual stockpiles of produce were affected, but I had no car and no Patrick at my disposal.

As things reached crisis point, President Babingida made a surprising speech to the nation in which he claimed to be on track with the transition he had planned all along. Abiola was not acceptable as his replacement, Babingida said, but he was resigning immediately and handing over to an interim government to be headed by Ernest Shonekan.

Shonekan, a civilian, was widely respected for his opposition to the excesses of the military government but the news caused confusion. Some people were delighted, others outraged that Shonekan would sell out in this way instead of continuing the drive for a democratically elected government. Once again Babingida had wrong-footed the protest movement sufficiently to buy time. The strike ended because people were hungry and desperately seeking a solution. They returned to work and Nigeria struggled back to life again. The crisis passed but not the hardship, because money and fuel remained in short supply.

Peter rang FORMECU to arrange our return to Ibadan, but he was met with the news that all the vehicles, including ours, were out of fuel. Peter decided that this was the emergency he had predicted so he rang IITA and authorised International House staff to give Patrick the key to our concrete storeroom. Patrick refuelled the car from Peter's stash and next morning there he was at our door, excitedly shaking our hands and bouncing around in high spirits. We agreed that it felt more like two months than two weeks, since we left Ibadan. Later, when we called at his office, Peter's colleagues were profuse in their praise of Sah's foresight in stockpiling a little fuel for emergencies. I felt obliged to tease him, only slightly unfairly, that he and Blind Freddie were the only ones who could foresee that yet another fuel shortage was on its way.

Next morning at the office, Peter noticed that Andrew looked unwell. At first the young man denied that anything was wrong but when Peter asked him again, he admitted that he had not eaten for four days. No government employees had been paid and, in any case, the banks where their salaries were paid, were still closed. They had been ordered to remain closed until extra security could be arranged, officials said, in case angry crowds tried to vent their spleen when the doors finally opened. Andrew gratefully accepted assistance in the form of a loan and in the months ahead, he was diligent in his repayments.

I went to the office and confronted Beatrice. She and Ayo and the children had a small amount of rice left, she told me, but no money to buy oil or kerosene for cooking. They were in a bad way, but, she assured me, not as bad as a family she had seen that morning, pulling leaves from trees and chewing them.

I was horrified and when I asked if we could help, Beatrice fell to her knees in front of me. The sight of a friend reduced to this appalled me and I hurriedly pulled her to her feet. She would not accept a gift, but she was comfortable with a loan. The amount was perhaps a month's salary to Beatrice, not a large sum in Australian terms and in the months ahead an occasion arose when it was appropriate to give her a gift and we were able to declare the debt forgotten. Peter and I were chastened to realise that although we'd made sure Patrick was provided for when we went away, it hadn't entered our heads that a professional man like Andrew or the double-incomed Bamadeli family, could also face hunger.

Life regained momentum, with IITA residents cushioned from the worries that existed only a kilometre away. But I was preoccupied, remembering the struggles of Nigerian friends outside that fence. Any help we gave was like offering a Band-Aid to an individual on a battlefield. It was one thing to have strong views on the effectiveness or otherwise of international aid. It was quite another to accept that it was the Andrews, Beatrices and Patricks of the world who suffered when the going got tough. I was as far as ever from knowing how best to help in a long term, meaningful way.

I distracted myself by preparing for our shift to 20 Tropical Crescent. I needed to contact IITA's Administration and request a transfer of the household's accounts to our name, and friends had to be notified of our change of address. Jeanette introduced us to David and Reuben and tutored me in how to supervise David's care of her beautiful garden. Having admired this house for so long, I was thrilled with the opportunity to live in such surroundings. All I wanted now was to be a fly on Bill's wall when he heard of our new address.

In contrast to Nigeria's woes, blessings seemed to be coming to us in bundles. As we finalised our packing, we received a phone call from Glen and Lisa. They had decided to marry and were announcing their engagement in the next few days. We were thrilled with the news but there was pain too, a longing to see them, to be physically present as everyone rejoiced.

Peter and I went about smiling happily at the thought of Lisa becoming part of the family, but occasionally we'd catch each other's eye and admit that we wished we were part of it all. Once-in-a-lifetime opportunities such as this stint in Africa surely came with a price.

1. Olawaye, Doctor O.O., Strength for the Battle, Faith Bible Publications, Ibadan, 1993 p 2

Chapter 10
WE MOVE HOUSE

The Kangs were leaving within the hour. They stood with us now in the lounge of our little unit chatting about departure and arrival times and we all blustered about the world being a small place and how our paths would cross again, but deep down we knew it wasn't likely. The ritual complete and with nothing else to say except goodbye, we thanked Jeanette and BT once more for their kindness, handed them the mail they had offered to post for us during their Australian stopover, and received in return, the keys to their house.

When the day had cooled, I walked down beside the golf fairway to our new home. I wanted to browse and soak up the personality of the house now that it was ours. I opened the front door and stepped across the enclosed porch into the large, cool lounge room and saw Jeanette's parting act of friendship. She had brought the garden inside with vases of flowers and their perfume filled the room. On the coffee table was a small package in gift wrapping. I sat down in a lounge chair and took it all in before I opened the attached envelope and read the Kangs' warm wishes for a happy stay. When I turned to the gift, I unwrapped a jewellery box, carved with Indonesian motifs. I sat there, admiring it and thinking back to that day five months ago when Jeanette had first made herself known to me. Her greeting had been spontaneous and generous, signalling the sort of person she was. I was going to miss her. Unexpectedly, I felt unsettled, almost sad. While we'd lived in the tiny flat, surrounded by the extra furniture which we had improvised and draped in bright African prints, I'd felt in holiday mode, temporarily away from home. Now, as I looked around this room, all I could see was permanence. It was the Kangs, not us, who would soon be on Australian soil. I longed to be in two places at once. I locked up and walked back to the unit, trying to make sense of my mixed emotions.

I woke early next morning, allowing the plaintive wails of the Muslim Call to Prayer to reach me. The early noises of IITA were so familiar by now that they usually just signalled how much more sleep I had coming to me, but not today. Before the bats began their early morning bipping, I was up and well underway with the last of the packing. Peter intended staying home today and when Patrick arrived, they loaded the car for the first of several trips to the house four hundred metres down the road. The results of all my visits to the markets were now painfully obvious, but Peter showed admirable restraint and held his peace. By evening we had unpacked again and rearranged the furniture to make the house more 'us'. We looked around with immense satisfaction and felt the urge to show off our new home.

Our IITA friends knew this house and furniture well. Not only had they been guests here, but also their own homes were almost identical, with most furniture supplied by the Institute. Only our location and garden made ours special and that was hardly of interest to those who had seen it every day for years. With no one but ourselves to enthuse over it, we felt a sense of anticlimax and began thinking of people many thousands of miles away who *would* be interested. We looked at each other glumly and recognised the danger signs - homesickness was looming. Peter took action to lift the mood of the evening. He mixed us each a generous gin squash and turned to the newly connected hi-fi system. Weren't we supposed to be celebrating?

He selected a Neil Diamond tape that was a gift from Glen before we left. As the music filled the room, we found ourselves talking, not of African adventures or new houses, but of twenty years ago and gifts we'd received from three little boys. The tube of underwater tank sealant from Mark to his father, a must for every home-handyman; a double-A battery from five year old Tim so we'd have power during a blackout; the gift of companionship from preschool Glen, as I iced a wedding cake in the morning hours, long before sleepy brothers woke and demanded a share of rejected icing-sugar flowers. At this moment, on the other side of the world, our family and Lisa's were celebrating an engagement while we sat wondering where all the years had gone. The music changed and Simon and Garfunkel moaned that they wished they were homeward bound. Mood music indeed.

But the Bard was right; sleep does indeed *knit up the ravell'd sleave of care*. We woke the following morning bright of eye and brimful of enthusiasm. Besides, it was Peter's 55th birthday and when the phone calls came from home, we were able to give a highly optimistic report on our chances of survival. Had we but known it, we had just weathered the final and most painful bout of homesickness and it was never to be as bad again. That evening as we relaxed in the lounge room, we looked not to the past, but to the future. Forty-eight hours into the future, in fact, because that was when we'd become Employers of Domestic Staff.

Peter waved his hands in front of his face in a gesture of submission. He could cope, he said, with vanishing forests and creeping deserts, but the thought of dealing with household staff was altogether too daunting. Before I could invoke my power of veto, I was appointed e*l supremo* of 20 Tropical Crescent. To prepare myself for the task ahead, I thought back several weeks to our initial meeting with Reuben and David.

Jeanette had invited us down specifically to meet the two men and as we knocked on the front door, we could hear sounds of energetic gardening nearby. Jeanette stepped out into the garden and called to David, using the title that indicates familiarity yet respect for a senior person.

"Baba. Please come. I wish to introduce Mr and Mrs Cranny."

A small, grey-headed man appeared around the corner, carrying a digging fork not much smaller than he was. He was barefoot, dressed in dark, ragged clothes, yet there was an air of dignity about the little man. He welcomed us quietly, with no sign of the disapproval he'd voiced to BT. When Peter and I went to shake hands with him, David apologetically showed us that his were covered in mud, so I jokingly reached forward and 'shook' his forearm instead. He glanced at me, surprised, then the hint of a smile touched the wizened face. I recalled Jeanette's warning that he was a bit 'strange' but I couldn't help but take a liking to the old fellow. A short time later, Jeanette led us inside to meet the steward.

Reuben was in his late-thirties, of medium build, dressed in long-sleeved shirt and heavy corduroy trousers. *How on earth do Nigerians tolerate the heat*, I wondered.

As we were introduced, Reuben's pleasant, square-shaped face lit up with a ready smile and he returned our greetings in clear English. I breathed a sigh of relief; I had enough to contend with in Patrick's thick accent, always spoken at top speed. As we chatted, Jeanette kept a relaxed conversation flowing. She commented that Reuben, like herself and BT, had been at IITA for many years and had seen a lot of changes in that time. Reuben had nodded in agreement.

"IITA is big now," he said, "but when I first came, many people were not around." I smiled and looked forward to hearing more of his expressions. I felt myself beginning to relax and even daring to hope that we'd done the right thing in continuing Kang's domestic arrangements.

Now, as Peter and I sat in the lounge room that Saturday evening, I realised that we'd soon know.

I spent Sunday swanning around, adding final touches here and there, inspecting the garden and making a list of all the groceries I would be able to fit into the room-sized pantry and large freezer. At times I simply stood admiring the scenery from the back porch. *Bill Powell*, I thought, *if you want us out of here, you'll have a fight on your hands.*

Chapter 11
ONE SAINT AND SEVERAL SINNERS

While we rejoiced in our new surroundings, our weekend was brightened even further. The Gulleys had returned from holidays and now invited us to dinner on Sunday evening. Nancy and I were the only females present because the families of the other guests hadn't yet returned. The evening fell into a familiar pattern of wide-ranging opinions and lively repartee, and I was struck by the influence upon personality of the different cultural backgrounds. Like a tapestry, the evening's conversation emerged in a variety of different shades as we revealed our individual viewpoints and humour, but always we used the colours of our own culture.

The story of our evacuation to Lagos led to speculation about IITA's plan of action if civil war broke out. One suggestion that was worthy of the cutting-room floor of a *Dad's Army* production, included the rapid changing of the flags that fluttered at the entrance to the Institute, in keeping with the political sympathies of any approaching threat. The news that Peter and I, mere interlopers, had moved into an IITA house also caused considerable interest. Had my wish been granted to be a fly on the wall of Bill Powell's office on his first day back after leave, I suspect that I'd have been one of a swarm sitting there.

Also at the dinner party was Rahim, our Afghani-New Yorker tennis-playing friend, who lived off campus and wished he didn't. His work-relationship to IITA was similar to Peter's and as yet the Institute's heart remained hardened to all arguments that he should be offered one of the vacant houses. As Rahim listened to news of our change of address, his handsome, swarthy face took on the glum expression that always preceded a bout of melancholic humour.

"I'm *really* pissed off," he said, going on to illustrate how his luck would need to change before *he* ever got into an IITA house. "On our way home for holidays, somewhere over the Atlantic, my daughter and I both came down with malaria."

As Rahim spoke, I tried to imagine being confined to an airline seat while the parasites romped through the bloodstream, and nausea, pounding head and aching joints being the only sensations letting you know you were still alive.

Rahim went on, "When we landed, the doctor wouldn't accept our word that all we needed was some chloroquin. Oh no, he had to play the hero and save America from some exotic disease by slamming us into an isolation ward for a week. Some holiday!"

The Friday evening ritual of sauntering up to International House for a few sets of tennis followed by suya and beer on the grass, continued. At the end of our second week in the house, I arrived to find that I had been paired to play with none other than Bill Powell. Judging by his dour expression, Bill was as thrilled as I was with the coincidence, but we survived the ordeal and even managed to win a game or two.

A few days later I received a phone call from Nancy to discuss the following weekend's social activities. Rahim was the only one of our gang whose television set was connected to a satellite dish so he had been invited to host a dinner on Sunday evening so that his friends could watch the finals of a European tennis championship. His family was still away, so Nancy and I had volunteered, apparently, to provide the food.

I leafed through the two recipe books I'd brought with me and realised that the ingredients for the main course were a worry. I picked up the phone.

"Nancy, do you have a chook in your freezer? And could you spare me a lemon?" I asked, intending to repay the ingredients of Lemon Chicken when I next shopped.

There was a stunned silence at the other end of the line, and then she spoke.

"A *chook*? What's a *chook*?" She turned my own accent back upon me and made it sound quite inedible. "Whatever it is, I'm not certain I'd want one in my freezer," she said warily. "But a lemon? Oh, my goodness, do I have a lemon!" she added with feeling, and went on to tell me the story of a very special piece of citrus fruit.

She had visited the children's home the day after returning from holidays and although she thought the children looked frail, their spirits were high. They were excited to see her again and when she left, the children who could walk had gone with her to the car. Those who couldn't manage the distance, dragged themselves along the concrete floor to a spot where she'd see them waving as she drove off. As she said *odabo*, goodbye, Bosiyo, an eight-year-old who was considered by staff to be of below-average intelligence because he didn't speak, ran to a nearby lemon tree and selected a piece of fruit from its branches. He came back to Nancy, kissed the lemon and offered it to her as a gift.

I was moved by the story and I didn't want to take the lemon, but Nancy insisted. She promised that Bosiyo would hear how a group of his friends shared his gift and thought of him while doing so.

Rahim proved a gracious host and the caterers acquitted themselves admirably. Before the evening evolved into a gathering of noisy armchair experts who would never have missed the shots that so troubled the opponents of Pete Sampras and Steffi Graf, we gathered around the dinner table. Jim said a brief prayer of thanks for the good things in our lives. As I listened to his words, I knew I wasn't the only one thinking of a small boy whose life was surely marked for hardship.

Nancy was right about the children's deterioration. I had been saddened and frustrated to learn that while Peter and I were in Lagos, Cielo hadn't been able to visit the home as planned. IITA had issued instructions that Institute cars were not to be taken off campus until the demonstrations ended. To make matters worse, the general strike had paralysed the city and food deliveries to the children's home were more unreliable than ever. The day before Cielo's car was confined to IITA's grounds, she had visited the kids and found them without food or adult supervision. No staff had come to work because of the transport strike and although Mahdi and Taju were with them, they were mere children themselves. Cielo loaded eight of the smallest children into her car and brought them back to IITA where she bathed and fed them and gave them a wonderful day. Later that afternoon, she drove them back, taking food for the others. If she had been involved in an accident, there would have been serious trouble because she was acting without authority, but Cielo was no respecter of red tape when the kids needed help. For the next week or ten days, the children had to survive with almost no adult assistance and only occasional deliveries of food. Their weight fell and their general health deteriorated.

Weeks passed and Ernest Shonekan's interim government had now been in power one month. For a brief period, the rioting stopped and political argument was conducted through the press. The fuel shortage eased temporarily and the IITA managers lifted the ban on vehicles leaving the premises. As the families returned, life settled down and our roster for taking food to the children resumed. Cooking the large quantities of food for the children was easy in my new, well-equipped kitchen and each Tuesday Patrick and I headed off laden with chicken or beef stew, scrambled eggs, rice and fruit.

One morning, as the children smiled and clapped happily at our arrival, I caught the eye of an attractive child of about three years of age, standing some distance off quietly watching proceedings. I went to him and he immediately raised his arms to be picked up, but his serious expression didn't change as he studied me closely. He looked the picture of physical health, but he wore the look of a grieving child. I asked Bose his name.

"'e says 'e is called Scent," she replied.

"Scent?" I thought this a strange name for a child, even in Nigeria.

"Nor Pum, *Scent*," she said, repeating the name carefully to help me get the pronunciation right. I tried several times, saying the word as I heard it, but she kept shaking her head.

"Nor, nor. Dat is not how *yo'* would say it. It's like 'Scent Joss-eph, Scent Mary, Scent Jude....'"

"Oh, you mean 'Saint'!" I exclaimed tactlessly, as light dawned.

My Australian accent sounded flat and unattractive compared to Bose's clipped tones. She beamed, pleased that I'd grasped the meaning of his name even if my pronunciation left a bit to be desired. Meanwhile Saint snuggled close, his arms around my neck.

The following week when we arrived at the home, Saint had a companion, another healthy, handsome child his own age. This little boy would not speak and had been dubbed Friday, because he had been brought in on that day and they were 'corrontly out o' Fri-dees'. I thought wryly of the stress that must be placed on staff's imagination if they ever received a child on a Wednesday or a Saturday. Saint and Friday went everywhere together, like two little old men who never spoke or smiled. At times they sat silently holding hands, lost and frightened, trying to offer each other some comfort in this harsh place. In my mind I called the newcomer Good Friday, an appropriate name, I thought, considering the suffering that this innocent child had endured.

A few days ago, he had been found beside the mutilated body of his mother who had been sacrificed in what appeared to be a ritualistic killing. Her vital organs had been removed, suggesting a black magic ceremony. It was probable that he had witnessed the atrocity although he was too young to tell his story. His face betrayed no emotion but he clung to me throughout my visit. All I could do was to hug him tightly and helplessly and my eyes filled with tears when he reached out with a small hand to turn my face towards the car, then indicated that he wanted me to take him somewhere, presumably to his home. When it was time for me to go, he clung so desperately that he had to be prised from me. When he realised that I was not going to rescue him, he turned a sad face to Patrick and extended his arms, only to be disappointed again. Patrick looked thoroughly wretched as he walked to the car. I paused and asked Bose to comfort Friday, but as we drove off, I saw that he was on the floor with his only friend, Saint, for company. The staff, untrained in childcare, didn't regard it as their role to touch the children unless to discipline them.

Patrick and I drove home in silence. I didn't trust myself to speak and all I heard from Patrick was an occasional sigh. When he finally spoke, it was obvious where his thoughts were.

"His chances of adoption are not good. I am worried dat many pepple will not touch 'im because of superstition," he said. "Wot will 'appen to 'im, I wonder?"

We were left wondering, because Saint and Good Friday disappeared after only a brief stay at the home. Saint was adopted out, we were told, and his twelve-year-old brother was to remain at the other institution. That was the first I had even heard of an older brother. My questions as to why the children hadn't been together at this institution, then adopted out to parents willing to take both, remained unanswered, for it was not my business. I heard nothing further of little Friday, except that he had been taken to live in a children's home in the southern city of Ogbomosho.

Juliana Asidu, a Ghanaian and wife of one of IITA's staff, had taken me under her wing soon after our arrival because she had fond memories of Australia. While her husband had been studying at Flinders University, the people of Adelaide had shown them wonderful hospitality and I was reaping the benefit. One day after returning from holidays, she announced that she had brought back a selection of Jane Fonda's fitness videos and intended working out in her own home. She was motivated, she told me, by her stomach, which was 'not in'. Word spread and soon the owners of many an 'out' stomach were clamouring for Juliana to start an aerobics group.

The idea developed into a circuitous debate about time and place but finally it was decided that we would meet three mornings a week at International House, although the venue later changed to Cappa Bar. A large screen normally used for seminars was connected to a video recorder in mysterious ways and soon Jane

Fonda, too svelte to be truly human, was gazing down upon us, urging us along the tortuous path to firm biceps and in tummies.

We pranced around with much enthusiasm and little grace. Wimps like me sought to deceive by wearing baggy tee-shirts and floppy shorts. We stole sidelong glances at those in form-fitting gym gear and smiled at their wobbly bits fore 'n aft, all the while hypocritically aware of our own secret caches of less-than-taut flesh.

And so began one of my most enjoyable activities at IITA, for our aerobics classes turned into wonderful fun as well as being physically and socially rewarding. At first I was the only white person to attend. Each session I would arrive punctually, eager to start, but everyone else operated on Afro-Asian time, so I'd wait, entertaining myself with books from the library shelves. Eventually the other seven or eight masochists would arrive and we'd move on to the next phase, the ritual of The Chat. At first, it was conducted in French as many of the African women were from Francophile countries, and I couldn't understand a word. I was determined to be included so I mounted a campaign of relentless friendliness. Each time they'd arrived and formed a scrum, I'd be there in the middle, asking questions or making statements that probably had little bearing on the current topic. In the end, I wore them down. The Cappa Bar became an English-speaking zone at aerobics time. I was one of the gang.

Maureen, Doctor Akintewe's Scottish wife, heard about the aerobics class and joined us, swelling the ranks of Caucasians by one hundred percent. After the sessions, she and I would sometimes sit, our beet-red faces making a mockery of any claim to 'whiteness'. On one occasion our conversation touched upon our individual places in the colour spectrum and Maureen decided she was 'beige with a tendency to become crimson under stress'. I was to learn more about others' perspectives of my particular hue during a later trip to the markets, but for now, I switched the conversation to Nigeria's problems.

Maureen felt unsure about the Women's Group involvement with the homeless children. Perhaps it was unfair to raise their expectations when, really, she argued, it was an illusion. In an environment like that of Nigeria, having a family was what made the difference, if anything could. What if we were merely breaking down their defences, stripping them of the protective shell they needed for survival? If this were so, the children would be even more vulnerable than before we became involved. Also, she reminded me, what looked horrendous to us would look normal to many people there because the physical conditions in which the children lived were probably no worse than those of a majority of West Africans.

I carefully considered her arguments because Maureen had insight denied to me, having lived in Nigeria for many years. She and Tom had not always enjoyed the cosseted environment of IITA. After their marriage they had stayed in Tom's home town for a while, and then lived 'on the job' at University College Hospital, Ibadan, for several years. Tom felt strongly that he should use his medical skills amongst his own people. It was only when their sons' secondary education demanded a higher salary that they came to IITA. I weighed up Maureen's reasoning and felt uneasy. Surely it is universally true that children are better for knowing that someone considers them special and loveable, even if the relationship is time limited? Maureen agreed with the special and loveable bit, but was unsure about the effects of time limitation.

With her concerns in mind, I regularly asked Patrick to remind the children that I would be going home to my own country one day, but while I lived here I would visit them whenever possible. I knew my attempts didn't really address the point Maureen was making, but I hoped I was reducing the impact of my going.

With her strong sense of social justice, Maureen also questioned the wisdom of providing so much assistance to the children that the government was under no pressure to meet its obligations to the underprivileged. On this issue, I accepted that she had a strong argument, but I continued to have difficulty with letting today's children go hungry in the hope of improving the plight of tomorrow's.

One day there was a firm knock at the front door and through the screen I saw the figure of Mr Titoloye. I had known that my tormentor would track me down. I had prepared mentally for the little Pork n' Prawn man's next visit and although I could see the humour of our previous encounter, I was determined that he wasn't going to get the better of me this time. I should have known better.

Unfortunately, he again came while Peter was at home, and knowing when high entertainment was imminent, my husband settled himself on a comfortable chair to watch the show.

As the little vendor and I negotiated, I recalled an episode in my childhood when I had tried to pick up the mercury that spilled from a broken thermometer. That had proved a simple task compared to managing Mr Titoloye. I knew I was doing badly when a furtive glance in the direction of the lounge showed the level of Peter's enjoyment. To make matters worse, he had a camera in his hands. Mr Titoloye noticed it too and that was all my companion needed to completely take over proceedings.

"A camera? Come, Madame, yo' sit dere and I will sit 'ere. Now, I mus' be holdin' a pen. Dat is good. Now we are ready, Sah. Tekk de photo, and I mus' get a copy," he ordered imperiously.

By the time he left, I had purchased some good looking prawns, a piece of pork and some 'bess-quality' fillet steak that was, I knew, only fit for a slow-cooking casserole. Mr Titoloye had also shamed me into increasing the amount of money that he held in credit for me.

"All de leddies on IITA 'ave given me bigger amounts dan dis so I can buy de best goods for dem," it was explained. *Oh, well,* I thought. *If that's how it's done around here...*

I had convinced myself that the visit hadn't gone *too* badly, when the phone rang and Indira's voice greeted me.

"I am just ringing to tell you that Mr Titoloye might call on you today because I gave him your new address," she said. "By the way, don't fall for his usual story about all of us giving him cash in advance, will you. Just be firm," she added breezily.

"Oh, that old story? Heh, heh," I said. "Yes, he *did* try that. Heh, heh." Beneath my breath I vowed to wring his scrawny little neck on his very next visit.

Shonekan's government could not withstand the withering attack of the press and the simmering resentment of the people. The military took the opportunity to reassert its authority and in a bloodless coup, General Sonny Abacha, reputedly the power behind the detested former regime of Babingida, took over government. Peter couldn't believe his bad luck in striking such an unstable time to try to influence government policy. We had been in Nigeria less than eight months yet he was on his third Minister for Forestry and each one had been more preoccupied with saving his own political neck than with administering his new portfolio.

Political, economic and social conditions remained unsettled, often changing overnight. One day there would be fuel; the next day chaos would reign as people queued for miles awaiting petrol or kerosene for domestic use. Rumours began circulating that the new government intended increasing the price of fuel by seven hundred percent and panic erupted as people clamoured to buy at the old price. Although circumstances were making Peter's job extremely difficult, he realised that his project would never be completed if he waited for political stability. He decided to go ahead with plans to visit Benin City for a two-day meeting despite the fuel shortages and riots.

Much of the last trip had been lost to me in a malarial blur so I decided to go too. We were to take the 4WD and after lunch on departure day, Patrick came back to IITA to collect two passengers - Pierre (a visiting forestry marketing consultant) and me.

Patrick was so frustrated when our route from IITA was blocked by a serious go-slow that he decided to take an alternative road but hundreds of others had had the same idea. Our vehicle stood nose-to-nose with oncoming traffic on a single-lane stretch that was lined by deep washouts. Pierre and I thought we had no option but to sit it out, but Patrick preferred action. He took to the eroded gullies and squeezed the lumbering vehicle between houses, stalls, light poles, people and cars. The vehicle scrambled up mounds then fell into mini-ravines on the other side, while we flopped around inside like sacks of potatoes. More than once the vehicle tilted alarmingly as it scrambled along, up and over embankments. It was a hair-raising experience, particularly as Patrick seemed to think it necessary to get it over quickly. My heart spent a lot of time in my mouth until I gave up all hope of getting through in one piece. I withdrew into fatalistic silence; if we tip over, we tip over and may God have mercy on our souls.

As we scraped ourselves off the ceiling one more time, Pierre asked Patrick in a voice that betrayed a pessimism similar to my own, "Do you know this vehicle's centre of gravity, Patrick? No, I didn't think you did..."

And so it went on until we were through. As we talked about it later in the subdued voices of genuine survivors, Pierre and I agreed that children, goats, houses, light poles and ourselves were all very fortunate to have come out unscathed.

We collected Peter at his office and headed for Benin City. By the time we'd arrived, my nerves had stopped jangling and we looked about us, enjoying the signs that fronted small businesses. Back in Ibadan we had chuckled about the *Uphill Driving School* and I often threatened to put myself into the hands of staff at *God's Will Beauty Parlour*, just to see what His plan actually was, regarding my appearance. Now, in Benin City, our attention was caught by *Why Worry Towing Service*, and there, offering hope to the unfortunates with specific problems, a large sign announced:

TRADITIONAL MEDICINE CENTRE
Gonorrhoea and Syphilis
Killed Here

We drove on to our hotel and when we were settled, I rang the appropriate number to place our breakfast order for the following morning. I asked for fruit, cereal and tea for the two of us, but the person at the other end of the line was loath to hang up.

"But 'ow do yo' want de heggs cooked, Madame?" he asked. I told him I hadn't ordered eggs and replaced the receiver. Five minutes later the phone rang. This time, a different voice quizzed me.

"Madame, I see dat yo' 'ave ordered heggs. Please, 'ow do yo' like dem cooked?"

I again denied all knowledge of eggs but said that I wished to add a large bottle of drinking water to the order. I finished speaking and the man at the other end suggested we clarify matters with one final check.

"So, Madame, yo' are cancellin' the heggs? And yo' want water?"

"Right. Eggs off, water on, OK?" I hung up, glad that we understood each other.

Next morning, having demolished the plateful of scrambled eggs that had taken pride of place on my tray, I walked down to reception and bought a large bottle of water, all the while pondering how to make my accent more intelligible to Nigerians.

Benin City was maintaining its fiery reputation and CNN reported that its streets were being vandalised by students protesting about the rumoured fuel hike. I was relieved when Peter and the team returned safely to the hotel that afternoon. We bowed to common sense and cancelled plans to eat out, settling instead for the services of the in-house restaurant.

We were driving dangerously late in the evening on our return to Ibadan and by the time we pulled into IITA, it was dark. We were no sooner inside our house than there was a knock at the back door. David had come over from his quarters and now stood there, obviously anxious to speak to me. He greeted me briefly then launched into the real purpose behind his visit.

"Madame, on de night before yesterdee, dat 'ouse over dere was brokken into and de security guards come 'ere and arrested me for stealin'!" David paused to assess the impact of this news. Satisfied that he had my undivided attention, he took a second to arrange his little body into its storytelling position; arms folded across his chest and one leg extended, splayed to the side. Suitably arranged, he continued, "I wuz tekken down to 'edquarters. De security men were angry an' shouted at me, 'Tell us what yo' did or we will keel yo'!'" David's eyes blazed with indignation. It was obvious that he relished the opportunity to tell his story.

"So I said to dem, 'I doan even know what I am supposed to 'ave done.' Den I asked dem if dey were goin' to keel *everyone* who lived in boys' quarters or jes me."

I hid a smile at the mental picture of the feisty old fellow giving cheek to the tough security guards. As he drew breath, I slipped in a question of my own.

"How long did they hold you, David?" I was concerned that they might have harassed him for a lengthy period.

The little man's eyes glinted.

"For *ten* minutes, Madame!" he replied, furiously. To my credit, I still didn't smile. David went on, "And den I said to dem, 'Jest because God has given yo' a position of a'torrity, yo' wear guns and threaten to keel innocent old men. Well, yo' are nothin' but wicked sinners!'"

David paused, obviously savouring the memory of his defiance and he marked its significance by arranging his arms into a different configuration and changing legs so that the other one took up point duty. He hadn't finished his story by a long shot.

"Den I said, 'If it wazzen for God's a'torrity, yo' wouldn't be able to do dis an' if Madame was 'ome yo' wouldn't be doin' it either!'"

Apparently David had a high regard for my influence, bracketing me in such company, although he fixed me with a reproachful look, making sure I felt guilty for being away when most needed. I was then subjected to a list of shortcomings to be found in security guards in general and Yoruba security guards in particular. I uttered conciliatory words until he eventually ran out of steam then, looking and sounding much happier, the old man said goodnight and returned to his quarters. As I headed indoors, I wondered if all my domestic dramas would be resolved with as little inconvenience to myself. Perhaps I could arrange to be away for the next one, too.

The issue of ethnic rivalry was never far below the surface when Patrick and David came face-to-face. They eyed each other with deep suspicion and a rigorous tussle for top pecking order seemed inevitable. I decided to quash trouble before it arose by reminding Patrick that he was a visitor to IITA and must behave accordingly. Issues of seniority simply didn't come into it.

"On IITA, you are seen but not heard, my friend," I told him firmly, because we knew that stirrers could easily be warned off the campus. I took the opportunity to expand my lecture. "And that includes horn-blowing," I added, because the accursed tooting had crept back into existence.

"But, Marm..."

I held up my hand and cut him off before he could launch into his usual excuse.

"No, Patrick, you *don't* need to let people know you are coming, because on IITA, you are going to drive slowly and let pedestrians have right of way *all* the time."

Patrick sighed, probably wishing Marm a speedy recovery from this quirky need for peace and quiet. It was not long before Patrick encountered an innocent soul walking quietly down an IITA street, a plastic container of water perfectly balanced upon her head. Suddenly the serene atmosphere was shattered by a blast of the horn and as the startled pedestrian jumped aside, the water container on her head teetered. It was time I resorted to unfair tactics.

"Ah, Patrick, you have played into my hands." I was almost enjoying this battle of wills. "I am reducing your tip to help you remember what I said," I told him, "and the fines will get bigger each time."

His rueful laugh told me I had landed a telling blow but the preoccupied tapping of his fingers on the steering wheel suggested he was already calculating how long he'd need to wait before testing my resolve. I sighed. Life would be so much simpler if some of Reuben's serenity would rub off on the other two, but, I had to admit, that would make life less interesting.

One day Philomena, an IITA resident, originally from the tiny West African country of Togo, invited me to go with her to the markets. The thought of shopping with another woman appealed greatly. Philomena loved clothes, always looked a million dollars, and could be relied upon to be as interested as I was in the wonderful fabrics on sale. It would be a change from Patrick, who traipsed around with me, stifling yawns.

Philomena drove and as we passed through Ibadan's streets, I pointed out sights that still amazed and amused me. I was watching a push-bike rider with a bag of grain on his head when a noisy toot caught my attention. A motor bike chugged towards us, cutting a wide swathe amongst the pedestrians who were also using this busy street, for balanced on the head of the pillion rider (fortunately a taller man) was a full sized garage tilt-a-door. I turned to Philomena to share the moment but she had already looked away. She had grown up in West Africa and such sights didn't even register.

At the markets Philomena bargained cheerfully, without the aggression I had come to expect whenever Africans did business. Our shopping was proceeding happily when a young woman asked her in English if her 'yellow friend' was going to buy anything. All eyes turned to me and when people saw that I had understood the words, laughter erupted.

"Who *says* I'm yellow?" I demanded, pretending to be affronted.

"Yo' har a *little* beet yellow, Madame," the stallholder said, holding her ground. A young man seemed unsure of my reaction and decided to mollify me.

"We know yo' are called a whart person, Madame, but de collar of yo' skin…it's…um…not really whart *or* yellow, but…grey?"

My howl of dismay made everyone laugh all the more. I held out an arm for inspection.

"Look at my arm. Is *that* what you call yellow or grey?" I demanded.

"Well, maybe not, Madame, but," and he paused, his confidence dwindling, then he went on, "What collar do *yo'* say yo' har?"

I studied my arm carefully, playing to the gallery as the circle around me grew. I chose the most flattering of the ideas that sprang to mind. "Tan, maybe?"

Philomena could contain herself no longer. As a West African educated in Europe, she knew how differently I would define and categorise colours. She also knew that 'yellow' was not meant as a flattering description, so perhaps that's why she decided to terminate all speculation.

"Haven't you people been to school?" she scolded severely. "Don't you know what 'yellow' looks like? Madame is *not* yellow. *That's* yellow," and she pointed to a young man's faded yellow tee shirt, which was uncomfortably close to what Caucasians call 'skin-tone'. I shook my head and clicked my tongue in mock disapproval of their poor colour discrimination and made my escape before I heard any more truisms.

Several kilometres from home we were caught in a go-slow near a 'fool' station where hundreds of women and children were queuing with their tins for household kerosene. The crowd spilled across the road, reducing the traffic flow to a frustrated, horn-tooting trickle. As we inched forward, a group of soldiers arrived. They pushed past our car and began yelling and gesticulating in an attempt to clear the road. A man in the crowd shouted back at them and in reply, a soldier stepped forward and viciously jabbed him in the stomach with the butt of his rifle. The crowd shrank back and we had an uninterrupted view from our car. When the man fell to the ground, the soldier kicked him. The women and children watched in silence, for there was nothing they could do. The man was hauled to his feet and marched off at gunpoint and the crowd, subdued and grim-faced, resumed their vigil beside their kerosene containers while Philomena and I continued our journey, feeling sick and shaky.

The morning was getting on and David had not appeared in the garden as usual, but before I could check on him in his quarters, he arrived at the back door, a picture of misery. He told me he felt 'eel in de stomach' and he invited me to come and see what he had 'brott opp'. I declined the offer and suggested that Patrick drive him down to the clinic but David would have none of it, insisting that Nigerian staff received second class treatment there.

"It's not de same treatment dey give yo', Madame," he informed me, no doubt blaming those wicked Yorubas again. I could tell by the stubborn look on the old man's face that I wouldn't convince him otherwise, so I saved my breath. Against my better judgement, I offered to pay for a visit to a doctor of his choice. My peace of mind was not helped when later, at aerobics, I described David's symptoms and one of the women reported calmly that her nanny had had something similar, had gone to a doctor in the village and the next day was dead. Had I known the statistics that were to be released for 1993, showing that twenty percent of all deaths in Nigeria that year were directly related to imported fake drugs (*The Nigerian Guardian*, 14 March, 1994), I would have been even more worried.

I scurried home, the weight of responsibility heavy upon my shoulders. First port of call was David's door as I checked to see that he hadn't succumbed to the same fate. He certainly looked sick but he welcomed the opportunity to describe in minute detail his visit to his doctor.

As I listened to the story of a complicated diagnosis requiring unconventional treatment (all of which depended upon regular injections of money from Madame), I decided that David and I had been assessed as potential bunnies. I discarded my principles of non-interference and told David that in future, I would pay only for medical attention received at the IITA clinic. To my surprise, he didn't argue and went that same day. He soon began to recover, although it was a slow process. As I watched him return to health, I also watched our lovely garden deteriorate.

There was nothing for it but to attack it myself so I got up early one morning and set upon the weeding and pruning with all the vigour of a newly-fit aerobics enthusiast. A couple of hours later I staggered inside and showered, well pleased with the uncluttered look I left behind. I was still basking in self-satisfaction when I was called to the back door by a loud knocking. David obviously felt better because he stood there tittering behind his hand, for all the world like a mischievous garden gnome. He reported that Madame had cleaned out a particular garden bed of Mrs Kang's most valuable imported specimens and that an eagle-eyed neighbour, whose garden was inferior to the Kangs', had pounced upon the pile of garden refuse and whisked much of it away for replanting at her place.

Back into the searing heat I went, scrabbling amongst what remained of the debris, trying to coax back to life the wilting remnants of Jeanette's horticultural treasures. David stood nearby offering advice. The reversal of roles caused a few jaws to drop as IITA residents drove past and observed me on my hands and knees with David standing nearby directing my efforts.

I decided to accept my limitations. The garden was too large and too beautiful to survive my forays so we employed a young man who worked well under David's supervision. Soon it was back to its former glory.

Life was a joy and I relished it, knowing this leisure was time limited. Eventually I would be back in Australia, caught up in a busy life, wishing I had time to relax. For me, the lazy days stretched into weeks and we loved our house and its view more each day. I walked, swam, went to aerobics, played tennis, borrowed interesting books from the library, visited the children and socialised with friends. And I watched with pleasure as my two tapestries revealed themselves.

Chapter 12
THE END OF A BEAUTIFUL FRIENDSHIP

I had been out for the day and when I arrived home, Reuben told me that the pork I had ordered from Mr Titoloye was in the refrigerator. I had not, of course, ordered anything, but there it was, a five-and-a-half kilogram leg of pork. Reuben explained the details. The vendor had arrived and told him that I had placed an order and had paid in advance. On that basis, Reuben had no hesitation in accepting it. As I gazed at the huge piece of pig, I decided that this time Mr Titoloye had pushed his luck too far. I eagerly awaited his next visit but he cunningly stayed away for some weeks. Unfortunately for him my feathers were still ruffled when I opened the door to find him standing there. I chose not to remember that the previous Sunday, I had served non-Muslim friends from a large, tasty, baked leg of pork.

"Mr Titoloye, I am very cross with you. You had no right to leave pork here without my permission."

"Oh, dat," he said, and waved a dismissive hand in the air, "Deese things 'appen when pepple are away an' I carn ask dem, Madame." Without invitation, he brushed past me into the house. "De other lady didn't want it, so I sold it to yo' instead." I took a moment to pay due respect to so much audacity contained in one small body, but I quickly hauled my attention back to the moment because Mr Titoloye was speaking again.

"We mus' now adjust de account to show dat yo' money is all used up, then we can..." He got no further.

"No, Mr Titoloye. Our business dealings are over." Then I

remembered those delicious prawns. "If I ever forgive you and decide to deal with you again, I shall leave word at the security gates that you may call. Until then, you do not visit this house. Is that understood?"

He looked at me, stunned, and the little shoulders slumped momentarily as he digested this unpalatable news. Suddenly he brightened. He reinflated, his eyebrows shot up and a bright smile lit his face.

"But, Madame, yo' promised me a copy of de photo. I mus' come and collect it, so I will call next time to see if it is ready!"

"You shall do no such thing," I snapped. "When the photo is ready, I will put it in an envelope addressed to you and leave it at the security gate. Goodbye, Mr Titoloye."

I had remained at the door and now, with a sweep of my hand, I indicated that he should leave.

He gazed at me for a moment as he collected his thoughts. Mr Titoloye was no quitter and he tried one more roll of the dice, this time revealing a creative streak.

"Hokay, Madame, I will go, but before I do, I mus' tell yo' dat when I saw yo' husband last time, he promised to borrow me N2000 to have my car repaired, because we are frens." His serious expression reflected the importance of the man-to-man relationship. Surely Madame wouldn't question men's business? He went on, "Yo' can give me dat now, to save me comin' buck."

I didn't even bother to reply, just pointed out the open door. He departed and as the little figure plodded down the garden path, even the green satin robes looked dejected as they hung limply, without so much as a flutter.

Peter's tours throughout the country continued and I decided to go north with him to the city of Kano. As Patrick guided the car along the pot-holed highway it began to rain and soon the heavy storm had water cascading down the bitumen. Conditions were more treacherous than ever, so we were moving slowly when we saw, through the blinding rain, a man kneeling in the middle of the road.

As we edged closer, we saw that he was doing his washing in

the cascading water. Admiring his ingenuity, if not his sense of safety, we waved, Patrick tooted and we manoeuvred around him and were on our way.

Further on, with the rain behind us, we overtook a man riding a small motorbike. Strapped securely to the pillion seat was a large, rather disconcerted pig. I have heard that the flesh of animals killed while stressed tastes different from meat obtained from those not quite so aware of their impending doom. By the wild look in this pig's eye, someone was in for some strange-tasting pork in the next few days.

I had read about Kano and knew of its interesting past as the southern destination for trans-Saharan camel trains. As we drove around the city, we couldn't see any camels, nor could we find the forestry office. As we crossed a busy intersection, Patrick nonchalantly halted the progress of dozens of cars by stopping in the centre of the road and asking directions from the traffic warden who was directing the afternoon rush. The 'yellow fever', as these unfortunates are nicknamed because of the colour of their shirts, promptly abandoned his post and, uninvited, climbed into our car.

"Turn right, den go straight," he instructed Patrick, while Peter and I exchanged incredulous looks.

A few more twists and turns and we arrived at our destination. We handed our guide a healthy tip, guiltily aware that we were encouraging dereliction of duty in this already undisciplined country. Meanwhile, back at the intersection, the evening traffic battled on unaided.

My days in Kano were spent sightseeing and shopping. Patrick's friend, Alfred, was also there, having driven Simon and Andrew in another FORMECU vehicle.

One day Patrick asked if Alfred could accompany us to the markets. He was lively company, with a good sense of humour and an interesting mix of friendliness and assertiveness. He added another dimension to the shopping trip because I had to contend not only with the bargaining process, but also with Alfred's innate dislike of the Hausa ethnic group, the main inhabitants of this part of the country. It was only a matter of time before the usual market banter became heated and on one occasion, Alfred and a stallholder stood nose-to-nose exchanging insults.

"Yo' call dat nice material? I wouldn't wear dat to de Kano yam festival!" Alfred shouted in the face of a vendor who was offering a piece of material for my inspection. It was the final straw and the man turned on me.

"Madame, yo' select and bargain with me if yo' wish, but I will no longer tolerate dis bud mun in my shop!" then he turned back to Alfred and resumed posturing like a fighting-cock.

I told Patrick to take Alfred away. They could keep an eye on me from a distance. To my surprise they didn't argue, but retreated to the shade of a tree until I moved on. When I rejoined them, I decided to find out what was behind their ready obedience. They admitted that the hostility between Yoruba and Hausa ethnic groups was such that this type of incident could well escalate and end with the two Yorubas getting daggers in the back.

I decided it was time we moved on. We crossed town to another market and I began my search for material suitable for long shorts, which I seemed to live in these days. Having heard me describe the garment I intended sewing, Alfred moved ahead, stopping at stalls to make inquiries on my behalf, unfortunately using a loud voice.

"Madame wants knickers. What material do yo' 'ave dat would be nice for dem?" he asked. I consoled myself that he was probably just using the Nigerian term for walk shorts, but I would have preferred that he mind his own business.

Next day, back in Abuja, we booked in at the Sheraton, an older hotel than the beautiful Hilton, but clean and secure. That evening we headed down to one of its restaurants to be greeted by posters promoting Switzerland as a holiday destination. The food and décor were appropriate to the theme and the Nigerian staff was friendly and helpful. When the two wines that Peter recognised were declared 'finished, sorry Sah', he again perused the list.

"What can you tell me about the Hungarian Chardonnay?" he inquired of the young man who was hovering nearby, beautifully attired in full drinks-waiter regalia.

"Ah...um..." He looked troubled for a moment then he brightened as the details came back to him. "It's med from greppes, Sah."

Peter nodded solemnly and accepted this as an excellent recommendation for any wine and he ordered accordingly. It was delicious. One can't beat greppes as an ingredient for wine.

We had an uneventful trip back to Ibadan and as we wheeled into the driveway of our house, we saw a new sign had been erected near the footpath: 'PT CRANNY', it read. I no longer felt like a hermit crab that had ousted another resident. The place was ours.

The price of fuel rose, not by the rumoured seven hundred percent, but sufficiently to put enormous strain on Nigerians. The cost of public transport soared and Patrick told me that people were feeling the pinch more than at any other time in his memory. We sent him to buy a bag of *gari* (cassava flour) for himself, to store in case things become even worse.

That week, when I greeted David while he worked around the garden, the old man took the opportunity of asking a question.

"Madame, may I buy a teabag from yo' because dat way I can have three cups o'tea today. I very much like de tea," he added poignantly. Then he went on, "Also, would it be possible for yo' to borrow me N30 until pay-day? I am out of food."

I went inside and stepped into my walk-in pantry and stood looking at the shelves. I gazed at things that I have grown to regard as essentials - plastic wrap, aluminium cooking foil, cooking spray, minerals; the list went on and on. My shelves were laden with frivolous things and outside the gardener was asking for $AU1.05 to see him through the two weeks till pay-day. I collected a handful of teabags and went and put them into David's hand.

As we parted, the old man smiled up into my face.

"I say thank yo' with words, Madame, but de *real* reward will come from a higher a'torrity." I didn't share David's confidence in the pulling power of half-a-dozen tea bags. It was time I lifted my game. I went in search of Reuben.

"Reuben, do you have enough money to feed your family?" I asked bluntly.

As I watched, his normally serene face was transformed by distress. He began to shuffle from foot to foot and his hands clasped and unclasped as he looked at me. When the words came, they were choked, interspersed with coughs of humourless laughter, trying to disguise the extent of his distress.

"I jes doan know what I'm goin' to do, Madame. I 'ave de choice of sending de kids to school or buyin' food for de table." Then he turned away, embarrassed, and began to wipe down the already clean kitchen bench.

"Did Mrs Kang tell to you, Madame, what she does when we doan 'ave any food?"

I asked him to tell me and he turned to face me again.

"She sends me 'ome with a tin of powdered milk, or if she and Doctor Kang catch fish in de lake, she gives me some. She wuz always doin' it, Madame."

My own voice was unsteady as I told Reuben that we would help in the way Mrs Kang had.

"I woan be askin' all de time, Madame," he said, quietly. I turned and went to the other end of the house while I regained my composure. *No Reuben,* I thought, *you shouldn't have to.*

Before she left, Jeanette had told me that she did not lend money to the men nor pay them more than the going rate because in the past that had caused friction amongst workers on IITA. Now I knew that she helped in other ways, just as the Gulleys, Philomena and others helped their staff.

That evening Peter and I talked it over and decided that we were less bound by IITA protocol than our friends, so we'd bring forward the men's scheduled wage rise, still a few months off. Also, I could ensure they always had milk, tea and eggs. I set about learning from Nancy and Philomena, ways of getting extra provisions to the men. I adopted the local idea of giving instead of receiving on one's own birthday or special days and by putting our minds to it, we found special days galore that could be used for the purpose. In the months ahead, we were able to mark our birthdays and those of our kids, Australia Day, Easter, etc., by asking Nigerian friends to celebrate with us by accepting a gift of food.

The day after Patrick took home his first supply of milk and tea, he greeted me with a beaming face.

"Thanks for yesterdee, Marm," he said. "Yi! Mercy called de neighbours an' we celebrated. I wuz able to give *five* friends a cup o'tea," and he rubbed the stubble on his head, awestruck at his ability to entertain on such a scale. He went on, "Now I leave de tin of milk on top of de fridge so everyone sees it when dey come in. Dey all say, 'Hey, yo' mus' be a big man, Patrick, to 'ave such a large tin o'powdered milk!' Our whole community said a prayer for de Crunnys, Marm."

I wasn't comfortable with the gratitude. "Thanks, Patrick, but I hardly think a tin of powdered milk is too much to expect..."

He wasn't prepared to have the matter dismissed lightly. "Nor, nor, nor. I 'ave not been able to afford to give my children milk for five years," he said, then added, "but now, dey have milk and whenever we've bin to Lagos, dey know I will 'ave bread with me. Even if I am late, dey hear me and dey are up, sayin' 'Duddy, did yo' bring any bread today?'"

As I listened I thought, may God forgive me if I whinge ever again in my whole life.

The year was wearing on and despite the on-again-off-again fuel shortage, Peter and his team needed to tour the extreme north. I was invited along too, on a trip which was to take in Lake Chad and the famous Sahara Desert. In preparation, I began reading about the north, its desert dwellers and the present problems caused by the creeping sands.

Then, as if looking forward to the trip wasn't excitement enough, our son Tim rang with an idea that had Peter and I anticipating Christmas with the eagerness of five year olds waiting for Santa.

Beatrice, Ayo & Family

David, Pam & Reuben

Mr Titoloye & Pam

Patrick, Mercy & Family

Gbade

Mahdi & Pam

Chapter 13
WHAT A DIFFERENCE A DAY MAKES

B efore leaving Australia, Peter and I had made an offer to our boys and girls that was based on pipe-dreams. If any of the couples decided to visit us, we told them, we'd share the expense. But it was a long way to come and the cost of even half the fare so high that we didn't hold out much hope that any of them would visit.

Only Mark, Glen and Lisa had ever travelled overseas and none had been to West Africa. In the past few months Tim and Louise had toyed with the idea of coming, but they'd been discouraged by Nigeria's transport and security problems. It didn't seem sensible to make the journey and then spend most of their time confined to IITA. Peter and I accepted that we were in line for our first ever Christmas not surrounded by family.

But what a difference a day makes! A simple suggestion from Tim turned the whole idea around. Why don't we meet in Europe instead?

The idea caught on like wildfire. By the following weekend, the other two couples had declared themselves in and Peter had considered it from all angles and had given the nod of approval. I pored over our inflatable globe and came up with a list of possible destinations. What about Paris? Miserable in December, said Glen. Rome, then? Lisa's voice betrayed her feelings as she remembered a bout of Italian food poisoning. Well, what about Spain? Mark cut to the heart of the matter.

Wasn't the whole idea of meeting in Europe, he asked, largely aimed at being together for a white Christmas? I happily retired from the discussion and left the details to the young ones. Before long Glen came up with the solution. We would go to Salzburg, Austria. Peter and I walked around grinning at each other, carefully avoiding doing any sums.

On Monday morning I hurried across to IITA's Travel Department and booked our flight to Munich, where we'd all meet, then drive to Salzberg. I chose to ignore the travel clerk's remark that the *harmattan* sometimes closed the Lagos Airport for days on end during December. That wasn't going to happen this year. I busied myself with preparations for the Saharan trip, glad to be occupied instead of sitting and counting the days until December 18.

We were to fly to the north of Nigeria and meet with Peter's colleagues who were stationed in the area, so when all the arrangements were in place, Patrick drove us to the domestic airport in Lagos. As we went, we looked around for evidence of President Abacha's promise of a massive clean up. The Acting Secretary of State Government had declared that 'the present military administration…is determined to remove filth in all areas and make Lagos one of the cleanest states not only in the federation but in the entire world' (*Nigerian Guardian*, 25 November, 1993). This was to be achieved by dividing the city into sections with teams of street cleaners employed to beautify their own patch.

There was some activity. Here and there men were shovelling rubbish from gutters and drains into wheelbarrows then, like a string of ants, they disappeared around corners with their loads. We hoped that more was happening between this street and the next than a futile exchange of rubbish.

We arrived at the domestic airport and as Patrick parked the car, Peter and I carried our luggage inside. I was stunned. Months ago, my first experience of the international terminal had been a culture shock, but by comparison with this, that had been a model of efficiency. Touts descended like flies, shouting, haranguing, grasping at luggage. We'd been warned that if we relaxed our grip, we'd never see our possessions again. I kept repeating 'No thank you, no thank you, no thank you,' but Peter used a more direct approach, ordering our tormentors loudly to 'buzz off'. Neither technique made the slightest difference.

We struggled through to a desk and eventually bought tickets for a flight that went direct to our destination of Maiduguri in the far north-east of the country. There were more tickets allocated than seats available, we were told, so we must keep an eye on our plane and move quickly to a barricade on the tarmac's edge at the first sign of activity. Then, having passed through the barricade, we must check that we had the correct plane by reading the blackboard at the foot of the boarding steps.

We found two rickety chairs and began our vigil. As we watched, our plane became one of an identical flock, as other aircraft taxied around and like giant birds, selected nesting spots near ours, before sprouting blackboards of their own. We were too far away to read the writing, so we were no longer sure which sign of activity should stimulate us into a competitive frenzy at the barricade.

A young man carrying a clipboard appeared in front of us and interrupted my dithering about the problem. In businesslike manner he informed us that we must pay an additional amount of N500 per person as departure tax. Peter asked to see some identification and the man ambled off, assuring us that he would return soon. He didn't, but a short time later another gentleman, this time in airport uniform, approached. He spoke to us, concerned that the man seen talking to us earlier may have tried to collect departure tax when, in fact, he was *not even an airport employee*. We managed to contain our astonishment. We were assured, however, that he himself *was* an official and as proof, he tapped the identification tag clipped to the inside of his shirt pocket.

Peter asked him to tell us more, so he bent closer in a confidential manner. It was possible, he said, that the shyster had exaggerated the amount of the boarding fee to maximise his ill-gotten gains. In fact, the amount due was only N250 per person. If we would just give him that amount, he would attend to the paperwork immediately, without us having to leave the comfort of our chairs.

Peter nodded slowly, obviously appreciative of the reduction and the kind offer of assistance. Just a formality of course, but could he have a closer look at that identification tag? The young man unclipped his tag and, talking all the while, waved it under our noses and put it away again.

Peter's hand remained outstretched and with great reluctance, the tag was handed over. It was indeed airport employee identification, complete with photo of our friend, but under his picture we read the words 'Assistant Cleaner'. We laughed out loud. The man huffily retrieved his precious tag and retorted that he was quite entitled to collect fees because "at dis airport, all de staff worked 'and in 'and."

Finally realising that Peter wasn't going to swallow the multi-skilling story, he turned on his heel and left, while I wondered uneasily which of his colleagues intended flying our plane. Peter then admitted that he had known all along that departure tax didn't apply to domestic passengers, but he had been unable to resist pulling a few legs.

Completely irrepressible, the cleaner reappeared to tell us it was time to line up at a barricade outside the building. He grinned cheekily as we tipped him for this assistance and disappeared into the crowd, no doubt in search of someone to help with boarding fees.

I was standing at the barricade, waiting for the nod to proceed to the plane when a hand reached across my shoulder and latched onto the airline ticket in my left hand. I held on grimly and turned to face a young man in his twenties, dressed in tout's regalia of slacks and loud shirt. He ignored my demand that he let go immediately and insisted that he would help me with 'de formalities'.

Just then a batch of passengers, including Peter, was allowed through and they were now hurrying towards the plane. Through clenched teeth I hissed at the man to get lost, but it was like water off a duck's back. Still tugging, he began a shouting match with the official who had stepped forward to stem the flow of passengers. The ticket tug-of-war continued as I lowered my hand luggage to the ground and clasped it between my ankles. One by one, I prised open the man's fingers with my free hand and while he was particularly distracted with his arguing, I jerked the ticket free. The two men stopped shouting and looked at me in surprise, then exchanged a few quiet words in their own language. It dawned on me that their discussion was about the division of the money they hoped to extract from me. The man at the barricade spoke.

"It's hokay. Give 'im de ticket," he instructed me, backing his words with a flurry of gestures that I interpreted as a promise that if I handed over the ticket, the two of us could proceed through. I could see Peter walking on ahead, unaware of my predicament, so I did as I was told and was released onto the tarmac. My flashily dressed friend accompanied me, my ticket in his hand. Just as we arrived at the foot of the boarding steps, a woman in uniform picked up the blackboard and strode off so we scampered after her, remembering to check for taxiing planes as we went. My self-appointed assistant was there, glued to my shoulder as we fell into line once more behind the elusive blackboard.

An attendant checked Peter's ticket, confirmed that this plane was indeed headed for Maiduguri and waved him aboard. Because I had been assessed as incapable of carrying my own ticket I stood watching as the tricky manoeuvre of handing it to the attendant was accomplished. But I was about to spring a coup of my own. As the passenger's copy was handed back, I intercepted it and strode up the steps, pausing at the top to look down at the indignant face of my right hand man. Where was my gratitude, he demanded to know. I owed him money for all de assistance he had given me. With a smile not totally devoid of malice, I disappeared inside.

Seated beside Peter in the decrepit plane, I recalled what I had heard about Nigeria's domestic airlines. It was, we were told by a wag much given to bleak humour, cheaper for Nigerian airlines to trade in a plane than wash it because Western countries sold them for a song once they no longer met noise and air pollution regulations at home.

This particular plane was of Russian origin and, judging by the accent of the captain, it must have been a package deal. I couldn't imagine a near-bankrupt Russia or a completely bankrupt Nigerian airline being particularly fastidious about maintenance. And why would a Russian pilot need to work in a country where payment of salaries was a hit-and-miss affair? I didn't like any of my own answers, so I hauled Saint Christopher out of retirement.

The pilot interrupted my supplications by announcing a change in the flight plan; we were to land at Abuja where there'd be a 'short delay' before we proceeded to Maiduguri. I had been in Nigeria too long to be fazed by such a minor adjustment. Resuming my prayers, I settled back for the journey.

As we flew north-east, I memorised the route we were to take once we were on the ground and the names and roles of the people to accompany us. Over the next week we were to travel from Maiduguri north-east to Lake Chad, then, retracing our steps through Maiduguri, head west through Damutura, then north to Gashua and Yusafari. Here we'd be standing on the edge of the mighty Sahara.

Of our companions, I was particularly keen to meet Mrs Le'an ('Lee-arn'), the Tropical Forest Action Plan's regional co-ordinator for the north-east and someone whom Peter regarded highly, considering her one of the most capable people involved in the entire project. She must have overcome high obstacles to gain such a senior position. Her headquarters were in the city of Jos and with members of her staff, she would now be driving to Maiduguri to meet up with us. She would travel with us all week, discussing with Peter aspects of the overall project in terms of her area.

Our plane touched down at Abuja, but without a major delay we continued on our way. In Maiduguri, the wide, sandy streets were as I imagined they would be, so close to the Sahara, but the intense green of the neem trees lining the streets came as a surprise. The species, originally from India, loved these conditions and flourished. Their shade provided wonderful meeting places where groups gathered to chat. Here businessmen brokered their deals, teachers taught chanting children sitting at their feet (the Koran grasped in their hands), women gossiped and men sprawled languidly on cane mats.

Unexpectedly, my attention was caught by a pleasant but unfamiliar perfume in the air, so subtle that I was unable to identify it or even describe it accurately. Perhaps it was from the neem trees, but the foresters in the group didn't strongly support my theory. In the absence of proof, I decided it was the distilled essence of this continent, the scent of Africa.

While Peter and Mrs Le'an discussed the week's itinerary, I studied the trim, quietly spoken lady and her eighteen year old daughter, Iisha, who was travelling with her mother during a break in her university studies. I watched and listened as Mrs Le'an briefed Peter thoroughly and although I didn't understand the technical details, I could see that Peter appreciated the thoroughness with which she handled her responsibilities.

As I listened, I looked at mother and daughter and I compared the lives of the Le'an and Cranny families. Mrs Le'an had tertiary qualifications, was employed in a senior position in a government department, and had three children with the potential to attend university. Superficially, our family situations had similarities, yet when the prospects of the young people were compared, the differences were stark. Again I wondered how much longer the people of Nigeria would tolerate the injustice of having their nation's wealth frittered away instead of being used to provide better opportunities for all.

As the days progressed, Iisha and I often waited under neem trees while the workers were tied up in meetings. Iisha would reach for a bottle of soft drink, casually apply her strong white teeth to the crown seal that would normally require a bottle opener, and then hand me the opened bottle. We would settle comfortably and for the next few hours, exchange stories of our different worlds. I spoke of family, social work and Australian society and she told me of university life, giving me insight into a world where culture and science collide. Iisha had inherited her mother's quiet manner and in a calm voice she described an annual ritual at her university, one that no amount of policing could eradicate. Each year a third-year medical student was killed, sacrificed by fellow students in a clandestine ritual, an offering meant to promote their chances of academic success. Iisha spoke with resignation, not hopeful that such superstitions would ever change, even in an environment dedicated to teaching scientific practices.

Our travels continued. We visited Lake Chad, which forms part of the border of four countries, Cameroon, Chad, Nigeria, and Niger, and we hired boats and were taken out to inspect its reedy waterways. At this famous landmark, I visualised a globe and pinpointed my location on this planet, enjoying my own incredulity each time I 'saw' where I was. We clambered back into the vehicles and headed south again, through Maiduguri, then west to Damutura. Finally we headed north, pushing towards the Sahara. We paused at tiny settlements and each time Peter and I became the focus of open-mouthed awe. The adults had known white missionaries some years ago but we were the first whites that the children had ever seen. At each stop, Peter was introduced to the Head Man of the community and he explained through an interpreter the reasons for the visit.

Meanwhile, I tried to communicate with the children. Any sudden movement from me and they screamed and scattered, but I was too fascinating a spectacle to ignore. Eventually, a brave child would respond to my outstretched hand with a tentative prod and when the sky didn't fall, a tiny fist would clasp each of my fingers. I was the Pied Piper, with dozens of fascinated children in tow, giggling, near-naked tots who stared at me with eyes only slightly less amazed than my own, for I was looking down at small faces covered in white ash, a local treatment for a skin condition, perhaps chicken pox. They began repeating my words and I listened to the echo of my drawl, "Har-low. Har-low…" *Is that*, I wondered, *how I really sound?*

Each day's travel was punctuated by stops to inspect shelter-belts, large plots of vegetation about five kilometres long and one kilometre wide. As part of an earlier World Bank project, they had been planted at right angles to the prevailing *harmattan* to anchor the sand and to provide protection for crops and animals. Left to mature, they were now producing firewood and building materials for local communities.

We stopped at a village where a dignified Head Man movingly told Peter, in English, how greatly he would appreciate any project offering employment for his young people. With quiet courtesy he invited us to inspect the homes of two families in his village. We felt honoured and we circled the round huts, inspecting the grass walls and thatched roofs as the construction was explained. I bent and stepped through the low doorway into the darkness of the first dwelling and as my eyes adjusted to the dim light, I found myself face-to-face with the family horse. It drew back in fright, but given time it nuzzled my hand, though it didn't seem overly impressed with this strangely pale being. The smoke from a small fire combined with the odour of horse manure. I stood looking around, trying to imagine for even a minute, the life of the wife and mother within this family. I tried to put myself in her place, to experience, briefly, her expectations and satisfactions, but I couldn't make the transition, so great was the divide.

In the second home, two calves were tethered to a wall and they stood rolling their eyes at me as I listened to an interpreter describe the family's sleeping arrangements in the one large hammock slung across the centre of the hut. I rolled my eyes back at them as I pondered the practicalities of the arrangement.

During this tour, our own sleeping arrangements called for a combination of self-control and sense of humour. Only the proportions varied. At times I knew that bed bugs were a distinct possibility and one evening I wouldn't retire until we had cleared the room of six lizards which ranged in size from forty to sixty centimetres. Actually we cleared the room of five, because number six flatly refused to leave and took up residence on the back of the lounge chair. Reptile and woman spent much of the night eyeing each other suspiciously across the room.

I applied my stock-in-trade technique for keeping things in perspective as the standard of our accommodation deteriorated.

What is the worst thing that could possibly happen to me here, I would ask myself. Each time I'd have to admit that the most serious threats came from bed bugs or lizards and really, neither posed a major threat to my continued existence. Even though I lacked a fondness for either as sleeping companions, I decided to accept them as the price of this trip. A look in a mirror, on the rare occasions when one was available, explained some of the nervousness of children, horses and lizards. In this climate, my hair stood in a crackling halo and the mere sight of a comb or brush was enough to send it into an extra frenzy of static electricity. I pulled my hat down over my ears and tried to forget what I must look like.

During the evenings, the temperature dropped to a comfortable level and for those hours at least, we weren't covered in perspiration. Peter and I would rise in the cool of the morning and, dressed in shirtsleeves, we'd step outside to hear our companions complaining bitterly that 'dis cold is too motch' as they huddled in parkas and beanies.

The sequence of novel experiences continued. Our vehicles paused to allow camel trains to cross the road; people in bright traditional costumes and elaborate head-dress sauntered by; always, we were aware of the restless sand as the Sahara moved on. There were other surprises too. We came upon fadamas, a system of agriculture in valleys where farmers used simple means to tap water that was not far below the surface. In places the water seeped through to form lush green areas surrounded by desert, wetlands where birdlife congregated.

At last we retraced our steps to Maiduguri. The wonderful north-eastern safari was coming to an end and as we said goodbye to our companions I was sorry to realise that I would not be seeing Iisha again. For a moment we daydreamed of her visiting Australia, but we knew the chances of it happening were infinitesimally small. We arrived at the airport, checked in, and set about waiting for our afternoon flight back to Lagos, where Patrick would be awaiting for us.

Eventually, we became concerned at the lack of activity out on the tarmac. There didn't seem to be any planes capable of flying anywhere, let along the length of the country. Finally airport staff had to admit that it didn't look as if our plane was going to arrive today. Perhaps we should book into a hotel and return the following morning? With few other options, it seemed like a good idea.

We returned to the hotel that we'd used a week ago and asked for the same room. Instinct led me to inspect the bed and there it was, the same linen. A large ink-spot near my pillow last week remained in exactly the same location and the sheets were creased, not taut and crisp, fresh from the laundry. Maybe, I told myself, there hadn't been many guests before or after our last visit? And if there had been, perhaps they were good types who bathed regularly? I looked around and couldn't see a single lizard so I pronounced myself lucky and fell into bed. My final thought for the day focused on how one went about fumigating oneself and one's spouse.

We returned to the airport next morning and discovered that at last our plane was honouring Maiduguri with a visit. Soon we were bound for Lagos and hoping that Patrick hadn't given up and gone back to Ibadan without us.

Chapter 14
GETTING READY FOR SANTA

Patrick was there, all smiles, waiting for us. We considered ourselves doubly fortunate. Not only was our transport home assured, but also with a few barks in the Yoruba language, he spared us the worst of the touts' attentions. He explained that last night, when told that no more domestic flights would be landing, he had slept in the Sheraton Hotel's carpark and returned to the airport at daylight to resume his vigil. His common sense spared us hours of struggling to arrange a new rendezvous and now, as we drove towards Ibadan, we brought ourselves up to date with an exchange of news.

Because we were to be away for Christmas, Peter and I were keen to have an outing with Patrick and his family before we left. When Nancy told us about the Ibadan Amusement Park, we knew we were onto a winner. The Park was only two years old so it was likely that the rides still worked, although we guessed that none of the machinery would have seen so much as an oil can since the day it was installed.

The following Sunday, when they arrived to collect us, Patrick and Mercy stepped from the car wearing traditional outfits. The three little girls lined up in identical dresses of harsh green. Patrick felt the need to explain. Although he and I had bought pretty dresses for Christina's and Margaret's birthdays in recent weeks, Gladys was still without a new dress because her birthday was some months away. The other two were refused permission to wear their new outfits today because it would make Gladys feel bad. I kicked myself for not foreseeing this problem, but secretly I commended Patrick's thoughtfulness.

Haute couture was the last thing on the children's minds at the moment. As usual, they were silent but today they couldn't stand still in their excitement. We piled into the car and headed for the Amusement Park.

Each ride would have cost the equivalent of half a day's pay for Patrick so we were not surprised to find that we were the only patrons wherever we went. The absence of people played havoc with the atmosphere. Surely blaring music, throbbing crowds and competition for rides are mandatory conditions at a fair? We made our way down deserted alleyways and across empty spaces, with no music, no crowd, no jostling and no laughter unless we provided our own. Occasionally a cluster of people strolled by and they glanced at the stationary equipment, but they moved on and disappeared into a large marquee standing in one corner of the Park grounds. Signs at its entrance wished someone a happy 78th birthday. Not much hope of infectious hijinks overflowing from there into sideshow alley, although the music was appreciated when it started.

But our guests had no preconceived ideas about what a fairground should be like and to them, everything was wonderful. The girls skipped from one ride to the next, missing nothing. Merry-go-rounds, a ferris wheel, a rollercoaster and a miniature train - everywhere we went, surprised operators sprang to the task of cajoling rusting machinery back to life. Patrick and Mercy forgot the traditional reserve between adults and children and they laughed, shouted and clapped hands with as much excitement as the girls.

We came to the dodgem cars and for a brief moment I was ten years old again. I stood there and remembered spinning and crashing, being jolted silly in contrived collisions and knowing beyond all doubt that it was not possible for a kid to have more fun than this.

A sign announced that children under twelve were to use the smaller cars nearby, so Patrick, Mercy and I boarded separate vehicles and prepared to blast off while the children watched.

The cameraman was spoiled for choice. Should he focus on the professional driver's astonishment as he whirred around backwards out of control, or Mercy's blindness as she speared through the 'traffic', her headscarf firmly anchored by two ears and the tip of her nose? Or perhaps three little girls helpless with laughter as they watched their parents' uncharacteristic behaviour?

The day continued as it began, full of fun. As the family licked ice-creams, we headed back to IITA to relive the highlights on the television screen.

Next morning, when I put my head through the doorway of the garage to say hello to Patrick, he got out of the car and smiled at me, his head on one side, fingers fluttering gently. The change from his usually effervescent greeting emphasised the feeling behind his simple words.

"Thanks for yesterdee, Marm."

IITA residents were not to be deprived of an Oktoberfest even though the appropriate month had escaped and it was now December. The Institute's band, The Cockroaches, promised lively entertainment at the Cappa Bar and we strolled across the grass from our house to enjoy again the advantages of living in a small community. There was no need to organise parties for these outings; people simply turned up and the evening's company was arranged by a cheery wave across the room. The Institute's population was the right size to offer variety as well as familiarity.

Tonight as we joined a table with five others, we could hear the Cockroaches warming up. We'd been warned tongue in cheek, that the band consisted of IITA residents who had not yet been offered sufficiently large bribes not to play, but that was too harsh. We enjoyed a lively tempo until, during a lull, a voice called us to order.

It was International Celebrity Time. 'Celebrities' of questionable talent were given a suitably hard time, but suddenly the standard took a turn for the worse. The voice on the microphone boomed across the room:

"...and the next number...(drum roll)...is...(drum roll)...*Waltzing*

Matilda!" A chant went up: 'Cran-nees! Cran-nees!' We needed to do something quickly to avert a riot. I had seen what people are capable of during the Beatles tour of Australia in 1964, so we kangaroo-hopped to the stage and gave it our best shot - noisy, woeful, but apparently amusing to those not being subjected to the same humiliation.

In the days following our return from the northern trip a large parcel had arrived from Glen's fiancée, Lisa. She was teaching Years One and Two at a school to the south of Brisbane and during the year she'd spoken to her small students about the lives of African children. As Christmas approached, her class decided to contact my little friends, sending greetings and soft toys that they'd made in class. Patrick and I now set out with the gifts and a camera to record the event, but our luck was out because every member of staff that I knew well was away and none of the casual employees was prepared to give permission to film. I was disappointed but accepted that the main purpose of the gifts was to give joy to the children, not to provide a photographic session. Besides, this was my last visit before leaving for Europe, so we presented the carton and invited the children to look inside.

They were entranced. First items discovered were the drawings of African animals. These were inspected carefully and declared by the ever-hungry waifs to be 'bush meat'. Then they found the soft toys made from stockings and socks. The children cuddled them and rubbed them against their faces tenderly. Some dolls were made from black stockings and twelve-year-old Mahdi hugged hers with fierce affection, not letting go until she was barked at to do some work. Gbade's curiosity got the better of him. Soon he was laughing at the faces painted on the paper plates, rubbing noses with the stocking dolls and holding up his favourites for me to admire.

I was sorry that Lisa and the children who had worked on the gifts wouldn't be able to see these initial reactions and I resolved to get photos at a later date, even if this degree of awe could never be recaptured. With the warden away, the older children from the remand section inched closer until they too were playing with the toys. I wondered if any of these young people now playing with the soft toys and admiring the drawings, were among the unfortunate ones that the warden ordered shackled at night.

To mark this visit, the last before Christmas, I had taken a chicken and a loaf of fresh bread for the adults to share and I was disappointed that Bose was away. I asked about her absence and was told that her husband had been killed in a motor accident and today was his funeral. Back at IITA, the news had already reached members of the Women's Group and Nancy had begun arranging financial assistance for Bose who would find it difficult enough to pay for the traditional funeral, let alone feed and educate her children on her minuscule salary.

But sadness could not touch me for long at the moment for there was no denying my excitement as the family reunion approached. With only days to go before we left for Europe, I launched into visiting the markets each morning, gathering items for Christmas. Gifts for the family had to be featherweight because the travellers were already bewailing the weight of their luggage. I enlisted Patrick's help with my shopping (as if I could have avoided it) and explained that Glen was about his height and size so I needed his assistance in selecting a pair of black leather shoes. Off to the markets we went and Patrick, after trying on a dozen pairs, finally selected some that he felt would be comfortable for Glen.

That afternoon when Reuben arrived to do the ironing, I noted that his shoes were all but falling off his feet, so I told him that I had a pair of shoes that weren't quite right for my son but maybe they would fit him? Reuben's quiet manner was transformed at the possibility.

"Dey fit me, Madame, dey fit me!" he declared, before his big toe even passed the laces on the way in.

He was right. That evening before he said goodnight, he paused at the back door and mulled over a topic of major importance.

"I bin thinkin' about where I will wear de shoes first, Madame. I 'ave decided on church first an' after dat I will wear dem whenever I need to," and with a happy smile, he departed.

Next day, I told Patrick I needed to borrow his feet one more time because I had changed my mind on the shoes we had bought. Whatever his thoughts about such an indecisive shopper, he kept them to himself and we set off for the markets where he carefully selected another pair.

We planned to give Christmas hampers to Beatrice, Reuben, David and Patrick. When our boys were young, I had loved shopping for bits and pieces for their Christmas stockings and had felt a sense of loss when they outgrew the tradition. This year I could let my head go. I bought wonderful baskets each costing N10 (30 cents) at the markets and stocked up on foodstuffs at the three supermarkets-cum-variety stores, while an unsuspecting Patrick waited in the car. I couldn't imagine well-fed Australians getting excited over a hamper containing rice, vinegar, tea, sugar cubes and other common pantry items, but I knew these were genuine treats for our Nigerian friends. There were festive items too; sweets, shortbread, nuts, bon bons, cordial and, in Patrick's, a bottle of beer.

At home, I piled each basket with food items then added a gift, wrapped and labelled separately, for each family member. Peeping through the foodstuffs, the bright parcels added mystery. Lurking in each hamper, too, was an envelope containing sufficient money for a chicken for Christmas dinner. When they were bursting with goodies, I encased each hamper in transparent cellophane paper and tied it with a big bow. I could hardly wait for the day when we could deliver them.

The morning before we were due to fly out, I greeted Patrick as he waited to take Peter to work. I needed help, I said, in carrying things to the car. He walked through the house, greeted Peter cheerfully, then listened carefully as I explained what I wanted done with the items on the table. The small packages were for IITA friends and I told him to which houses they must go.

Then I put on a bossy voice.

"And when you have done that Patrick, come back for these hampers. They are to be delivered to the people named on the labels."

Patrick nodded, walked over to the table and bent to read the writing. His eye fell upon the words 'To Patrick and Family'. He froze for a moment, then straightened up, his eyes not leaving the parcel. He put his hand on his chest and stood for a second as if trying to make the link between himself and the name he had read. He bent to look again.

"Yi!" he shouted, straightening up, then he turned to us to make sure he was interpreting it all correctly. "Dat says 'Patrick'...is dat for me?" He saw from our smiles that it was. "Yi, Yi Yi!" he said and then pirouetted, laughed, bowed from the waist and straightened again to scrub his head in astonishment. Completely forgetting his usual reserve in our home, he pulled out a chair and sat in front of his parcel, peering at its contents.

"I am a 'appy mun!" he shouted, then buried his head in his hands. Suddenly he jumped up, apparently forgetting that he still had to take Peter to work and he scooped up the hamper and started to run out the door, perhaps to take it home to Mercy. We called him back.

"And this, Patrick, is from Mark and Michelle. They sent you a gift to thank you for looking after us so well." He stared at us open mouthed as he digested this bit of information.

"Dey doan even know me, but dey sent me a Christmas present?" The gesture silenced even Patrick for a while, then another batch of 'yi, yi, yi's broke out. He had to sit down again. I walked over to him and put my hand on his shoulder to get his attention and to emphasise the importance of my next request.

"You may want to use some of the food items before Christmas, Patrick, but there is one thing I ask. Please leave the parcels that are wrapped in coloured paper until Christmas morning. They are Christmas Day gifts, OK?"

Patrick agreed wholeheartedly, breaking out in yips and delighted laughter as he ran his hands over the crackling paper. To add to his excitement, today he was taking home a dress for Gladys, an early birthday gift, so all the girls would be able to dress up during the festive season. We waited until Patrick had calmed down before making our final request and he listened carefully. We wanted him to deliver to driver Alfred, the addressed envelope that contained enough money for a chicken for Christmas dinner.

Later, Reuben and David accepted their hampers with smiles and quiet dignity. We thoroughly enjoyed their reactions, which were as different as the men themselves. Noisy, excitable Patrick who wore his heart on his sleeve; quiet, unflappable Reuben who was an oasis of calm around the place; and stroppy little David who felt life's ups and downs intensely but always voiced even strong feelings in a quiet voice - provided, of course, the downs didn't include being pushed around by a Yoruba. That the little man would *not* accept quietly.

On the day of our departure for Europe, the hours dragged unmercifully until it was time to leave for the Lagos Airport. As we headed south, Patrick chatted happily about the hamper.

"Our frens all gathered when dey saw me carry it in," he told us, "and I shared de bottle of beer wit' dem immediately." Waiting for it to cool in the refrigerator was out of the question, obviously.

Suddenly, he smacked the steering wheel as another thought occurred to him. "Ahh, Marm, yo' pretended de shoes were fo' yo' son, but dey were for me!"

I leant forward from the back seat and prodded his shoulder with an accusing finger. "How do you know you have shoes?" I scolded. "You were not supposed to open that parcel until Christmas Day!" and as I spoke, he clapped a hand over his mouth and had the grace to look guilty.

"Um...um...well de rice is *defin'ly* gonna be kep' for Christmas Day," he said lamely, "an' de money for de chicken, dats for Christmas, too."

Although we tut-tutted, our hearts weren't in it and Patrick took this as an invitation to describe in detail every item as if we had never seen them. They had enjoyed the hamper as much as we'd hoped, even if a trifle prematurely. Still bubbling with excitement, he described the gifts from Mark and Michelle and the delight of his little girls as they'd tried on the necklaces and bracelets with their new outfits.

"And," he announced importantly, "I know dat January 26 is Australia Day!" The Aussie calendar that Mark and Michelle had included in the parcel had been thoroughly inspected, it seemed.

Today's plan was to go to the airport and check in our luggage then double back to the Sheraton where we'd have dinner and wait in comfort until it was time for our flight. As we made our way through the throng at the airport, touts, beggars and staff kept up a chorus of requests.

" 'Ave yo' somethin' for me for Christmas, Sah? Madame?"

We battled our way through, almost overcome by the hot, stale air inside the sealed building where the air-conditioning had not worked for years. I couldn't recall such discomfort in my life. It seemed hard to believe that within hours we would be scrabbling for the winter woollies that, hopefully, our sons had remembered to bring from Australia. At last we reached the point where we were to check in our luggage but we were greeted with the news that our particular plane had been unable to leave Munich and the replacement plane was five hours late. The young man was sorry, but no luggage could be booked in and no seats allocated for at least another five hours. He delivered the bad news with a sympathetic click of his tongue, a suggestion that we find somewhere to sit, and a request that we give him something for Christmas.

Peter had had enough. He wasn't going to stay in this hellhole of an airport a minute longer than necessary. He decided we'd go to the Sheraton (at least the car was air-conditioned), and there we'd eat a decent meal and put in a couple of hours in relative comfort. When check-in time approached, we'd return and *then* find a seat and wait.

The Sheraton, less than ten kilometres away, took over an hour to reach in the chaotic traffic. As Patrick let us off at the front door, we asked him to meet us at the same spot in four hour's time, then we made our bedraggled way into the hotel foyer. I noticed an airline passenger service desk nearby so I detoured en route to the dining room to tell the attendant the whereabouts of Passengers Cranny should anything else untoward happen. Before

I finished speaking, the ominous tongue-clicking drowned me out.

"Madame, I am sorry dat dey sent yo' away from de airport," she said, shaking her head apologetically. "I 'ave jest been talkin' to dem an' it is important dat yo' go buck straight away. De replacement plane is much smaller an' if yo' don't book in, yo' will miss out."

Cussin' fit to bust, we found poor old Patrick and spent the next hour enduring more of the same agony before we joined the now lengthy queue in front of the check-in desk. The young man who had sent us away spied us and called us to the head of the long line. He had been warned that we were on our way and were less than impressed with him. Our flight was still several hours away, but this time he accepted our luggage, allocated our seats and after checking departure times, told us to report back in *another* five hours.

We climbed back into the car. By now I was convinced that I'd died and for my past sins was condemned to an eternity of travelling to and fro between Lagos Airport and the Sheraton Hotel in peak hour. I wondered feebly what heinous transgressions Patrick must have committed to earn the extra punishment of being the driver.

Ahh. At last, food, wine and salubrious surroundings; balm for wilting body and spirit. After an excellent dinner, we were sitting in deep, soft lounge chairs of the foyer, feeling less like murdering anyone than we had in hours, when a cultured English voice drifted through the nearby potplants.

"It's a pity that Leventis[2] had to abandon the experiment of putting Santas in their stores this year," a man's voice said to an unseen companion, "but they felt it just wasn't appropriate to have the jolly old gentleman asking the people who passed if they had something for him for Christmas."

Maybe it was particularly amusing or maybe I was just so tired that my funny bone was dangerously exposed but I was overcome with laughter.

A few hours later, in the middle of the night, we drove back to the airport, the journey this time taking twelve minutes. After a final round of thank-yous and Merry Christmases, we sent Patrick on his way and girded our loins for another stint in this dreadful place. We finally reached the Immigration desk where the official took an unprecedented interest in my passport. After flicking through it several times, he looked up at me and his facial expression changed to one of menace. His eyes narrowed to mere slits as he gazed at me malevolently.

"Yo' peppers are not in order," he said, continuing the peculiar stare that was meant to intimidate me. The ritual required me to ask in what way my passport was deficient, then offer an amount to have the 'error' remedied. Before I could implement my own cunning scheme to scuttle the extortion attempt, Peter reached from behind me and tapped the desk with his blue Lassez-Passez passport, issued by the United Nations.

"Madame is travelling with me. I think you will find that her papers are in order, after all," he remarked coolly. The man shifted his gaze to Peter's face and for a few seconds the men eyed each other off. In a scene worthy of David Attenborough footage, the challenge continued until one of them capitulated. The Nigerian allowed his eyes to resume their normal contours and with a shrug and a resigned thump, he stamped my passport and handed it back to me.

We joined the next queue and when the African traveller ahead of me presented his hand luggage for inspection, the official held it in front of him, unopened. His eyes, too, narrowed into mere slits, indicating impending trouble.

"Your 'and luggage is not in order," he growled. The traveller took a moment to digest this information, then pulled a N20 note from his wallet and placed it on the counter. This amount, apparently, was an insult. A N50 note was added and was pocketed. The luggage, without being opened, was declared in order. When it was my turn, I glared at the official, willing him to try the same thing on me, but the heat and the overall dreadfulness of this airport had ruined Peter's sense of fun. He tapped his blue passport on the desk as my luggage was presented and we were waved through without inspection.

We shuffled along the tunnel to the plane, getting ever closer to the reunion. We were welcomed by cool, sophisticated smiles and invited by cultured European accents to ignore our boarding passes and select seats anywhere because airport staff (tsk, tsk, these Nigerians!) had experienced some confusion in the seat allocation process. I stashed my luggage overhead and dropped onto the seat beside Peter, sighing with relief. At last we were in the hands of a reputable airline. Nothing to do now but relax and begin mentally recording every sight, sound and emotion of the next two weeks. I wanted every moment to remain available to me whenever I needed it, sustaining me over the remaining six months away from Australia.

Yes, I could relax at last. The highly trained crew would soothe away every care and ensure an inconvenience-free trip.

Wouldn't they?

2. Chain of stores located in many of Nigeria's major cities.

Chapter 15
TIME OUT WITH FAMILY

I sit, knowing that at last I can let go and wrap myself in the joy of knowing that we are on our way. Soon I will sleep, but not until after our touchdown at Accra, only a short flying time away.

As the plane taxies to a stop on Ghanaian soil, we are told to collect overhead luggage and without leaving the plane, proceed to the seats nominated on our boarding passes. How do hundreds of people swap seats without disembarking? Nonplussed, people rise and begin to delve in overhead compartments, sending showers of parcels and bags down upon heads.

But not everyone has risen. Peter sits, serene. He is convinced that eventually a voice beside him will say, 'Excuse me Sir, but I think you are in my seat? Perhaps that vacant one over there is yours?'

Passive measures are not for me and I join the fray. The man with whom I was standing cheek and jowl in the aisle turns and bends over, his ample rump sending me nose-diving back into my seat. I struggle upright but my indignation is lost in the armpit of a neighbour whose laden arms are trapped above his head. We form two aisle-wide rivers of humanity, swaying to and fro but like seaweed anchored to the ocean's floor, we go nowhere.

People are getting angry, and mutterings ebb and flow. Advice being offered over the loudspeakers does little to soothe tempers. Someone has achieved the impossible. A robust matron looks down at Peter, wanting her seat. She doesn't look like one to trifle with so the master tactician rises and stands in an 'S' configuration, unable to go anywhere. We push and are pushed, shove and are shoved. Chaos reigns.

Please forgive me, Nigeria, for ever thinking you have a monopoly on disorganisation.

A man's voice, affecting the piping tones of a child, calls out in mock distress, "Mommy, I gotta go to the bathroom!"

We smile, wondering what we'd do if it were true, then someone laughs and good humour ripples down the congested aisles.

"Let's leave the overhead luggage," someone calls. "We can get it later."

Things simplify and a surprised voice paraphrases Henry Higgins: "By George, I think we've got it!" and eventually we have.

Chaos subsides and we take off for Europe, allowing ourselves to be slightly mollified by a hot supper. Eventually, sulky looks ease and we settle down to sleep.

We are landing and the captain, with ironic laughter in his voice, trusts we had a comfortable flight and looks forward to our company in the future. But five hours'delay in the world's worst airport and a suffocating game of musical chairs are not to be forgiven lightly.

"Dream on, buddy," a voice responds, and even though the captain can't hear us, everyone joins in the general chorus of "Never again!"

We traipse into the airport and as we stand watching at the circling luggage carousel, an Australian voice rings out across the gathered multitude. Again I think of barbed wire being dragged across a sheet of tin as my ears are assailed by a voice I had hoped never to hear again. It describes the trip in obscenities that make me cringe on behalf of eighteen million Australians. Is this the best Australia can do for diplomatic staff?

We are the only ones left at the carousel and it is still circling, offering us nothing. As seasoned travellers we accept rehearsed apologies, hand over suitcase keys and disbelieve assurances that our bags will be delivered to our hotel by evening. But nothing matters because through the glass we can see Mark and Michelle, faces beaming and arms laden with warm clothing for us. We hug then dash to the hire car and away. We chatter nonstop and learn that Glen and Lisa will fly in this evening and Tim and Louise will arrive tomorrow morning.

Mark is battling a cold that he caught in Egypt, so he spends a quiet afternoon while we sightsee with Michelle. Time flies and soon Glen and Lisa walk in, giving the Africans their first chance to greet the newly engaged couple. Everyone is full of news so we continue our talkfest in a little restaurant near the hotel. In its cheerful atmosphere, amidst many *Guten Appentits*, we devour *leberkaese* with onions and wash it down with steins of German beer, raising our glasses to toast those present, those coming, and those who delivered our luggage this afternoon as promised.

Next morning we wake eager for the day's events and we spend breakfast making plans. Peter and Glen will take delivery of the second hire car and collect Tim and Louise at the airport, then drive into Austria, meeting us in Salzburg for lunch. Lisa, Michelle and I shop for groceries, trudging up and down aisles, peering at unfamiliar packaging and unintelligible labels. Where is Louise with her secondary school German when we need her? *Staub zyzker* the package says - but is it cornflour or icing sugar? We want something special to drink with Christmas dinner, but what is *Sekt*? Every step of the way we have to make uneducated guesses so we anticipate some strange meals. One worry is that the Christmas turkey has short legs, but maybe that's how turkeys are in Europe? We pay, load the car and are off, bound for Salzburg.

Michelle drives and Mark, wedged in with parcels, sits beside her navigating. In the back, Lisa and I have only our eyes showing above the luggage piled on top of us, and we look and feel so ridiculous that we laugh whenever we peep at each other. As we come in sight of the Austrian Alps, Mark, with his usual sense of theatre, slips a tape into the cassette player and turns up the volume. The hills and our car are alive with the Sound of Music.

Our accommodation is just as we wanted it to be; three apartments which snuggle together like mother hen and two chicks. They are new, well equipped and perched high on a hill overlooking the city. We are still admiring everything when the other carload arrives and excitement breaks out again as we greet Tim and Louise. We are complete. Amid the chatter, I hear sneezes. Tim and Louise are making their contribution to this international summit of germs, with colds brought in from Ireland.

Our landlord checks to see that all is well and we tell him that the only thing we need to make it perfect is snow. In clear English, he prepares us for disappointment. The snow usually reaches Salzburg about mid-January, he informs us, but visitors can always drive to higher ground if they want snow. I decide that we will do just that because I must have a snowman on Christmas Day.

The afternoon is talked away and in the gathering dusk, we go for a walk, postponing the challenge of producing a meal from mysterious ingredients. We make a jovial group and the repartee fires back and forth as the quick wit of the young ones gathers momentum. Peter and I soak it up, not minding when the humour is turned on us; sometimes we even turn the tables.

Back at the unit, to a background of sneezes, I play it safe and serve grilled spareribs with familiar-looking vegetables. In the background I hear the younger generation negotiating cooking and cleaning rosters, proof at last that it was worth persisting through years of teenage scowls as we insisted that boys too must learn household skills.

Our first evening meal together ends and Mark and Michelle appear with two Christmas gifts that cannot wait until December 25. The first is a plum pudding from my sister in Toowoomba and we vote to begin on it immediately. The other, a small, flat parcel is addressed to Peter and me. Mystified, I unfold the tiniest tee shirt in the world and read the words printed on its front: "My grandma went to Nigeria and all I got was this tee-shirt."

We are to be grandparents. The room erupts into whoops of excitement, hugs, moist eyes, but also quiet moments aside while I digest the news. Our grandchild is due ten days after Peter's African contract ends and immediately I abandon all thoughts of a detour through East Africa to see the animals. I have to be in

Brisbane by July 10.

Later, I go to bed but cannot sleep. The excitement has caught up with me so I get up and give myself over to the sensation of being with family. I am puzzled that someone who feels as young as I do, can possible be a grandparent. Where have all the years gone? I also wonder how many others have asked the same questions on hearing that their child is to be a parent.

It is morning and the weather is bad, cold and drizzling with rain. Six of us go to explore the town and end up in a warm restaurant, sipping hot soup and talking, talking, talking. Evening comes and after we devour Glen and Lisa's lasagne, Mark organises a game of Celebrity Heads. The undisciplined players make it a noisy, laughter-filled evening. The colds are spreading and Peter and I punctuate our goodnights to everyone with sneezes. There is no insomnia tonight and I sleep like a tired grandmother.

I look at the time and can't believe it is eight o'clock because it is so quiet. As I rise, Peter asks if it is still raining so I draw back the curtains and stand speechless, looking out at a fairyland of white. Who would have thought that a scene could be made more beautiful by removing all colour? A wisp of smoke drifting from a chimney further down the hill only emphasises the stillness and reminds me that this is real, not a Christmas card. I find my voice and my cries bring a bleary-eyed Glen running, thinking something is wrong. Isn't this just the best organised Christmas ever?

Days and nights pass, forming a kaleidoscope of memories. Finally it is Friday, Christmas Eve. This swarm of locusts must replenish its food supplies and we decide to shop after our Sound of Music tour. We return hours later, well pleased with our morning and head off to the grocery shops. As we stand puzzling over signs that hang on closed doors, Louise struggles to make sense of the words; something about closing at noon because it is Christmas Eve.

What are we to do? In desperation, we divide up and go on scavenger hunts to buy whatever we can that looks like food. Peter and I don't have much luck and as we make our way towards the bus stop, I notice that the rain falling and hitting my face is strange, sort of soft and floating. I glance at Peter's shoulders and they are white. This is the first snow I have seen falling. For a week it has only snowed at night, as if to ensure our pleasure every morning when we look out at a pristine world.

Peter wants to hurry back to the unit before he gets wet and cold, but I loiter, lost for words to describe how much I love it.

During the Julie Andrews tour, Mark has stayed home and, unaware of impending famine, he makes a hearty stew into which he throws everything he can find, reducing our provisions even further. It smells wonderful and we consume it with gusto as we discuss the possibility of starving to death on Christmas Day. Then I remember my little orphans, a world away.

We have difficulty in finding a church for midnight Mass and drive around crazily until we end up at one within walking distance of our units. The place is packed and we stand at the back, cold and *nein sprechen si Deutsch*. Only when the choir raises its voice to the beautiful strains of *Stille Nacht, Heilige Nacht*, Silent Night, Holy Night, do we relate to the ceremony. I feel strangely sad, made emotional by the music. My mind sneaks ahead; only three more days until the first of the departures. Perhaps I am not the only one afflicted because everyone is subdued as we trudge home.

Back in our unit, Lisa tries to ring her parents but cannot get through. This is the first time in twenty-three Christmases that the girls haven't been with family and they feel homesick. With subdued goodnights, we head off to bed.

When we gather next morning, everyone is refreshed, feeling the Christmas spirit coursing through our veins. Amidst noisy Yuletide greetings, we begin the phone calls to Australia and munch on a breakfast of plum pudding covered with slices of banana. One by one the telephone calls are connected and we describe the view from our window; laden trees, smoking chimneys, white fluttering snow. It couldn't be more wonderful and we tell The Exaggerator of the family to go his hardest - even he cannot overstate how lovely this is. We boast about the snowman that we will build and we tease sweltering Queenslanders at the other end of the line with talk of our approaching snow frolic. But Louise gets a faraway look in her eye and talks fondly of perspiration and watermelon; she is howled down and threatened with an extra bombardment of snowballs later.

We turn our attention to the tree in the corner. It seems that this year Santa has demonstrated his sense of humour, no doubt inspired by the need to travel light. A special moment arrives when we present the boys and girls with a gift from Beatrice and Ayo Bamadeli. Everyone is touched by their generosity and we take a photo of the six young people holding the length of material. They sit discussing ways it can be used so that it can be shared around. A wall hanging, perhaps? Michelle, the skilled seamstress, inherits the task.

As we dress for the serious business of snowman construction, I realise that I have no waterproof shoes. I put on two pairs of socks then encase my feet in plastic cling-wrap and ignore all predictions that I'll spend most of my time in the car with frozen toes. It is my turn to drive and I concentrate on the slippery road while remembering to stay on the 'wrong' side.

We find the ideal spot. It is snowing as we leave the car and move into an open field, trudging through six inches of snow. For a moment everyone stands in silence, hands outstretched, watching the feathery flakes as they fall. I want to capture this moment, to relive it over and over. It is so quiet, so peaceful.

Whoosh! The first snowball finds its target as Mark succumbs to the small boy in him. No one is safe. I hear Peter's stern instructions that he is immune because of the camera. Whack! What was that you said Dad?

It's no use. Mark and Louise just won't respect seniority. Peter puts the video away and gives as good as he gets. Don't throw snowballs at Michelle, she's pregnant, someone calls. No nephew of mine is going to be a wimp, says a future uncle. Whopp!

Snowman time and I begin to scoop up the snow as if building a sandcastle. Others, also children of the sub-tropics, join me and like kids on Kings Beach we gather, pile, pat, gather, pile, pat. This is slow work. Doctor Tim, bent double, is running around in circles pushing an ever-growing ball and he calls "Hey, Gang, I think I'm on to something!"

Trust the mathematician to work it out, but we don't give credit, just christen him the Dung Beetle and pepper him with snowballs. Soon Snowman Cranny is complete, a fine addition to the family.

Two hours pass in minutes and my feet are still warm and dry, good for another two hours, but I am outvoted. It has been snowing steadily and others are getting cold so the vote is for a hot cuppa. It is the right time to leave, longing for more. By noon we are in a warm eatery sipping hot soup and biting into crusty bread. All we have back at the unit is a thawing turkey and Christmas-night treats so we turn this into lunch, a most acceptable solution to the food crisis. Like everyone else, we are noisy and happy. I say a little prayer of thanks. May I always remember this Christmas and know that life is sweet.

By unanimous vote, I am elected turkey-person. As I marvel again at its short legs, Louise salvages the wrapper and announces that we shall be dining on goose. I hope my friends on the lake at IITA never get to hear of this. I harden my heart and decide that if this one was prepared to masquerade as a turkey in the supermarket, the pretence can continue. It is renamed a gurkey and with traditional forcemeat aboard, it is consigned to the oven.

We eat, and very tasty it is too. Poor old Mark succumbs to his cold and goes to bed, so we put his portion of gurkey aside while the rest of us enjoy a quiet but a happy dinner. This morning's exercise has left me feeling relaxed and pleasantly weary so I go with that sensation, my mind sliding away from the thought that tomorrow, Sunday, is our last full day together.

We attend early morning Mass and the choir is even more beautiful today. These carols must have been born here, they seem so at home. Later, almost without discussion, we decide to spend the day quietly, making the most of the time left together. It is a good day, spent talking, resting, reminiscing and, in the afternoon, finalising plans for the departure tomorrow of Mark and Michelle by car, and Glen and Lisa by train. Peter and I are delighted that Tim and Louise will remain with us until our departure for Nigeria.

Four suitcases are packed and stand ready for tomorrow morning. Everyone retires for the night but I cannot settle. Near midnight I tiptoe upstairs to the family area where we have spent so many happy hours over the last ten days. I stand in the darkness, looking out as the snow drifts down. How can it be over so quickly? I know I am going back to Africa of my own free will and that I wouldn't change anything even if I could. Also, it's only a matter of months until we will be home for good. But in spite of everything I tell myself, the fact remains - tomorrow we say goodbye.

"Mum?" Glen is standing at the door and has guessed what is in my mind. He crosses the room and I feel my son's arms around me as I shed my tears, a mother's privilege.

Mark and Michelle are first to leave. It is still dark and I am glad that they drive off quickly because it helps me to be brave, though my heart is heavy and the memory of the red taillights disappearing down the road will bring tears to my eyes all day. Next, we drive Glen and Lisa to the train station. They hurry through the customs' gates while we find a vantage-point and watch until they are out of sight.

And now we are four. We depart next morning, pleased to be moving on because Salzburg was for everyone, not just half of us. All four must experience the scenery so we change drivers regularly. At times we just pull over and sit there spellbound. Never have I seen anything as beautiful as sun on snow-laden, leafless trees. No camera can do it justice but we can't resist taking photos. Louise has set her heart on seeing Innsbruck and soon everyone is glad she did. We park the car to explore and a life-long ambition of mine is fulfilled when Tim and Louise produce a bag of hot chestnuts to munch as we trudge through the snow.

The days pass, full of breathtaking scenery and roadside picnics of salami and crusty bread held in frozen fingers. We have a few hair-raising moments of slipping and sliding, of (almost) getting lost, of (almost) despairing of finding accommodation, but things work out every time, thanks to Louise's smattering of German and the friendliness and kindness we encounter everywhere we go. Sometimes our Bed and Breakfast accommodation is distant from

177

the towns so we feast in our rooms - on crusty bread and salami.

New Year's Eve is here and in a cosy restaurant we mark the end of 1993 and our once-in-a-lifetime Christmas holiday. As we talk of the coming year, Louise shares a confidence and makes a solemn pledge. She will never, ever again eat salami.

Next morning it is all over and we say our goodbyes at the airport. Tim and Louise depart through Gate 9 and with leaden heart I turn away. We move towards Gate 24 where the plane for Lagos awaits.

Below, I watch as the snow of Europe becomes the sand of the Sahara but I am too sad to appreciate the spectacle. Usually the *harmattan* blocks the view of the desert but today is as clear as crystal and every sandhill and ravine is visible from thirty-thousand feet.

We land at Lagos, pass through customs without problems and in the crowd, see Patrick's smiling face. We spend a comfortable night at the Sheraton and next morning we set out for Ibadan through the early morning traffic. We are chattering about our respective Christmases when our attention is caught by a strange truck in front of us, a mini-tanker of some sort, bristling with hoses and pumps. There is elaborate, colourful writing adorning the back of the truck and Peter asks Patrick to interpret the Yoruba words. Our driver hardly hesitates.

"Dat truck is for cleanin' out de drains," he explains, "and de writin' says 'Money for shit. Yo' mess is my job'."

We must be back in Nigeria.

Chapter 16
BACK TO EARTH

I couldn't face going to the markets or anywhere else for that matter. My retreat from the world was not due to great unhappiness, though as I recalled the wonderful reunion, I was swept by an ache of regret that it was over. I simply needed time to sit quietly and adjust to the fact that what I had looked forward to for so long, was over.

Such adjustments had better happen quickly, though, because people and things weren't allowed to stagnate with Nancy around. Within days she dropped by with a bright idea, and Nancy's ideas usually led to action.

As I would be aware, she informed me as she breezed into the kitchen and deposited a bunch of her home-grown carrots onto the edge of the sink, the annual party for International House staff had been postponed until now to avoid the Christmas rush. How about four or five of us volunteer to carry on the tradition of waiting on table to give the staff a complete break for the evening? By the end of the day, Nancy had lined up five women from five different countries to report for waitressing duties at four o'clock the following Thursday afternoon. My period of reflection was over.

We were at the ready when the guests began to arrive. They had been transformed from workers to partygoers with the shedding of uniforms and in no time the Cappa Bar buzzed with talk and laughter. Everyone had worked together all day, but now they greeted each new arrival with such backslapping, hand-shaking enthusiasm that I wondered what they did to mark a twenty-year reunion.

All refreshment was ignored until after the Call to the Top Table. To a deafening, foot-stomping welcome, the ten most honoured guests were accompanied to places of honour. When these worthy gentlemen were seated (no female made the top ten) the remainder of the guests took their seats. It was now the turn of the waitresses to be acknowledged. At first I thought there must be a misunderstanding because the chairman welcomed and thanked Doctor and Mrs Gulley, Mr and Mrs Cranny, and each of the other women and their husbands. Perhaps the ranks of helpers had doubled with the unseen arrival of our spouses? I turned a questioning look upon Nancy. She was smiling in acknowledgement of the welcome but I could see that something had raised her ire.

"Chauvinists," she muttered, when able to do so without being overheard. "Nigerians can't address women without first mentioning their husbands. A fat lot of washing up Doctor Gulley and Mr Cranny are going to do today, but they still have to be thanked!"

Guests who were not hungry on arrival had time to develop hearty appetites during the blessing. At regular intervals throughout the comprehensive prayer, guests were incited to join in with rafter-arising 'Amen!'s until at long last, the party began. It started to swing immediately. It was impossible not to contrast this with parties in my own culture. In Australia, this level of jocularity would have required hours of partying and social lubrication, but not so here. Crates of beer stood nearby, largely ignored in favour of soft drinks. We moved between tables doing our waitressing duties and were greeted wherever we went, as laughter and tomfoolery swirled around us. Everyone was talking top note, swapping tables to catch up with friends they hadn't seen for at least an hour, and telling jokes that required table-thumping acknowledgement.

Music struck up and added to the cacophony of noise. Dancing broke out and the festive mood continued for a couple of hours. When it was time for the party to end, someone rose and led the gathering in thanking the Lord for such a wide-ranging list of blessings that it became too much for one adolescent guest. A stifled giggle escaped and infected others until Ben, the usually mild-mannered clerk from behind the desk at International House, was forced to intervene. Like a teacher hurling chalk at cheeky students, he turned on the culprits and pelted them with prayers.

"Praise de Lord...Amen?" he bellowed, leaning forward accusingly. If the upward inflection wasn't sufficiently intimidating, the responding roar of "Amen!" from other guests, certainly was. The spluttering laughter ceased for about five minutes until another sobering dose of 'Praise de Lords' was required.

The prayer eventually ended and quite spontaneously, an informal guard of honour formed. Starting at the Cappa Bar end, people processed between the rows, dancing, singing and hand-shaking, to burst out the other end of the line, to begin their walk down the avenue of IITA towards the front gates and home. I had enjoyed the experience of seeing Nigerians at play. Patrick often referred to weekend parties that he and his family enjoyed with others in his street; now I could more easily picture the scene.

Involvement with the staff party was exactly what I'd needed to jolt me back into action, which was fortunate because Nancy had other activities lined up. She had told the children that when Mrs Cranny returned, we would take them to the Ibadan Amusement Park. On Tuesday morning when Patrick and I made our usual visit to the home, they were abuzz with excitement. As Funcho informed me happily, the planned outing was to take place on Thursday, 'the next tomorrow'. Still preoccupied with Christmas, I produced photos and they were inspected with great interest. Then I held out a picture of Tim, Louise and me standing in deep snow beside a beautiful lake, the background formed by a steep mountain where trees glistened in mantles of white. Bose studied it carefully then looked back at me, her eyes wide.

"Look at de snow," she said in awe. "Isn't it 'orrible!"

Sorry, Austria.

Matthew, the youngest Gulley, had mustered a band of volunteers to help with the children. The young people, all home at IITA on vacation from boarding schools around the world, joined us in the Institute's bus when we headed off to the orphanage.

The children were ready and for once they looked spic and span. Many were bubbling with excitement and those who could jump with excitement were doing so. Others looked back at us solemnly, not letting us into their silent, unfathomable world.

We noticed two new children whom we had never seen before and when we made enquiries, we were told they belonged to the warden. He had left them there earlier, then disappeared. Taking them on the outing would add considerably to the cost, yet we couldn't leave them behind because there was no one to mind them. Nancy was displeased at such chicanery and vowed that the children wouldn't be allowed on any rides, but of course, they were. Nancy was not one to punish little ones even if they did belong to the disliked warden and they took their place with the others.

Nancy, the teenagers and I were one-on-one with the smaller or more disabled children all afternoon. Kimi and Bosiyo were a joy to watch. The wilder the ride, the more they revelled in it and asked for more. I watched Kimi's round face glowing with excitement as she whizzed down the giant slippery slide, firmly held by one of the teenagers. I saw no shadow lurking over her that day, no sign that one day after I returned to Australia, Nancy would write and tell me that Kimi was dead. Years of malnutrition and neglect had taken too great a toll and even her wonderful spirit proved no match for the damage done since birth.

But there was no hint of sadness today. As befitting the occasion, the day ended with ice-creams and soft drinks before the weary little band was taken home. As we drove on to the comfort of IITA, we tried not to think of the children going to bed on rancid cane matting strewn on the hard concrete floors, nor of the beatings and deprivations that we were powerless to prevent. It had been a wonderful day and we consoled ourselves instead that we had given them a happy memory.

In order to have sufficient funds to see us over the last few months, Peter had instructed the Washington Credit Union to transfer a significant amount of money to our bank account in Lagos. Disturbing rumours were circulating so our plan was to get our hands on dollars before the Government made it impossible to withdraw anything but naira from banks. I hurried down to Lagos but was too late. The teller informed me that all foreign accounts were frozen.

I knew better than to accept this without a fight and insisted on seeing someone in a position of authority. After multiple security checks (designed to make me suffer because I had already established my identity with the teller), I was taken upstairs. Here I was handed over to Ebi, an Afro-English bank officer of some seniority. In a beautifully cultured English accent which suited her statuesque appearance, she explained that every application had to be considered individually and she asked me to return later that day for the decision. Ebi's manner suggested reasonableness and efficiency and as I picked my way along nonexistent footpaths to the World Bank office around the corner, I felt confident that she'd do her best for us.

Later, when I was shown into her office, Ebi smiled comfortably and I breathed a sigh of relief. We had not discussed the size of my intended withdrawal, nor was the subject openly referred to now as she addressed me.

"Mrs Cranny, I have obtained clearance for you to access your account," she said in her delightful voice, as she handed me a slip of paper. She paused ever so slightly then added, "And as yet, I have not been instructed to limit the amount you can withdraw."

I got the message. With a special smile of thanks, I hurried downstairs where I handed the teller my note of authorisation.

He was highly indignant when I requested that the account be emptied of all but a nominal amount, and he became even more incensed when I called his bluff regarding a substantial 'service charge' for doing so. Faced with my counter-threat to again enlist Ebi's assistance if he tried any such thing, he grudgingly handed over the full amount.

Now we had dollars but our cache of naira was running low. Until now, we'd been able to convert our dollars quite legally at the Bureau de Change at an unofficial rate (parallel rate) that was much higher than the official rate of exchange. When we'd arrived in Nigeria, the official rate of N22 per US$1 lagged behind the parallel rate of N29, but recently we were getting about N56 per US$1 at the Bureau de Change. They had to be watched, though, because if we weren't vigilant, the staff would short-change customers with a series of tricks. The slippery moneychangers, who strolled the streets in their flowing white robes, their wrists dripping with gold bracelets, were another option, although we were loath to mix it with them.

We were in a quandary when the military government announced that in future, there would be no parallel market. Instead, all foreign currency had to be changed at the official rate of N22 per US$1. Sellers and buyers of foreign currency who used higher rates were to be treated as 'economic saboteurs'. But debate raged as to the legal basis of the Economic Intelligence Committee's authority to make this declaration, because it was not a decree and it contradicted statements made the same week by the chairman of the Economic Committee of the Federal Executive Council. The chairman had indicated that the Government would take its time before passing specific laws that would make the parallel market illegal (*Nigerian Guardian*, 21 January, 1994).

Although international agencies paid lip service to the circular's instructions, an official blind eye was turned when United Nations' projects continued to use a higher rate of exchange in order to complete projects within budget. When an IITA acquaintance entered a Bureau de Change in Ibadan he was told that inside the building he could only be offered N22, but if he went and spoke to the driver of the white car parked outside...Seated in the white car was a member of the Bureau's staff and when approached, he offered an attractive rate of exchange. The practice was tolerated because dollars were drying up and something had to be done to attract more.

I didn't relish the thought of jail, deportation or robbery but if there was still no actual law against getting the best rate, how was it illegal? We talked the matter over with Patrick who insisted that getting a better rate would be a breeze. Just leave it to him, we were told.

With my heart in my mouth, I watched him depart. I remained in a state of near nervous collapse until he returned with an overnight bag bulging with money. I asked if he had had any trouble.

"Nor, nor, nor," he replied nonchalantly. "De only other person dere was a policeman, an' 'e was changin' money too."

As we drove through the centre of Ibadan a few days later, I saw a group of flashily dressed men, gold dripping from wrists and necks, waving to me enthusiastically. I turned to our driver.

"Patrick, please tell me that they aren't the moneychangers you used!" I pleaded, horrified when I saw that I was being greeted openly as a long lost friend.

"Yes, Marm, dat's dem," said my companion cheerfully, as pictures of myself languishing in jail swam before my eyes.

That evening I attempted to distract myself with my needlework, but it was a mixed success. I was finding similarities between the Nigerian tapestry in my head and the scene unfolding in my hands. To get the result I wanted on the front, I had to use stitches that left me dissatisfied with the back.

I loved the days when I had no commitments other than to select a cool spot and read or write. Aerobics too, continued as a favourite activity and nothing was important enough to prevent me joining my colleagues and Jane Fonda three mornings a week. Well, almost nothing. One afternoon I was forced to ring IITA's Housing department to report that my kitchen tap had snapped off level with the sink. I was promised that the plumber would call me back and before long, the phone rang.

"Is dat 20 Tropical?" asked a voice at the other end of the line. Knowing what he meant, I assured him that it was 20 Tropical speaking.

"Dis is de plumber. Is anyone at home, please?" I overcame the obvious temptation and assured him that I was at home. I was told that he was coming immediately to fix the tap.

A short time later there was a knock at the back door and in marched a young man in overalls. Halfway across the kitchen he stopped mid-stride.

"But, Madame, it is brokken!" he said in a shocked voice, peering at the stump of the tap.

I couldn't help but agree. He gingerly picked up the severed tap and shaking his head in awe, he walked out. Under the impression that we were in the middle of some sort of plumbing activity, I remained at home for the rest of the day. Much later, I heard a note sliding under the back door and I read that the plumber would be back to complete the job at eight o'clock the following morning.

This coincided with my aerobics class so I phoned immediately and got the man himself.

"I have an appointment between eight and nine o'clock so please, could you come after nine?" I asked sweetly, but to no avail. Plumbers are busy people, I was informed, especially Muslim plumbers on Fridays.

"It is not possible to come later, Madame. I 'ave to go to de mosque after lunch, so I mus' come to yo' at eight or eight-t'irty."

He regretted that there was no room for negotiation regarding Friday, but perhaps I would prefer to postpone the whole job until Monday? Knowing I'd be having the same conversation next Friday if I agreed, I sighed deeply and decided to forego my aerobics.

At precisely half-past nine the following morning, the plumber breezed in. I crossly reminded him of yesterday's conversation, pointing out that I could have gone to aerobics after all. My tirade must have lacked something in its delivery because all it achieved was to establish me in the plumber's opinion as a humourist. Faced with his unabashed good humour and total lack of repentance, I found myself losing momentum as he laughed in a chummy way and slapped his thigh in appreciation of my wit. I gave up and retreated grumpily to a chair from where I watched, from under beetled brows, his cheerful attack on the tap.

I made up for the missed exercise at tennis that evening and as

we enjoyed the usual suya and beer afterwards, we were
introduced to an Englishman who was visiting IITA friends. Brian,
a giant of a man, sprang to his feet, clicked his heels, and greeted
us in a deep, melodious voice.

"Greetings, salutations, and felicitations!" The voice boomed
out of him with a sound as interesting as his choice of words.
Here, I thought to myself, is a 'character'. When I was told that
he worked for an oil company in charge of security in the south
east of the country, I readied myself to hear strident criticism of
Nigeria and Nigerians. I knew that there was little love lost between
the international oil companies and the villagers, the haves and the
have-nots, at the drilling sites in the Delta region of the country.
As the evening progressed, though, I noticed he was friendly and
relaxed in his interaction with IITA staff as they served his food,
although his lapses into quaint terms often left everyone bemused.

Brian was still sufficiently new to the country to be intrigued by
all he saw and like Peter and myself in our first few months, he
had seen enough to expect the exotic at every turn. The big man
continued sharing his experiences. Recently, he told us, in a market
in Port Harcourt, he'd come upon a man standing near a pile of
blue, shimmering powder. Not sure what to expect, but alert to its
potential as an ingredient in some mysterious ceremony, he'd
inquired discreetly what the substance might be.

"Dat's Omo. We wash our clothes in it," came the reply.

On Monday morning, Nancy appeared at the back door and the
determined look on her face told me that I was about to be launched
into a new project.

"How would y'all like to come with me to UTH?" she asked,
referring to Ibadan's University Teaching Hospital. "I've heard
that one of its paediatricians does a lot of work for the poor. Maybe,
if we asked, he might come and see the orphanage kids on a
voluntary basis."

The thought of the children receiving specialist attention was
almost beyond our wildest dreams. I happily joined Nancy on her
mission.

Chapter 17
HOSPITALS AND HOSES

With Nancy at the wheel, we made our way through Ibadan's streets to the hospital. As she mixed it with other road users, I asked if she found it difficult to modify her driving behaviour when she was back in the States. She laughed ruefully.

"I don't know about my driving behaviour," she said, "but last time I was home, I found myself putting on a fine performance when I was short-changed in a supermarket." Nancy laughed again at the memory. "Matthew was horrified. He stepped in and said, 'Mom, cut it out. Y'all aren't in Africa now!'"

As Nancy muttered fiercely at a wayward Nigerian driver, I wondered if research would someday show that road rage as well as AIDS had its origins in Africa.

At first glance, University Teaching Hospital looked impressive enough. Four three-storey buildings, the heart of the hospital, stood around a central quadrangle and other, single-storey constructions branched out in all directions behind these. Around the perimeter of the quadrangle was an uncovered concrete drain which we gingerly stepped over and headed towards a ramp that zigzagged its way to the upper floors.

First port of call, Nancy told me, was the office of a nun, Sister Canty, who was head of the Social Work Department. She had been instrumental in arranging our appointment with our intended target, Doctor Nottidge. We introduced ourselves to the small, elderly woman with tired eyes and a slightly defeated air. In a soft

Irish accent she explained that she had come to Nigeria as a young missionary and had been here ever since.

As she spoke, a man tapped at her door and entered. He was introduced as a member of her staff, a welfare worker. When he heard my accent his dark face sprang to life and with immense enthusiasm, he focused all his attention on me.

"Ah, Madame, I think yo' must be from Australia?" He rubbed his hands in satisfaction as I stood tall with national pride. He was speaking again.

"I once 'ad a geography teacher who loved dat place." His face was awash with memories. Suddenly, his hands formed paws in front of his chest and he began to hop around Sister's office in resounding bounds. He came to a halt near me. "My teacher was a harsh disciplinarian," he confided, "and when he beat us, he'd shout: 'Yo' are no better dan an Australian wallaby!'"

Sister rolled her eyes in embarrassment, I tried not to laugh and Nancy's expression betrayed her conviction that she knew exactly onto whose head the most damaging blows had fallen.

Leaving Skippy to attend to other matters, Sister Canty led us along the veranda to Doctor Nottidge's office. As we went, she explained the disorder around us. We could see that not all the beds were full yet there were people everywhere. We were told that the latest crisis had started when nurses, kitchen staff and cleaners (who had not been paid for months) walked off the job. The people crowding the verandas were relatives of patients who were too ill to be discharged even in these circumstances. They brought in food, then stayed to attend to as many basic nursing duties as possible. Between doctors and family, a degree of medical attention was being provided, but in near-intolerable conditions.

The nun knocked on an office door and when it opened, a thin, middle-aged man invited us in. He was tall, with a slight stoop and as he shook our hands, I saw a glimmer of amusement in his eyes.

"Mesdames Gulley an' Cranny. What a geological pair yo' make!"

His easy manner appealed to me immediately. In spite of the occasional twinkle in his eyes, I could see he was exasperated by the chaos around him. He held up the letter he'd been reading. It was from the Ibadan City Council, he told us, and in it the Council had dismissed his complaint about the unreliable water supply to the hospital. Ibadan was a big city, the letter argued, too big for a Council to be expected to provide a water supply.

"How do yo' counter such nonsense?" he said in disgust.

We soon got down to the matter that had brought us and for the next half-hour we spoke of ways of helping the children. We learned that Doctor Nottidge had been involved in their care several years ago but for a variety of reasons he had stopped going. He asked if we could drive out to the home while we talked, and once there he took time to walk around, speaking to the children and noting the changes that had been put in place. Later, as Nancy and I once more sat in his office, he put a question to us.

"Would yo' be able to organise any investigations I request and get prescriptions filled? If I can get dat support, I will comm," he said. He offered to start the following week, "provided Ibadan has fool," he added as an afterthought, obviously worried about the ever-present queues at the petrol stations.

I was rejoicing as Nancy and I made our way down the ramp, but my Nigerian-wise companion turned and fixed me with a cautionary look.

"I'm gonna wait until I see a stethoscope on a kid," she said flatly. "Promises, we've *never* been short of!"

But I liked the cut of his jib and felt sure he'd turn up. Engrossed in our debate, neither of us batted an eyelid as we detoured to avoid walking in front of a man urinating into the drain around the hospital's quadrangle.

The following Thursday, when Nancy swung the car through the gates of the orphanage and up the long driveway, I could see an ancient Peugeot parked in our favourite spot under the shade of a tree. Doctor Nottidge was already there.

The doctor's eyes crinkled in greeting and he invited us to sit in on the examinations. We'd brought a tape measure, bathroom scales, tissues and other bits and pieces that Doctor had requested, including folders and paper for the medical charts. We'd felt sad as we'd written on so many, the surname of 'Unknown' or "Abandoned". Now, one by one, the tots were brought in and the list of required investigations grew. Shaking his head over the neglect the children had endured, Doctor ordered X-rays and blood tests and prescribed medication.

It was Gbade's turn to see Doctor. Although he looked about three years of age, he claimed to be eight, while his poise and resilience put him at about thirty-eight. He gingerly released the doorframe and set out to walk unaided to doctor. To keep his balance, he locked his swollen knees together and on matchstick legs that splayed to each side, he tottered across the room, determination written all over his face.

Doctor quietly murmured, "Rickets," then gave his attention to the child who finally reached him and like a little old man, extended his hand towards the doctor in greeting. The two spoke in Yoruba during the medical examination, then, visibly moved, Doctor Nottidge touched Gbade's face before solemnly shaking hands again. As Gbade made his way to the door, Doctor Nottidge sent him on his way with a message in English. "You are a first class little man!"

Nancy had several commitments involving travel to Jos in coming weeks so by the end of the morning, I had undertaken for Patrick and myself to take four children for X-rays, two for blood tests and one for a liver function test. Doctor Nottidge gave me the necessary referrals and a sheaf of prescriptions to get filled, and departed. Nancy had brought Bournvita and fruit and as the children demolished the unscheduled treat, I caught Gbade's eye and he smiled. At the time I was delighted. It was only later that I wondered if that smile marked the loss of just a fraction of the outer shell Maureen felt he may need some day.

During the next week Patrick and I took the four children to a clinic in the city for X-rays. A technician asked me to hold each child while the procedures took place but I declined and advised Patrick against doing so either, so the staff made other arrangements for steadying the children's limbs. The equipment was old and probably inefficient and I didn't want us subjected to multiple doses of radiation.

After delivering the children home to the orphanage, our journey back to IITA was interrupted outside the gates of the Ibadan University. Patrick was forced to slow the car to a crawl as we nosed through an agitated crowd that had gathered around a burning vehicle. Several young men near the fire turned their attention to us briefly, but we weren't stopped and I promptly forgot about the incident. Patrick delivered me home and left to go back to FORMECU.

I was no sooner in the house than the phone rang. It was Nancy, saying that she was relieved to discover that I hadn't gone out after all. She had just heard of a serious riot out on the streets, with two people being killed and a car burned near the gates of the University. I reassured her that I had been there and that although there was a burning car, there was no other indication of trouble.

That afternoon when Patrick delivered Peter home from work, the driver put a glum face through the kitchen door to tell me of the afternoon's adventure. On his way back to the office after dropping me home, he had been stopped by the youths at the burning car and they had demanded fuel from our car's tank. Being Patrick, he had refused and was threatened with the car being torched.

"But I told dem dis car is British and it wouldn't 'urt de military one bit if dey torched it, so dey jes kicked at de door an' let me go," said Patrick, as he pointed to the sizeable dent left by the frustrated protesters. I smiled at the ease with which Patrick changed the nationality of our car to suit the needs of the moment. Patrick also confirmed that two people had been slain nearby so I had to admit that I had underestimated the state of affairs.

Some of the children's medical tests were to be done in the outpatients' section of the hospital. On the appointed day, Patrick and I arrived with a carload of kids, only to be told that there was no water today so hospital technicians were unable to do any of the tests we'd lined up. There was not even water for the doctors to wash their hands.

There was nothing for it but to take the children home. As Patrick and I carried some and guided others slowly towards the ramp, we met Doctor Nottidge who was walking along the veranda with a colleague. He introduced the Head of Paediatrics, Doctor Sodeinde, who pricked up his ears at the mention of IITA. Before I left, he had recruited my help in arranging a meeting between him and a member of IITA staff. Doctor Sodeinde wanted suggestions for a simple and cheap source of nutrition for the chronically malnourished children in his ward. He hoped to demonstrate to parents what a difference even a little protein could make to a child's health. I promised to make inquiries about a contact person and to let him know.

"See how it works here?" Sister Canty was nearby and had caught the end of our conversation. She fell into step beside me as we continued shepherding our little group down the veranda.

"In Nigeria, it is always a case of 'I'll do something for you but I expect you to do something back for me'," she said. Then she smiled a mite sheepishly as she continued, "Is there any chance that you could come one afternoon and speak to my staff on the topic of *Social Work in Australian Hospitals?*" We set a date there and then.

Obtaining the tests for the children developed into an epic. The next two trips to the hospital also proved futile because of no water. Because of unreliable phones, it was impossible to check with the hospital before coming.

I was still feeling jaded after several fruitless attempts when the phone rang one morning with a message from the hospital. Delighted that they had been able to reach me, I listened as I was told to 'comm quickly because de water is honn'. Patrick was available so away we went.

When we arrived, the water was not only on, it was cascading over the balconies of the upper storeys in silver curtains. Standing in the middle of the quadrangle, my ambition to see the Victoria Falls was rekindled. I met Sister Canty in a corridor and she smiled at me with satisfaction.

"We're very blessed," she said. "Yesterday the water was on for half an hour and we were able to flush all the toilets then too!" Blessings are relative, I decided. To my satisfaction, I noted that the drain around the quadrangle was swirling with water.

My little friends had their tests at last. Now Doctor Nottidge could prescribe the treatments and medications best suited to their needs. Provided fuel supplies remained on, things might begin to look up for the children.

It had been an exhausting week and I looked forward to a quiet day at home. My habit of self-indulgence had been sorely neglected of late. After Peter's departure for work, I sat watching the self-important geese on the lake below me and musing over how I was handling my employer responsibilities.

True, I lacked the aplomb of my IITA friends in conducting the household, but Patrick, David and Reuben seemed happy in our service and I certainly appreciated the extra assistance. As I poured my second cup of coffee, I decided I was not managing the role too badly at all.

I was still daydreaming when Patrick returned to help in what I thought would be a simple exercise. He was to drive David and four decrepit garden hoses across campus to IITA's Housing Department to exchange them for four new ones. Ours was a huge garden and we had been issued with twice the usual number.

They loaded the hoses and I watched the two men drive off, David's head of steel-wool curls barely visible over the window-ledge of the car. The uneasy relationship between the driver and the gardener had settled somewhat since my lecture to Patrick, although I suspected that mistrust still lurked beneath the surface.

Pecking order remained an issue. David, who proudly described himself as 'a very old mun' was entitled to respect, but Patrick was a senior driver, hauling in an impressive salary of US$30 per month and he wasn't about to be subservient to a gardener, especially one of different ethnic origin. As they drove off, I fancied that Patrick sat just a little taller than usual in the driver's seat, as if to clarify the issue.

In no time they were back and as they tumbled from the car, they seemed barely able to contain themselves. Obviously something had gone awry with their plans and I was about to be drawn into it.

David busied himself crossing his arms and arranging his short legs into the pose that usually meant a long discourse was on its way. This took time so Patrick grabbed the initiative and burst into an unintelligible gabble accompanied by much hand waving and finger-pointing to all points of the compass. I'd known Patrick for ten months, yet I still found him difficult to understand when he was excited. All I caught were his closing words, "So, if yo' will comm, Marm, we'll go buck and see dem."

With that he hurled himself back behind the steering wheel and started the engine.

David had given up all hope of getting a word in and had stalked off in disgust. I called him back and asked for an explanation but first I had to wait until he was again physically arranged to his own satisfaction. When all was ready, the tiny firecracker of a man spoke in scathing tones.

"Dat evil mun at Housing said dat we could only 'ave TWO hoses instead of four so I said I would not accept dem. I will never speak to 'im again!" The words came out, stamped black with indignation. And just in case I hadn't already got the message, he added, "I am not goin' buck dere, ever!"

Patrick, on hearing this, flew out of the car.

"What? What yo' mean, yo' never goin' buck dere again? Yo' *got* to go buck. Now!"

Knowing the Nigerian penchant for shouting matches, I knew it was time to step in.

"Patrick, I'll handle this."

I turned back to David and suggested that two hoses were better than no hoses and that I'd appreciate his co-operation in getting them. Meanwhile Patrick was in an agony of frustration, stymied by my injunction. He stood at my elbow, hopping from foot to foot and opening and shutting his mouth soundlessly. His hands fluttered, pointed, clasped and unclasped in agitation, as he was forced to listen.

David, his little nose pointed skyward, spoke.

"Mr Godwin at 'ousing Department is evil, Madame, but for yo' sake, I will comm. But," and here he wagged a finger in the air, "I will not speak!"

Thank goodness for that, I thought. Not knowing whether to laugh or tear out my hair, I got into the car and we drove off in silence.

As David and I got out and headed towards the building, Patrick made as if to accompany us.

"Patrick, you stay here," I instructed. "The last thing I need is you in there, yelling and screaming."

He looked crestfallen. "I won't say anythin', Marm. Carn I jes comm an' listen?"

I relented, but because I knew how easily this could degenerate into chaos, I levelled a finger at him.

"OK, you can come, but not *one word* out of you!" I said, and he doubled up with laughter at my words.

We entered the wide doorway of the storeroom and walked inside, threading our way between piles of gardening equipment and boxes of all sizes. In a far corner of the long building, I could see a tall, lean man with a clipboard in his hand. This must be the evil Mr Godwin. I guessed from his tall frame that he was probably a Hausa and if this was the case, it would partly explain David's condemnation of him. Mr Godwin watched our approach from beneath lowered brows.

David accompanied me until he was sure of being within earshot, then stopped and struck the pose that he was to maintain for the rest of the visit; arms folded high on his chest, lips pursed and eyes fixed on a spot on the ceiling. His right leg was thrust out at a particularly defiant angle and a bare, leathery old foot tapped at the concrete floor. When I reached Mr Godwin, I introduced myself and was immediately and stridently informed about 'certain gardeners aroun' dis place who like to be deef-icult'.

Mr Godwin was polite but furious as he confirmed that only half an hour ago, he had ordered David and Patrick from these premises and had told them that in future he would speak only to Madame on the delicate subject of hoses. I heard an intake of breath from Patrick as he prepared to comment, but I turned and fixed him with such a fierce glare that he clamped his mouth shut again, prudently deciding that, even in Nigeria, there are times when silence is golden.

I asked Mr Godwin if we could continue our discussion in the privacy of his office and when I followed him in, I turned and shut the door firmly in Patrick's face, which by now was alight with the happy expectation of witnessing black and white fur flying.

I was subjected to another litany of David's sins over a twenty-year period. The tirade finally ground to a halt as an exhausted Mr Godwin repeated that he was merely doing his job. Because of a shortage of stock, we could only have two new hoses, but would that gardener listen?

I had heard enough of David's imperfections for one day so I steered the debate towards possible solutions. A few minutes of calm discussion led to a compromise, and in no time we were on our way home with two new hoses and some connections for joining useful pieces of the old ones.

In the back yard, Patrick and David set about the repairs, using the car's tool kit for the purpose. As I worked inside the house, I could hear their voices raised in occasional argument as to how best to do things and I had a distinct sense of déjà vu.

The years rolled away and I expected at any moment to hear Glen's voice calling to me: "Maarmm, tell Mark to stop being bossy!"

Chapter 18
THE REST OF THE WORLD ON MY DOORSTEP

I closed the door behind the last visitor and walked back to the lounge room, sighing as I went. I saw Reuben shaking his head and smiling.

"Ah, Madame. Yo' are like Mrs Kang.Yo' have too many frens!"

I knew that 'too much' or 'too many' simply meant 'a lot of', but the expression always amused me. But today I had good reason to sigh. If Reuben only knew the reason for the latest influx of visitors, he might be forgiven for thinking that at the moment, Madame had little need of enemies.

A few days ago, Juliana had decided that all aerobics enthusiasts should meet to discuss our future direction. Perhaps we should each pay a subscription and be able to buy extra videos and equipment? Also, several members were concerned that their silhouettes still bore little resemblance to that of Jane Fonda, so maybe we should upgrade to a more difficult programme? Half our number looked depressed at the thought of more difficult exercises, the other half looked depressed at the thought of losing the battle of the bulge. It was decided that a serious gabfest was called for and that it would commence at three o'clock sharp the following Thursday at 20 Tropical Crescent.

Immediately after agreeing to host this gathering, I'd hurried off to the next meeting of the Women's Group. On the agenda was the planning of the main fund-raising event of the year and with surprisingly little debate a consensus was reached. We were to hold an International Dinner Party and a sumptuous meal representing global cuisine would be provided. I listened as the world was divided into three zones: Asian, African and The Rest of the World and I smiled at the eagerness of some to be appointed co-ordinator of their own division.

Judging by the heat rising from under Asian and African collars as people lobbied for the job of co-ordinator, I gathered that there was a certain prestige attached to the position and I shook my head in amazement. The election process was such an emotionally charged issue that Chairperson Juliana suggested that Asia and Africa call individual meetings so the matter could be resolved elsewhere. The matter of a co-ordinator for the third zone still had to be addressed.

Suddenly Nancy's voice rang out over the hubbub.

"I nominate Pam to co-ordinate the Rest of the World."

My mouth opened and shut in speechless protest. By the time I found my voice, my non-acceptance was lost in a tide of thanks. I was a source of envy to Asians and Africans and, I am sure, an object of pity to the Rest of the World. I couldn't believe how quickly it had happened. One moment I was sitting there, carefree and unfettered, the next I had the worries of a large portion of the world upon my shoulders. I spared a thought for Boutros Boutros Ghali. Mine was the responsibility of forging the Rest of the World into a catering force; somehow I must avoid us being shamed by wily Indians or outclassed by flamboyant Africans.

Juliana smiled at me from the official table and I detected a glimmer of sympathy in her African eyes. Obviously she recognised panic when she saw it.

"Is there anything we can do to make it easier for yo', Pum? Anythin' dat yo' would like resolved at dis stage?" she asked kindly.

I nodded mutely and, folding my hand to resemble a revolver, I placed it against my right temple. The African women laughed aloud, but I was fixed with unamused looks from Indian eyes. Perhaps they thought I was not taking the matter seriously enough. Little did they know.

Later that afternoon Nancy put her head through our kitchen door. Judging by her expression, she was far from contrite. In fact, she was highly amused at my panic-ridden state and she waved aside my high-pitched protests that I was not up to the task. She would have taken it on herself, she explained, but she intended travelling quite a bit in the next two months and couldn't possibly volunteer. As a peace offering, I received yet another bunch of carrots and extravagant promises about the level of assistance that she intended giving me - whenever she was home.

"Anyways," she said, and she even managed to inject a note of self-righteousness, "Y'all should be thankful that I didn't nominate you to co-ordinate the African section. You'd *really* have had prarb-lems then!"

I decided to get all my extraordinary meetings over in the one afternoon and scheduled a Summit Meeting of the Rest of the World at my house at four o'clock Thursday. That allowed an hour for the aerobic enthusiasts to resolve the issue of outstanding stomachs before the catering heavies arrived.

Of course, the result was chaos. I should have known that the aerobics group would be late and that when they *did* arrive all we'd do was talk, laugh and plunge ourselves into deeper crisis by plying ourselves with tea and scones topped with butter and jam. The Rest of the World joined us at four o'clock and the afternoon degenerated further into a pleasant but totally unproductive shambles. Eventually each Madame had to dash home to check on Nanny's progress with the evening meal and I was left on the receiving end of airy waves from my team of chefs and cries of 'Just put me down for whatever you think...'

Nanny-less, I stood at the sink and tackled the pile of cups and saucers.

Golf fever was sweeping IITA. The Women's Group had been bitten with the fund-raising bug and in addition to the wretched International Dinner Party, they had another scheme afoot, a golf tournament. Everyone with two legs was somehow cajoled into competing, after paying an entrance fee for the privilege. Teams were arranged so that each experienced golfer was paired with an inexperienced team-mate.

The day came and Peter and Nancy teamed up for the mixed competition. All was going well until they prepared to hit off from the tee near our lake. As Nancy stood addressing her ball, hips and club head wiggling in the required manner, a foolhardy duck decided to take a short cut across the fairway some thirty metres in front of her. Peter facetiously offered to chase the moveable hazard but Nancy interrupted her swing only long enough to fix her partner with a withering look before she launched into her drive. It was her strongest shot of the day. The ball sizzled off the tee along a low trajectory, giving Nancy her first birdie - a duck hit amidships. Bird and golfing opponents alike were overcome - one by indignation, the others by laughter.

My performance in the women's competition rivalled Nancy's for embarrassment, with several trees and rocks being defaced by wayward golf balls. That didn't stop me unashamedly taking my place beside my partner Lec Atkinson when we were called forward to receive second prize.

The day ended with several of us gathering for a barbecue at our place and with everyone contributing, we were soon sharing a feast. As the laughter and banter wafted towards the lake, we spared a thought for our feathered friend and hoped the noise wasn't disturbing the recuperative rest of one very sore duck.

It was Monday morning and I had just returned from aerobics, when there was a tap at the kitchen door and soon I stood face-to-face with a woman whom I had never seen before. A teenage boy stood beside her and judging by their smiles, they expected me to guess who they were. The woman bobbed a greeting and spoke.

"Good mornin' Madame. I am Cecelia." I continued to look blank so she added quietly, "I am Mrs Reuben, an' dis is my son, Emmanuel."

Cecelia, a tall, slim woman with a beautiful face, was dressed in *bouba* and wrapper. She had a quiet, self-possessed air and I soon decided that in choosing his partner, Reuben had shown his usual good sense. We moved into the lounge room and when we settled, Cecelia explained that she had brought Emmanuel to the IITA medical clinic and had decided to call on me while here. I boiled the kettle and as we had morning tea, I turned my attention to Emmanuel who hadn't spoken yet, although he met my gaze with an alert, inquisitive look and a bright smile.

I asked him about school and he replied readily that he was in Year Two of secondary education and that his favourite subjects were English and Geography. I took our inflatable globe from the shelf and showed him where Australia is in relation to Nigeria. He looked so totally mystified that I asked Cecelia if my accent was causing either of them difficulty. She assured me that she could understand me well, then she spoke to her son in their language before turning back to me.

"He understands yo' words, Madame, but he does not grasp what yo' mean about this ball."

I paused as the realisation hit me. Emmanuel, a bright-eyed fourteen year old, did not know that the world is round. I sat beside him and shared with him the basics about the movement of the sun and planets. As I spoke, I realised how bizarre it must all sound to a teenager hearing this for the first time – how different for those of us who could hardly remember a time when we didn't know that the world was round. With the globe in our hands, I pointed out some countries he may have heard of and showed him the route that Peter and I had taken to get to Nigeria: Brisbane, Hong Kong, London and Lagos. Emmanuel seemed to understand most of what I said and he began to ask questions. The large patches of blue on the globe fascinated him. Does the sea really move all the time? Why? Why does it taste salty? I brought out books on Australia and we turned the pages together, finding pictures of the ocean and beaches and talking about the moon and the tides.

When Cecelia and Emmanuel left, I realised how much I had enjoyed their visit but I was stunned at the secondary school boy's lack of knowledge. I went to the IITA library and photocopied articles about the things we'd discussed: the solar system, oceans, animals and dinosaurs and other things that I imagined would be of interest to boys everywhere.

Who knows, I thought, *a little stirring of the curiosity now and this young man might continue wanting to learn more.*

Whether his world would ever provide the opportunity was another question.

It was my birthday, a happy day that began early with the opening of gifts and a sheaf of mail that Peter had been hoarding since the arrival of the latest DHL parcel. Yesterday we'd given Patrick, Reuben and David treats to mark the occasion and this morning, when Patrick arrived, he got out of the car and approached me.

"Thanks for yesterdee, Marm," he said and his fingers fluttered in front of him as he cleared his throat for a little speech. "We shared de food with de compound an' we want yo' to know dat everyone said a prayer for yo'. We asked dat yo' may see yo' grandchildren's children grow opp."

I asked him to pass on my thanks to his family and friends for the thought, but as I spoke, I did some mental arithmetic. I'd be about one hundred and five years old by then and I suddenly pictured myself on the sun porch of an aged persons' home with my octogenarian sons in nearby recliners. What if they were cranky old codgers? Suddenly the idea wasn't quite as appealing as at first thought.

We had to go to Lagos the next day and because Maureen Akintewe was coming with us, we decided to postpone part of the celebration until then. One of the pleasant little restaurants on Victoria Island would do very nicely as a birthday luncheon venue.

Early next morning, just before we departed, Janice Olawoye knocked at our side door. She was due in Lagos for the same round of meetings as Peter but had been unable to buy sufficient petrol for the trip. Peter had a reputation for not being caught without fuel so she had used her dwindling reserves to get to our house in the hope of catching us before we left.

We introduced Maureen and Janice and listened as many interesting coincidences came to light. Both had met and married

Nigerians while at University in Scotland and the USA respectively. Now they discovered that the men came from the same area and the families were certain to know each other. As we headed south, the two women spoke about the decisions that had shaped their lives and as I listened, I learned much about the Yoruba culture.

Maureen had known at the time of her wedding twenty-two years earlier that they would be returning to Nigeria, but she hadn't fully realised how much Tom's love of his homeland had rose-tinted his descriptions of their future home. When they arrived back in Nigeria, the young couple had at first lived in a typical Yoruba environment. Maureen had eventually adjusted to many cultural differences, though some customs were vastly different from her own. The relatively low status of a new wife meant that relatives could, in theory, require Maureen to prepare food whenever they wanted, or arrive without notice and expect to be accommodated for as long as they wished. There were times when such things happened, but Maureen pointed out that in practice, relatives mostly tried to be considerate.

She went on to explain other areas of adjustment. Her unusual appearance tended to be an object of curiosity, outside the family. Reactions were usually friendly, especially when people realised that she was a wife. However, not all responses were favourable. At the time, there was a lot of publicity in Nigeria about the situation in South Africa and the dreadful things white racists were doing under the apartheid system, and unfortunately some of this reputation rubbed off on innocent white non-racists. But, Maureen went on to assure us, the animosity shown to her was nothing like the racism experienced by blacks in Europe.

The question of personal privacy was sometimes an issue, too, particularly with female relatives. Maureen's reservations could be difficult for family members to comprehend, and even Tom did not at first fully understand his young wife's resistance and unhappiness. However, being somewhat of a cultural rebel himself, he was determined not to let the needs of the extended family overwhelm those of his wife and children. Maureen and Tom shared a common characteristic; both regarded social norms with a certain degree of scepticism and neither was inclined to conform unquestioningly. *No wonder those two made a match of it*, I thought as I listened.

As we travelled, the conversation strayed to a related topic. Polygamy is traditional and considered quite normal in West Africa, so any (female) foreigner marrying into a Nigerian culture would naturally have a lively interest in her future husband's views on the subject. Maureen, who had the knack of making others think, posed a question: how can Western countries, with their high rates of divorce and large numbers of children growing up within serial marriages, regard the African tradition of polygamy as strange and perhaps morally inferior?

Maureen's parents-in-law both came from traditional polygamous backgrounds but had been early converts to Anglicanism and their monogamous marriage stood as a mark of their strong Christian faith. Their dismay at learning that their only surviving son intended marrying a foreigner and eventually living and working overseas, was understandable. In such circumstances, suggested Maureen, giving me something else to think about, would not a second daughter-in-law, a Nigerian who, with her children, would remain physically close to the family, be a blessing?

Janice's in-laws must have felt similar concerns at their son's plans for an inter-racial marriage but again, the young people had known their own minds. As I listened, I realised that each couple had used a different approach to making a success of their marriage. Janice had been prepared to go against the tide in the United States by entering an inter-racial marriage, but once in her adopted country, she fully embraced the social norms and expectations of her new husband and environment. In this part of West Africa, a woman began her married life with low status, but as she gained seniority with age, position in the family, or position in society at large, she could become quite dominant. Janice was a competent professional in her own right and held senior positions at the University of Ibadan and within her husband's church; she obviously felt fulfilled. As I listened, though, I gained an inkling of the intensity of the negotiations and compromises that must have been necessary for both women.

As my companions spoke, I wondered about the concepts of choice and reaction to difference. What allows some people to embrace difference, and find it rewarding, not terrifying? As we travelled, we talked on, exchanging beliefs and opinions carefully packaged in anecdotes. Suddenly I noticed Patrick's posture. His ears weren't exactly flapping, but he had his head tilted none-too-subtly so as not to miss a word.

We invited Janice to join us for lunch and she accepted readily. In another coincidence, it was her birthday, too, so lunch was to turn into a double celebration. While Peter and Janice worked, Maureen and I spent the morning at the nearby Nigerian Museum, learning more about the country's past.

Lunch was a comfortable, chatty meal taken in an Indian restaurant on Victoria Island. With generous servings of *Jigha Gucci Biryani* and other spicy dishes, the birthday girls were suitably feted.

As we headed back to Ibadan, we agreed that it had been a pleasant and successful day, something that Lagos didn't always provide. Even when Patrick pointed out that we were low on fuel and suggested we turn off the air-conditioner to reduce consumption, we didn't feel badly done by. Windows were lowered and hot air whipped at our hair.

I thought about the fuel crisis and the impact of yesterday's announcement that petrol would continue to be scarce. I thought of the queues and the prospect of Doctor Nottidge's car being immobilised by an empty tank. And I thought of the children as yet again, circumstances seemed to conspire against them.

Chapter 19
AUSSIE REINFORCEMENTS

Several times each week the IITA bus, complete with police escort, travelled to Lagos Airport to deliver departees and to collect returning residents and incoming visitors. Because it was not safe to travel at night, incoming airline passengers spent the night at IITA's own guesthouse on the outskirts of Lagos, then were taken north to Ibadan the following morning. Today I was on the bus as it pulled out of the gates and headed south, for I was going to the airport to meet an Australian friend who was flying in from Botswana.

Margaret and I had met about six years earlier when I'd applied for a job in the hospital where she was the Social Worker in Charge. I was given the position and Margaret became my boss for three years. After her retirement, she applied for and was accepted into the Australian Volunteers Abroad Programme, to work in Francestown, Botswana. A few months into our Nigerian stay, she made contact and we happily planned for an exchange of visits to maximise our opportunities of seeing Africa. It was agreed that she would come to us first, so she launched herself into the tortuous process of obtaining a Nigerian visa.

Margaret worked with a Nigerian doctor in Francestown and one day she blithely remarked that when she reached Lagos, she intended making her own way from Lagos to Ibadan. Her medical friend had shaken his head and smiled.

"Yo' friend has been in Nigeria for twelve months? In that

case, I am sure she knows enough about de place to be at de airport to meet yo'," he assured her.

And so I was.

I had to admit that things had improved since we passed through the airport at Christmas time. The behaviour of airport staff then had been so appalling that pressure had begun for a tightening of discipline. Then, a week after our return from Europe, there had been an armed robbery within the airport. Robbers had held up the Bureau de Change and four bystanders had died in crossfire between thieves and the police. This debacle finally forced the government's hand and now, ten weeks later, there was still some semblance of order. Touts were kept outside the arrival area and armed soldiers stood around looking menacing - a strangely comforting sight.

Joshua, the IITA bus driver, was experienced in the ways of the airport and installed me at one customs exit point and, armed with a description of Margaret, he stood at the other. Passengers streamed through and my eyes were still scanning each white face when my attention was caught by Joshua who came pushing his way through the crowd to me.

"I 'ave found yo' sister, Madame," he informed me, "but de customs officer wouldn't let 'er go in case I wuz not really me."

He had been told to first produce Madame Cranny. Only then would the passenger be allowed through to face Nigeria in the raw.

Margaret was an experienced traveller but she found this a unique introduction to a country. As a seasoned Nigerian, I merely found it reassuring and I thanked the customs officer for her prudence.

We spent a comfortable night at the guest house and next morning as we entered Ibadan, I watched Margaret's face to note her reaction to all she saw. The acres of rusted tin roofs caught and held her attention. Forming an ugly, blotchy blanket, they covered the valley below us and climbed up and over the hills opposite. These were the homes of hundreds of thousands of people, the totally poor. Compared to those who lived here, Patrick was a rich man. As always when I saw this sight, I tried to imagine the heat under that tin at midday.

We pressed on through streets congested not only with cars but also with garbage that had spilled onto the roadway in ever-increasing mounds. I became aware of a change in my own perception of everything around me. I had been here dozens of times, but now as Nigeria exposed itself to my guest, I felt ashamed of the poverty, of the rubbish and its odours, of a government that took everything and gave nothing. I had been here long enough for these problems to become mine. The diversion of millions of oil dollars into private Swiss bank accounts was no longer an interesting explanation for what I saw around me, it was a personal affront. I felt like apologising but I couldn't find any words that made sense.

While I was digesting the shift in my perspective, we passed through the Institute's gates and I watched as Margaret, like everyone else, was touched by IITA's charm. As always, the manicured grounds, the beautiful gardens and the cool, well planned houses offered respite from the outside world.

Our IITA friends were keen to offer hospitality and on the first evening, we dined with the Atkinsons. Lec produced the bottle of wine she and I had won during our moment of near-glory on the golf course. As usual, her culinary skill shone through and we enjoyed a wonderful Thai meal. The dinner party was a success in another sense, too. As the evening progressed, I detected a definite thawing in the attitude of the guest on my right. It seemed that Bill Powell, who had been opposed to us renting an IITA house, had decided to let bygones be bygones.

I was confident that Margaret would be interested in my involvement with the orphanage, not only because of the children, but also for the light it shed on Nigeria's welfare policy. The children's home spoke volumes about the government's (and perhaps society's) view of the appropriate level of assistance for those unable to help themselves - always a source of interest to social workers.

Fuel was scarce and a tired Patrick had spent fourteen hours of his weekend in a queue filling the car's tank and replenishing the little cache in our storeroom, but Peter decided that some of the precious liquid could be spent on our weekly trip to the orphanage.

It was a subdued band of little ones that greeted us on Margaret's first visit. Once inside, we heard that the smallest child, two-year-old Akinyemi, the one I had dubbed the 'tear-drop baby' because of the shape of the markings on his face, had been taken to a small hospital not too far from the Home. He had been refusing food for days, staff told me, and now seemed to be dying. Only last week I had spent an hour feeding him because he had difficulty in swallowing. Every mouthful had been painfully slow but each time he swallowed, his mouth had opened for more. I suspected that when we weren't there, nothing like that amount of time would have been spent feeding him and his malnourishment would have worsened.

Today, as Patrick, Margaret and I were finishing up, the staff member returned who had taken Akinyemi to hospital. The news was not good. He urgently needed to go on a drip and to be given oxygen, but staff at the small state-run hospital had said that he must be taken away unless a fee of N300 (AU$6) was paid immediately. When I offered to go to the hospital and pay the money, the warden and a female staff member got into the car to accompany us. *So much for our plans to minimise fuel consumption*, I thought.

The warden spoke as we walked into the hospital's compound.

"Madame, don't pay anything yet. I will check at de hoffice to see if de child is still alive. It would be a pity to waste de money," he said, as he motioned for us to wait outside a tumbledown area marked 'Administration'. He was told that Akinyemi was still hanging on, so we walked towards the one large ward that constituted the hospital. As we stepped onto the veranda we disturbed several chickens as they pecked away at the grubby floor and with indignant squawks, they scattered in all directions. Patients lay on canvas stretchers, rested on mats on the floor or sat propped against walls. In the centre of the room was a high canvas stretcher-cum-bed and on it I saw the doll-sized form of Akinyemi. He was unconscious, so close to death that he breathed in gasps that came every six or seven seconds. I had sat with enough dying patients to recognise the pattern of breathing that precedes death.

A nurse came and began trying to pump air into his lungs with a squeeze-type pump. I asked to speak to a doctor and a thickset young man joined us. His frustration at the conditions under which he was expected to work was evident. He answered my question about the child's chances by telling us that he would recover if given a glucose drip and oxygen.

"And I 'ave neither. I 'ave pleaded with de government for supplies, an' all I get is, 'Dere is no money.' De only t'ing wrong with dis child is malnutrition. He could be saved like dat!" and he snapped his fingers angrily in front of my face.

"He needs to be at UTH where he will get better care," he went on. "If yo' want to save 'im, yo' must take 'im dere."

Ye gods, I thought. *Have you seen UTH lately?* But the doctor was still talking, explaining that if we took the child now, stopping at a pharmacy *en route* to pick up tubing and syringes, doctors there could save him. Left here, he would be dead within hours.

I had gained the impression from the warden's attitude before we drove to the hospital, that he thought the child should be allowed to die. I was in turmoil. My head acknowledged the futility of using extraordinary means of saving him just to send him back to that orphanage where the same crisis would be allowed to develop again, but my heart knew that we couldn't give up without trying. I thought back to little Friday. A doctor's visit and a few dollars worth of medicine had saved his life then two months later he had been adopted into a family where he was now doing well. The choice was not ours to make.

Remembering to address my offer to the warden, I suggested we take the child to the other hospital. He fixed me with a level stare as I spoke.

"No. De child stays 'ere," he said. "It is not convenient for my staff to be goin' to UTH all de time to visit."

The doctor reacted with disbelief. He switched to speaking Yoruba and his voice grew angry. The hospital's social worker had joined us and soon she, the doctor, and the nurse were all arguing loudly with the warden. For once Patrick didn't wade in, but stood listening quietly. Perhaps, like me, he could see that the child's case was being argued strongly enough by others, not that that would be sufficient to inhibit Patrick normally. Suddenly the doctor, still staring into the warden's face, spoke in English.

"But Madame has said she will meet de costs. Why are yo' refusing permission? What's yo' real reason?"

There was a pause, then with a shrug of his bony shoulders, the warden walked out. We took this as agreement and Patrick stepped forward and gathered up the child who lay like a rag doll in his arms. At the car, Patrick leaned forward and handed him over to the woman who had accompanied us from the home. We stopped briefly at a chemist shop where I bought the items on the list the doctor had given me, then we hurried on to UTH.

We were directed to a crowded ward and because there were no spare beds here, the woman was shown to a chair and told to continue holding the unconscious Akinyemi. A doctor and several medical students turned their attention to him immediately, took the supplies we'd brought and went to work. Within minutes of the drip going into his arm, Akinyemi's breathing became more regular.

'Tsk!" I turned to look at the worker from the Remand Home as she clicked her disappointment that the child was going to live. Initially I felt a flash of anger towards her but then I wondered if her regret was a close relative of the uncertainty that I'd gone through earlier. I too hoped that our intervention wasn't merely saving this child to face further misery.

With the drip safely in, the doctor looked up and spoke to the warden.

"Dis hospital is cash and carry, yo' know. I hope yo' 'ave been able to borrow money to cover de costs?" I guessed that the comment was directed at me, as everything else had been spoken in Yoruba. The warden replied with a wave of his hand in my direction.

For the next three hours, Margaret, Patrick, the warden and I were kept busy with red tape concerning the admission. We queued to buy vouchers, then we queued to spend them on necessities for Akinyemi's stay while the warden lined up to fill in the child's details at the office. The formalities were endless. I didn't trust the warden with the money needed for buying milk and medication for the child, so I enlisted Sister Canty's help. She introduced me to Stella, a member of her staff who was to prove wonderfully supportive over the next week. Between us, we worked out a satisfactory arrangement for covering Akinyemi's expenses and she offered to keep a special eye on the little boy.

By now it was four o'clock and Patrick, Margaret and I hadn't eaten nor had a drink since breakfast. It was time to collect Peter from his office and as we hurried towards FORMECU, Patrick remarked that we were getting first hand experience of 1-0-1, or perhaps 0-0-1. I had heard the expression before but didn't fully understand, so our driver explained. In recent years people who couldn't afford to eat three times a day (1-1-1), cut out the midday meal and lived by the 1-0-1 rule. In particularly difficult times, it became 0-1-0. With his words fresh in my mind, I felt a twinge of guilt that afternoon as I carried inside several limp blocks of chocolate that had spent the day in the car. I had pounced on these treasures when I'd seen them in a shop earlier, before the day's drama began. Each block was now a glutinous mess, no longer suitable to offer as a gift to a future hostess.

Tomorrow we were due to return to the hospital to meet with Sister Canty's staff. I cunningly had scheduled the talk on *Social Work in an Australian Hospital* to coincide with Margaret's visit so Sister and her team could hear about the practice of our profession not only in Australia but in Botswana as well.

But for now, we were exhausted, badly in need of a shower, a meal and an early night. By nine o'clock as the IITA guards with ancient guns slung casually over their shoulders chattered their way through our garden towards the lake where they'd spend the night, we were already exchanging goodnights and heading off to our beds.

Next day's talk went well. Our Nigerian colleagues seemed interested as we compared and contrasted social work in the three countries, but they were also intrigued by the easy interaction between my former boss and myself. Here, such a relationship would require formality and deference on my part and they listened with a mixture of amusement and awe to our informal exchanges and occasional teasing about some aspect of our former working relationship.

Afterwards we enjoyed morning tea with the staff, then headed off to the children's ward. Along the corridor we met Doctor Sodeinde and he brought me up to date on his discussions with IITA scientists regarding a high-protein dietary supplement for his little patients. Doctor Sodeinde, who had been considering how to educate parents on the benefits of adding inexpensive protein to the diet of their children, had made a decision on how to proceed with his project. It appealed as such a worthwhile scheme that I was sure Peter and I would want to be involved. We made plans to meet to discuss the project further.

When we moved on to Akinyemi's ward, we found Patrick standing beside the cot, so lost in thought as he looked down at the child that he neither heard us arrive nor responded when we spoke to him. It was only when Margaret touched his arm to get his attention that he slowly came back to us from wherever he had been. Discussing his total absorption later, we could find no other explanation than that he was deep in prayer at the time.

The baby looked very ill. Oedema had set in and he was so bloated as to be unrecognisable. Only the tattooed tear-drops on his face convinced me we were looking at the same child. He was unconscious, but lay clean and cared for in his cot. I recalled the words that I had overheard Doctor Nottidge speaking to his medical students when he examined Akinyemi after his admission.

"Even though de nurses are on strike, dis is one child we must keep in de ward. His family and his government have already abandoned him – he will not get de same treatment from us. You will feed him and care for him yourselves."

Now as I looked at him, I knew it was not going to be enough.

I felt sad and helpless as we turned to leave. We met Doctor Nottidge on the veranda and he confirmed that Akinyemi's chances of survival were slim. He was not responding well; help had come too late.

The little boy clung to life for a week but one day at IITA I answered the phone to be told by Sister Canty that Akinyemi was dead. When I next spoke to Doctor Nottidge, he put my own hope into words.

"Perhaps de little boy sensed a difference. Hopefully 'e knew dat 'e wasn't abandoned at de end."

Having a houseguest gave me an opportunity to see aspects of Nigeria that hadn't yet caught my attention, as friends came up with ideas and invitations that promised to keep Margaret and me busy for the length of her visit. Maureen suggested a trip to Abeokuta, a city about one hour's drive from Ibadan, where traditional fabrics were printed and tie-dyed, and an aerobics friend, Clarice, offered to take us behind the scenes in an Ibadan market.

I was looking forward to introducing my visitor to Clarice. She was a Nigerian of royal blood, a princess of the Bini royal family in Benin State. Unfortunately for Clarice, her status cut little ice with other women on IITA and they treated her with the same informality that was extended to everyone else. She and her European husband had lived on IITA for perhaps twenty years, but she still had difficulty in accepting this lack of deference. Although she wasn't Yoruba, she spoke the language well and her status meant that she was regarded as a person of significance within the local community.

A complex relationship existed between Clarice and Maureen. Both were married to British partners so Maureen, despite her fair skin and auburn hair, was Clarice's 'sister' in the African context. Not only was she a sister, but she was a *junior* one and a certain amount of deference was appropriate if not always forthcoming from the independent-minded Maureen. All told, though, Maureen found it a reciprocal relationship, with Clarice proving generous in her friendship and insights.

On the day of the trip to Abeokuta with Maureen, we set off with loaded picnic baskets and soon were wandering around a typical Yoruba town, the sort that Maureen and Tom had lived in when they first came to Nigeria.

We visited the part of town where women toiled over boiling coppers, dyeing fabrics for the markets. At first, children ran from us, the sight of three white faces just too overwhelming. Illogically, I expected them to accept Maureen without question - her own children were Nigerian after all, but today she was as fearsome as Margaret and I were. As we walked between the mud-brick houses, Patrick pointed out a family grave, strategically placed beside the back steps, the location, during my childhood, where my mother always kept the mop and bucket. *Different culture, different priorities*, I thought in awe.

The heat of the day was incredible. This was the hottest time of the year and as we returned to Ibadan, we decided that tomorrow must be a rest day. Margaret assured me that she was enjoying everything she saw and did, but I was concerned that Botswana was perhaps not as hyperactive as this and, after all, she was supposed to be having her annual break from toil.

A few days later we were refreshed and ready to do over the markets with Clarice, but to my disappointment, she was stricken with malaria. Instead, she offered the services of Rebecca, a young, stylish Nigerian woman, who also held the title of junior sister. With Rebecca's excellent knowledge of Ibadan, we visited weaving factories, craft shops and tiny markets where *Oyinbos* rarely go. My stockpile of items to be carried back to Australia grew alarmingly.

While in the markets, Margaret and I decided to share the cost of a carton of powdered baby milk formula to leave with Sister Canty because we had noted how often poor families asked for her help. Rebecca led us through the cacophony of noise, odours and congestion of Bodija Market until she found the stall she was seeking. After spirited bargaining a deal was struck, (AU$13), then Rebecca insisted that the carton be unsealed, the lids prised off and every tin inspected.

I asked what we were looking for.

"Often de stallholders try to sheet yo' by fillin' every second tin wit' stones," was the simple explanation.

We delivered the milk to Sister's office and it was locked away safely. Taking me into her office, Sister filled me in on developments since Akinyemi's death. She had just had a visit, she told me, from one of the workers at the children's home, requesting receipts for all amounts that Mrs Cranny had spent on Akinyemi during his hospitalisation. Just for the home's records, it was emphasised. Sister had refused, saying that she would give the receipts into Mrs Cranny's hands only. When the worker got up to leave, angry at the nun's refusal, she'd dropped her purse and items scattered everywhere. She retrieved her belongings and departed. Later, Sister Canty had found a sheet of paper on her office floor and had read it, thinking it had fallen from her desk. It was an application to the Health Department for a refund of the amounts associated with the hospitalisation of one of their residents, Akinyemi Abandoned. On the page was listed every procedure I had paid for plus all purchases associated with his special needs. All that remained to be added to the page were the amounts that coincided with the receipts that Sister was holding.

I was still furious when we got back to IITA, my indignation feeding on itself as I recalled every episode, either real or imagined, where attempts had been made upon my person or my purse since I'd been in Africa. The first person I ran into was Agnes Uryio, one of my favourite people on IITA. In Agnes' veins flowed equal quantities of African blood and the milk of human kindness, and just as had happened on past occasions when I was confused or frustrated by the local scene, I found myself talking things over with her. As always, she heard me out before gently leading me to a different perspective. As she spoke, I realised that I was allowing personal indignation to cloud my vision.

"Ah, Pum. Just think it through. Sometimes people resort to lying and cheating so that their own kids get to eat and eventually it becomes a way of life. It is accepted as a method of getting money out of a government that owes them anyhow. Try to understand..."

I calmed down. Later when Nancy visited, I teased her that thank heavens I had met Agnes first instead of her, otherwise we might have marched off, machetes in hand, to confront the would-be fraudster. When the opportunity arose, I spoke calmly to the woman, letting her know that I didn't appreciate her attempt to involve me in the dishonest application. My words were met with silence and a steady gaze; not one word did she say, nor did her facial expression change. I was left with little satisfaction other than in knowing that I'd had my say.

One day as we were driving past the children's home on another outing, I suddenly asked Patrick to turn in the gateway. I wanted Margaret, (a trained nurse as well as a social worker), to look at a nasty gash on Ibimie's forehead and, if necessary, change the dressing. I was dismayed when I saw the littlies line up at the table as if to receive a meal, because this was an impromptu visit and I was empty-handed. Patrick explained and most of them readily accepted the situation, but predictably, it was Gbade who took me to task and as I said *odabo*, he gazed at me with cool reproof. One small shoulder said it all, causing the staff much amusement. His point was taken. Never again did I blow in without something to offer the children.

My fears about the effect of the worsening fuel shortage on Doctor Nottidge's visits were justified. After three visits he ceased to appear and no further action was ever taken following the tests the children had undergone. As Nancy described it, we couldn't win for losing.

Our social engagements continued. We were invited to bring Margaret to a dinner party at the Gulleys and an afternoon tea with Juliana so 'Pum's sister' could meet the other women on campus. This function turned into a wonderful afternoon and I was touched by Juliana's gesture. African and Indian guests in their impressive outfits, the laughter and chatting; it was a wonderful opportunity for Margaret to meet a wide range of people, and typical of Juliana's generosity in organising it.

On the day of Margaret's departure, we had time for a quick

trip into Ibadan to visit an exhibition of West African crafts designed for the export market. We were impressed with the displays and shopped accordingly. On our way home I asked Patrick to stop at a chemist shop and soon I was standing in an establishment not unlike a small pharmacy at home. An attractively groomed young lady approached and asked if she could be of assistance.

"Could I have some hairspray please," I asked, as clearly as I could. The assistant nodded and returned with a can of Airozone air-freshener.

I put my hand up and tugged a lock of my hair.

"No, I mean spray for my *hair*," I clarified.

Her eyes had followed my hand and now she looked at me in surprise.

" 'airspray, Madame? Yo' *did* ask for *hair*spray!" she chided, as she moved to the other end of the shop and took a can of Sunsilk SuperHold from a shelf. Silly me.

Moving on, we sat in traffic behind a car that sported several empty plastic drink bottles dangling from string tied to the bumper-bar. On the roof rack a twisted squash racquet was mounted at a jaunty angle. Margaret turned to our driver.

"What is the significance of the bottles and the racquet, Patrick?" she asked innocently. I smiled in anticipation of the answer.

"Doze bottles? An' de racquet?" Patrick was puzzled that she should ask. Margaret nodded.

"Dey are for decoration!" he said, as if the matter should really be quite obvious. Silly Margaret.

Margaret was due to fly out mid-afternoon and because the IITA bus was going direct to the airport, there was no need for me to accompany her to Lagos. She sought out Patrick before he left. Our driver looked tired because we had kept him very busy, but his eyes shone when she gave him a substantial gift to thank him for his assistance over the past days. Likewise, David and Reuben were soon beaming too. As she gave each man his gift, Margaret described the ways in which he had contributed to her enjoyment of the visit.

With plans in place to meet back in Brisbane when our contracts ended, Margaret boarded the bus and was off. IITA was back to two Aussies.

Next morning I remembered the blocks of chocolate that had melted and reset into uneven lumps. I couldn't give them as gifts and I respected my love of chocolate too much to leave them any longer within my own reach. I approached Patrick with two blocks in my hand and explained why I was giving them away, but I made a tactical error in my wording.

"Perhaps you would like to take these to work to share with the other drivers, Patrick," I said, intending it as a statement, not a question. Patrick, who knew all about chocolate from earlier tastings, gleefully hugged the misshapen blocks to his chest.

"Thank yo', Marm. I think I will like even more to take dem 'ome and share dem with my children!"

My next visitor was Sule, the little vegie vendor. He was always in dire financial straits yet never asked for handouts. Anyone less like Mr Titoloye, I could not imagine. Week after week the quiet young man would visit, pushing his wheelbarrow of rapidly wilting vegetables through the searing heat. He got into the habit of having a cool drink at my place and on some occasions, especially during the Muslim season of Ramadan, when he would also be weak with hunger, he would rest in a cool spot at my back door. But this was not fasting season and when he called, I bought some items then handed him a large block of chocolate.

He took it in his hands and thanked me but as he walked away, he stopped, put his barrow down and turned back to me with a puzzled look. He indicated the chocolate that now rested amongst his vegetables.

"Thank yo', Madame, but what do I do wit' it?" he asked.

When I explained, he unwrapped it and gingerly nibbled a corner. His eyes lit up almost comically and a smile spread across his thin face. As he walked off, he was munching his next mouthful, making appreciative noises as he went. I shut the door but a minute later remembered that I should warn him not to eat it all at once.

Too much chocolate on a stomach so unused to rich fare could have dire consequences. I went out and looked up and down the street but he was nowhere to be found. I just hoped he wasn't curled up somewhere with an upset stomach.

Right on schedule the following Friday, Sule appeared at my backdoor. Before I could inquire, he thanked me profusely for last week's wonderful treat, the first time he had tasted chocolate in his life. All was well.

At last I admitted that I had no further excuses for postponing my responsibilities to the Rest of the World. Picking up the phone I began a series of calls around the campus. We really had to meet to sort ourselves out once and for all.

Chapter 20
THE DINNER AND THE DELTA

The members of the Rest of the World sat facing one another, knowing that the time had come to make decisions. Several of us would be away next week and there would be no time for planning when we returned, so we attacked the topic of the dinner party with determination. In no time we had things under control. We decided that we might not be as exotic as other global zones, but we sure could make decisions.

Good Food in Casual Settings, was to be our theme - somehow it suited our style - and with a minimum of fuss we formed into groups and divided up the menu. First courses from Germany, Italy, Switzerland; mains from USA, Ireland and Israel; desserts from France, Columbia and Australia. Why, as I opened my mouth and volunteered to make pavlovas, didn't I pause to think where I was? Pavlovas and humidity don't mix.

I was blissfully unaware of the problems I had just embraced so we moved on to discussing plans for decorating the venue. By the time we dispersed, I knew that a veritable army of workers would be busily working in the interests of the Rest of the World while I toured the south east of the country.

Our trip was to take in an area that was under consideration for a biosphere reserve. The delta region of the Niger River consists of an extensive marshy jungle which floats upon a sea of oil; black gold that makes up ninety-five percent of the nation's wealth. This part of the coastline is dotted with rigs on land and offshore, monsters erected by multinationals Shell and Chevron Oil. The love-hate relationship between Nigerians and their oil is legendary. There are those who ask where would the country be without it and others who believe that the discovery of oil was the beginning of the end for the nation's integrity. Since its discovery, virtually all other export industries have been neglected while corruption has taken hold in the more easily manipulated environment of a single-industry. Those with political power were able to siphon off vast sums of money for their own use while the nation's poor gained few benefits from the windfall. Anger and resentment simmered amongst those who were being dispossessed of their farming land and amongst those who saw and felt the environmental damage being done by rigs, burn-off points and spillages. The oil companies argued that included in the royalties they paid the government was a component intended for the local communities and if this money was being diverted, there was little they could do about it.

The Tropical Forest Action Plan (TFAP) that Peter was helping develop, was concerned not only with forestry but also with general conservation of natural resources so it was important that he visit the area prior to finalising his report.

The fuel shortage was by now continuous and Patrick had to queue for twelve hours to fill jerry cans with petrol to ensure that we wouldn't be stranded in the south east of the country if we were unable to buy fuel in Delta State. We set out with petrol containers concealed in plain cartons, hoping that all robbers and rioters had head colds and couldn't smell the obnoxious fumes wafting from of our vehicle. We were a travelling petrol-bomb and I shuddered to think of the consequences if we were to have an accident.

We had an extra passenger on this trip, the TFAP's regional co-ordinator for the south-east of Nigeria. I liked Frank Faleru the moment I met him. He was a quiet man, not at all inflated with his own importance although he was young to be in this position. His company and quiet humour were appreciated during the drive to Sapele. Multiple roadblocks punctuated the trip and a tired Patrick was becoming increasingly irritated. As we were stopped yet again, he wound down his window and confronted the police. "Are yo' blind? Can't yo' see we are in a CC car?" he demanded, referring to our car's numberplates. As we moved off, Peter suggested to Patrick that he calm down because he knew that there was little advantage in antagonising police. Between the enforced stops, I continued my favourite pastime of watching the never-ending human parade that walked or traded along the roadside.

I had packed a set of linen because I had no desire to share sheets with previous guests ever again, but when we settled into our hotel room, I carefully inspected the bed and found crisp white linen that smelled like sunshine. My petrol-scented specimens were returned to their box in the vehicle.

Next day began with a trip to Forestry Headquarters, where we were introduced to a team of smartly dressed Forest Guards. Peter, every bit the visiting dignitary, was led down the line of men, stopping occasionally to shake hands and address individuals. He congratulated the men on their role in protecting the forest from those who plundered the stands of timber without thought of conservation. The Head Guard was asked to respond and he outlined the dangers his staff faced in the battle against these illegal loggers. The main problem, the man explained, was that the guards were no match for the ruthless thieves. They needed firearms if they were to do their work effectively.

"Without guns, we 'ave to run away because we carry nothin', while dey are armed to de teet!"

The thought of pitched battles between gun-toting guards and robbers who were armed to de teet somehow didn't immediately appeal to me as a solution.

Next, we were to visit a plywood factory whose management was keen to outline the benefits to the region if the World Bank were to subsidise their operation. The owner had provided a boat for the journey because the site was inaccessible by land. We made up a party of ten but the boat could carry only eight, so the lucky ones stepped aboard gingerly, leaving the two drivers standing on the shore looking forlorn. The only life jackets on board were offered to Peter and me and as I gratefully tied the straps of mine, I looked up and caught Frank's envious eyes. He smilingly admitted that he couldn't swim so we made a deal with my having the better of it; I promised to throw the jacket to him the minute my feet touched the shore.

I looked down at the water and pictured parasites lurking in its brown depths, just waiting to cause river blindness and other nasty ailments. Although I appreciated the snug fitting life jacket, I hoped not to test its buoyancy.

In the powerful boat we sped down the Forcados River heading towards Burutu, an island at the river mouth, roaring past fishermen, creating bow waves that set tiny canoes rocking and fish fleeing.

Tumbledown sheds, jetties and houses were squeezed between the jungle and the river. They were ugly, fragile constructions, their walls a muddle of iron, timber and mud. Roofs were rusting tin or, sometimes, disintegrating thatch. It was as if the buildings were caught between two worlds and suffering the worst of both, for they had lost the charm of the old culture but lacked the funds to satisfy the other.

At times we paused in our journey to pull into the riverbank for inspections or meetings to do with Peter's project. On the second of these we trekked up a narrow path to a village to meet with local leaders who wanted to put their case for World Bank funding to set up an employment-creation scheme. We trudged past a peeling sign which announced that we were entering the realm of *His Royal Highness, T Okpe Ogbon, The Ebenana Owei of the Obotebe Clan.*

At the village, we were shown into a reception area, where a serious-faced young man dressed in slacks and sports shirt, waited. As we filed in, I wondered if I was the only woman to cross that threshold because the local women, who had joined us as we walked up from the boat, remained outside.

His Royal Highness, a handsome young man with alert eyes that missed nothing, nodded a serious greeting. He sat in the position of honour, his casual attire at odds with the deference being shown him by attendants. When the state co-ordinator, Mr Onocha, asked permission to take a photo, the King stood and without word disappeared through the curtain-covered doorway behind him. For a few anxious moments I feared that he was offended but he soon reappeared, no longer dressed casually but looking most regal.

He made an impressive sight. Although not a tall man, he looked suitably majestic in a flowing white garment. He wore a short red cape over his shoulders and several bright, hoop-like necklaces encircling his neck. Covering his close-cropped hair was a beaded headdress gathered into a topknot, and in his hand he carried a small staff decorated with animal hair.

Once seated, he inclined his head towards all would-be photographers and the ceremony began. An aide delivered his Royal Highness' speech outlining plans for the development of employment in the area and Peter responded in terms of his project's involvement.

Later we gratefully accepted the offered bottles of minerals before heading back to the river and resuming our journey downstream.

At last we reached Burutu, one of the oldest settlements in Western Africa, originally settled by the Portuguese. By now it was half-past two and we hadn't seen food since an early breakfast at our hotel. Undaunted, the men inspected every log and piece of machinery at the plant and engaged in spellbinding discussions about the drying properties of the glue used in the plywood industry. When every map of the region was unfurled and no topic remained undiscussed, the workers drew breath, and the Italian manager and his Nigerian wife invited us to lunch. It would have been appreciated under any circumstances but today with the sweet sauce of hunger, it brought sighs of enjoyment from all. Unfortunately it was a hurried meal because it was important that we get back to Warri before dark, and amid invitations to return for a social visit, we said goodbye.

Darkness was closing in as we roared our way upstream, the boat's engine tearing at the peaceful twilight until we pulled into the jetty and found the two drivers waiting anxiously. It was not good to be on this road after dark and it was a relieved carload of travellers who finally arrived back at Sapele.

Showered and refreshed, we gathered for dinner. I noticed Frank was absent. He appeared later in the evening and told me quietly that he had taken Patrick out for a meal because he had been having difficulty getting food. I was disconcerted because I knew that money wasn't the problem, nor was transport. Until Frank spoke, I had forgotten that a Yoruba might feel vulnerable in this part of the country. The Biafran war might have ended almost twenty-five years ago but ethnic distrust still simmered.

The war had been triggered in 1967 when regional hostilities had led to the massacre of an Ibo minority in the north. Ibos in the homeland area of eastern Nigeria were bitter about the killings and, encouraged by the prospect of oil revenue, they responded by declaring a separate Republic of Biafra. Oil meant that instead of being the poorest region the East was now potentially the richest and the existing Federation of Nigeria had no intention of being cut adrift from that wealth. But even within the new Biafran Republic, there was discord. Some of the smaller ethnic groups within its boundaries preferred to be part of the larger Nigerian Federation than be a minority within Biafra. In the west of Nigeria, the Yorubas had been ambivalent about the power of the northerners but when the Biafran regime invaded the Mid-West, the Yorubas began to see them as a threat. [3] As a result, the Yorubas rallied to the Federal cause, an act that was seen by the Ibos as a betrayal. In later years, relationships between the Ibos and Yorubas fluctuated, with co-existence proceeding happily when all was well, but suspicion flaring if political tension mounted. At the moment, there was tension aplenty and Patrick had decided that discretion was the better part of valour.

As well as seeing to Patrick's food supplies, Frank also invited him to use the spare bed in his large suite rather than sleep in the car, as drivers were expected to do. I was accustomed to the "Big Man" syndrome that permeated the ranks at FORMECU and was surprised at Frank's gesture. I regarded him with more respect than ever.

Next day as we drove towards the headquarters of Chevron

Oil, the foresters were talking shop when tertiary-trained Frank turned to Peter and asked, "What do yo' make of our sacred trees? If de spirits of de gods enter a tree, it can be cut down one day but de next it is grown again. Nothing can kill a tree if de spirits have entered it."

Mr Onocha took up the theme. "Dere is a certain tree dat no matter how big a bulldozer dey used, it could not be removed. Den it was realised dat de tree was sacred. De road now is divided, leavin' de tree in de middle."

Sceptic that I am, I wondered if it said more about the bulldozers than about the trees, but later it was pointed out to me that the tree probably owed its survival to a nervousness about violating it. Peter, respectful of imponderable beliefs, listened but did not express a scientific opinion on the phenomena.

When we arrived at Chevron Oil, Sonni, their Nigerian public relations officer, took us in tow. As we walked through the office I was struck by the difference between this and a government-run agency. The place buzzed with activity and the influence of money. Equipment was in good condition and staff knew how to work it. Even the toilets flushed at the push of a button.

Sonni, a dapper little man with gold jewellery that peeped discreetly from below the open neck and cuffs of his designer shirt, led us to the company helicopter. We were to be whisked away to Chevron's tank farm at Escarvos, where the crude oil is held in huge storage areas before it is chemically cleansed for shipping out. As we lifted off, I looked down at Patrick's upturned face and I fancied I saw relief that his feet were remaining firmly on the ground. It was a fascinating flight. Below, the river divided into fingers that reached out to the ocean, and all the land in between was covered with the tight green carpet of coastal vegetation.

When we arrived, we were driven around the complex. I was overawed by the size of even one of the tanks yet here stood two rows of five each. We were taken to the administration area and introduced to the American manager, a man with ideal credentials for the job. He was personable and relaxed and in an open manner he discussed the industry's problems and its own contribution to them. All the while he was tactful and discreet when apportioning blame to others. He showed us a section of pipeline that had been punctured from the outside, presumably by villagers. When maintenance men had arrived to repair the damage, an angry crowd had demanded not repairs, but compensation for the damage being done by the seeping oil; desperate acts by desperate people who obviously felt they had no other way of sharing in the oil millions.

The locals vented their spleen on the visible foe, the oil companies, and they had plenty of evidence in the form of environmental damage to back their claims.

Having been in Nigeria for over twelve months, we had not seen the BBC television programme, *The Drilling Fields* which was filmed at a site less than 160 km from where we now stood, because such documentaries were banned in Nigeria. It told of bloody confrontations between Nigerian Mobile Police (whose intervention was requested by Shell) and the Ogoni people who had gathered in peaceful protest against their treatment at the hands of the multinationals. Their leader, Ken Saro-Wiwa, was arrested and after years of imprisonment, was executed for treason in spite of strident international protests.

With much to think about, we lunched in Chevron's impressive dining room, then were taken on a boat ride to inspect the effects of drilling upon mangroves. It was obvious that large canals, created to allow huge oil rigs to travel into the marshy hinterland, were allowing in salt water that was now killing the freshwater vegetation. At close quarters we saw the scars where the intense heat of the burn-off points killed surrounding plant life and baked the soil to rock-like hardness.

Some damage appeared at first to be due to natural forces. Our boat slowed while Sonni pointed out an island-village that was losing its battle against tidal erosion. It was only later that I wondered about the consequences when people are forced from their farms and move to vulnerable sites and clear away vegetation. Today, the anger of the people from the island-village when they saw us was palpable. I felt anxiety grab my throat as men took to small boats to chase us, waving their fists and shouting abuse. I turned to look at Sonni, but his face showed complete unconcern. As our powered boat pulled away from our pursuers, I realised that he must face that type of animosity daily.

Later, as we flew over the area on our way back to Warri, I felt overwhelmed by a surfeit of information and conflicting arguments.

After our final night at Sapele, we rose early for our journey back to Ibadan. Patrick had a full day's driving ahead of him, so I arranged with the hotel's manager for him to be brought to the dining room for a full breakfast. As I did so, I mentally thanked Frank for his example in consideration.

At no stage of our excursion had we been able to purchase fuel, so the jerry cans proved useful. At one stop it had appeared that Patrick could do a deal with a black-marketeer but the man reneged at the last minute, fearing that if he was seen supplying us with fuel, the locals might riot, demanding a share of the precious liquid.

It was good to be home again, although the challenge of the dinner dance loomed ever closer. I checked on the progress of my troops and found that I was the one most in need of a prod to action. With grandiose plans for whipping up several pavlovas, I booked Nancy's 'food mixer' for Saturday, having drawn an uncomprehending stare when I had asked for her Mixmaster. On the next shopping trip, I collected the extras for decorating the potential masterpieces. As well as forgetting the humidity, I had also overlooked the fact that Nigeria does not have fresh cream; the whole scheme was turning into an exercise in madness.

The morning dawned with the air heavy and sticky. So was the first pavlova. It was consigned to the bin. Numbers two and three should have met the same fate but I dared not. Bathed in a lather of perspiration, I battled on, the high-pitched scream of the electric beater accurately expressing my panic and self-recriminations. Suddenly there was a knock at my kitchen door and Nancy put her head around the door.

"Can y'all come with me to see the kids? Jim is away and I

don't like driving out there by myself. Please, I beg, Madame," she said, ending her request with a typical Nigerian plea. The thought of the kids waiting for food that never came was too much for me and soon we were on our way. I calmed myself by calculating that I could still cook two more pavlovas - just - if all went smoothly this afternoon.

At the orphanage I forgot my own problems as we talked to the little ones. It suddenly hit me that I would be leaving in ten weeks. On my next visit I must begin preparing them for my departure.

Nancy and I arrived home at one o'clock, by which time it was raining. I dashed up to keep an appointment with the decorators and between downpours we collected armloads of flowers to fill the upturned umbrellas that we'd decided upon as a decorative feature. A band of workers were swarming over the venue, setting up and finalising arrangements. The Rest of the World section was looking good, holding its own with the other zones. Dropping off the flowers, I explained my culinary crisis and fled to oversee further battle between egg whites and atmospheric conditions.

My creations were barely visible under the copious amounts of mock cream, tinned peaches and fresh passionfruit pulp as I slunk into the hall that evening. With mournful specimens clutched in each hand, I took an inconspicuous route to the dining area and hid my offerings amongst the rest of the food.

The evening was a social and financial success. The food was interesting and plentiful. The twenty unfortunates who succumbed to curiosity and polished off a slice of pavlova must have been mellowed by other good food and wine for I distinctly heard lamentations that there were not more pavlovas. As we headed home after midnight, I was heady with relief that the wretched function was over at last.

3. Ajayi, J.F.A., *Milestones in Nigerian History*, Ibadan University Press, 1980, pp 42 - 43

Chapter 21
SALMONELLA POISONING

David needed to speak to Madame urgently, Peter reported, as he returned to the lounge room. There was no way that Sir would do instead and judging by the look on David's face, I was in for a long discussion on a serious topic.

I went to the door and stepped out into the garage area, taking a seat on the low table that stood against the wall. David remained in front of me, not in his usual talking posture, but with his hands clasped almost nervously in front of him. He spoke softly and urgently.

"Madame, I 'ave to ask a favour, an' it is a matter of life an' death." The old man's face was crumpled with anxiety. "I need monny, Madame, six month's salary in advance. I 'ave given de matter serious thought and I 'ave no option."

I asked for more details.

"I need N3000 because my church wants its members to contribute money so a large temple can be built in de forest. Unless it is built, a calamity will overtake oss." He was plainly distressed.

"David, what you do with your money is your own business, but you're asking me to place you at risk. Do you completely trust these people?"

I had grave doubts about anyone who would ask someone to surrender his total income for six months.

"I trust dem, Madame. It is better for me to suffer physically than spiritually. I will survive some 'ow."

"Oh, David! You know that we won't let you starve, so are you being fair?" My words were tinged with impatience partly because I didn't know how to handle the matter. I suggested we both take twenty-four hours to think it through. David thanked me for listening and with a nod of farewell, he turned and disappeared into the darkness.

I fretted until the small hours, imagining the old man in dire circumstances. If I refused to pay him in advance, was I being motivated by a paternalistic attitude? If I gave him the money, was I being irresponsible in exposing him to exploitation? After more tossing and turning, I could come up with no better solution than to break not one principle but two. I'd give him two-thirds of the money due to him from now until the Kangs returned, and pay him the remainder in monthly instalments so he'd have some income. We intended giving each of the men a gift of money before our departure so he would be OK. In the meantime, I could be alert for opportunities to give him food. Consigning the philosophical debate on the rights and wrongs of the decision to the too-hard basket, I turned over and fell asleep at last.

Next morning David and I finalised our financial arrangements and our comfortable co-existence at 20 Tropical Crescent resumed. That is until Friday morning, when I walked outside and noticed that the old gardener had forgotten to put out the rubbish bin for collection. Although inconvenient, this was no hanging matter, but I felt a wave of annoyance at his carelessness and I set out around the garden to find him, intending to chastise him. I stopped in my tracks when I realised that I was trembling with rage, an unusual sensation for me. I needed to pull myself together. I was quite unnerved by the intensity of my anger as I went back inside the house and sat down, waiting until I had myself under control. Only when I could trust myself to be civil did I go and find David and ask him to deal with the overflowing garbage bin.

The day progressed normally until late afternoon. Suddenly I felt extremely tired, my head throbbed and I began to shake. I was in the grips of another bout of malaria. Suddenly I understood why I had been so unreasonably upset that morning. I dosed myself with chloroquin and panadol and took to my bed. I was only vaguely aware of Peter checking on my wellbeing throughout the evening but when the alarm went for my early morning tablets, I could tell that the medication was beginning to work. Thankfully, it was not another resistant strain of the disease. For the next twenty-four hours my time was spent sleeping for long stretches and swallowing tablets. As Peter left for work, he whispered that David had been coming to the door at regular intervals for progress reports on my health. As I drifted off to sleep again, I offered a little prayer of thanks that I had not vented my malarial spleen on the kind old fellow.

Once I was well, I decided it was time to speak with IITA's accounting section. We'd been told that, over the years, expatriate accountants had installed convoluted accounting systems that discouraged fraud and efficiency in equal proportions. It was now April, yet we had not received a supposedly monthly account this year. I had visions of chaos if we left the finalisation of our account until the week before our departure. Besides, Peter needed details of official phone calls for submission of his expenses to Washington.

"Don't worry, Madame. Yo' will receive de account for January in two or three week's time," I was informed by the clerk who had told me the same thing now for eight weeks.

Hoping to arouse some sense of urgency and to remind him that ours was a more complicated account because we were not IITA staff, I asked how the matter was to be handled.

"Madame," he explained patiently, "When yo' first moved into Kang's house, yo' paid a substantial deposit to cover expenses. Soon yo' will make another big deposit, then after yo' have been home in Australia a few months, yo' will receive a cheque for the balance remaining in yo' account."

I was shaking my head as he spoke and explained that we needed statements now in order to finalise our dealings with the World Bank. I knew that I would get more action if I did a bit of stirring, so I suggested that if it was impossible for him to give me an up-to-date statement, it would be best if we simply continued on as we were. Then, when he had prepared the account, he could sent it to Australia and we'd send back a cheque for the amount owing.

"Madame, dat is *not* how we do things." He almost doubled in size as indignation welled up inside him. He informed me sternly that I must pay another substantial deposit immediately. I decided to continue pressing for an account.

"How about I close our Personal Account today? That gives you two and a half months to get a statement to us."

"Nor, nor, nor, Madame!" He seemed even more horrified. How could he make this dense Madame understand? "We cannot close your account because yo' might want to come buck to IITA some day. Please wait here. If yo' insist, I will get yo' de current balance," and he disappeared, taking with him the copy of our December statement that I had brought with me.

He eventually returned and with a flourish, he produced my December account and another photocopied document. I was still thanking him when I glanced down and saw that I was now holding two copies of our December account, my original and a still warm photocopy. Determined not to give up, I suggested that I speak to someone in authority. I was led to a nearby office and introduced to the Head Accountant, Mr Sunday Udoh who, in a matter of minutes, devised a sensible plan to cover our departure. I was promised statements for January, February and March by the following day.

As promised, the documents were waiting for me when I called and if one judged by the proud smile on the face of the young clerk, the solution had been his idea all along. With the information I needed clutched in my hand, I headed home to begin tidying up our financial affairs.

Excitement was in the air back home in Australia. Cranny Junior was due on July 10 and with this in mind I went to see IITA's travel office to make our bookings. We had promised ourselves stopovers in London and Hong Kong on the way home and because July 1 was the earliest we could depart, the animals of East Africa would have to wait until another time. Unfortunately, we were also to miss our return visit to Margaret in Botswana. We were to leave Nigeria on July 1 and touch down at the Brisbane airport at ten o'clock on July 10. We instructed Michelle to wait until after noon at least, before going into hospital. If all arrivals were as scheduled, it was going to be a busy day.

Of more immediate importance than the day we were to leave, was the need to ship home our excess luggage. A trip to Lagos was necessary to start the process so when the car was next due to go down, I was on board. First port of call was the World Bank office where I went to see Sunday, the staff member who had worked wonders when we were having visa problems. When I described the items we wanted to send home by surface freight, Sunday recommended we deal with Panalpina World Transport. He also informed me that I needed a clearance permit showing that our cargo didn't include antiquities. This was necessary because Nigeria was taking sensible precautions against the nation being stripped of valuable artefacts. The required permit could be obtained from the National Commission for Museums and Monuments and I was assured that the Ibadan Museum would handle the matter. Sunday suggested that I list the goods we intended taking home before visiting the museum. In all probability, the permit would be issued on the strength of the list after the payment of a small fee. I decided to begin the process as soon as we returned to Ibadan.

Leaving the World Bank office, I asked Patrick to drive me across Lagos to Panalpina's headquarters and in no time I was being helped by an efficient staff member. Between us, we estimated the size of the job; six cartons, one suitcase and two wooden chests (one large and one small), all to be shipped to Brisbane in one container. It promised to be a straightforward consignment and a small removalist truck from Panalpina's fleet would visit IITA in ten day's time to collect our goods. I would supervise the packing and the goods would be transported to Lagos, then shipped to Brisbane without delay. I enquired about insurance and stressed that nothing was to leave our house before the necessary forms had been signed. I was assured that the packers would bring the necessary paperwork and when they confirmed the exact extent of the shipment, they would complete the forms, accept our payment, and issue a receipt before departing with our possessions. It all sounded most efficient. Once again, I was reminded to get the clearance permit from the Museum.

Back in Ibadan, I tried unsuccessfully to phone the Museum but the phones were not working so I compiled a full list of the items and had Patrick drive me there. With luck, I might even have the matter attended to immediately.

As we drove, Patrick and I talked about the Cranny's departure. Patrick rubbed his head and sighed.

"Not long now, Marm. Last night Mercy said she could hardly believe dat it is time for de Crannys to go. It 'as gone so quickly. I explained it to my family; 'If yo' have bitter soup it seems to last forever, but sweet soup, ah, it is soon gonn!'"

I sat in silence, my concern for Patrick's future on hold while I adjusted to being seen as a bowl of soup.

When we arrived at the Museum, we saw an impressive building, or at least it would have been, had it ever been completed. Situated in an open area, it must have been an ambitious project when commenced, but like so many government undertakings, construction had ceased halfway through when money dried up. Armed with my list, I picked my way over a tangle of grass growing up through concrete blocks and piles of sand. The rear section of the building had been completed and there I found the office I was looking for.

I explained the reason for my visit and indicated the list of items I wished to send to Australia. The young clerk heard me out, his eyes fixed on my face with what I hoped was a comprehending stare. Encouraged, I ploughed on and when every last bit of information was delivered I paused, expecting him to initiate the next move. He did.

"De man yo' must see is not on seat. Come buck later, Madame."

I was not to be fobbed off so easily. I asked to see someone who could at least confirm that I was following the correct procedure to gain the permit. With a sigh, the young man wandered off and returned with a more senior-looking gentleman who listened to my request, studied my list and shook his head sadly.

"Nor, nor, nor, Madame. Yo' 'ave it wrong. Yo' are to bring de items in so we can see dem. Also, yo' must wait until de correct senior person is here. No, I cannot tell yo' exactly when to comm buck. Just bring de items and if he is on seat, he will see yo' and tell yo' what yo' must pay."

Later, at Peter's office, I was relating my frustrating tale to Simon.

"Nor, nor, nor, Madame. Dey are settin' yo' up to sheet yo'. Leave it to me. I will try to find out who yo' must see and get confirmation about how much yo' must pay."

I thanked him profusely. Simon was an astute young man and his intervention on my behalf was sure to save me aggravation. I returned home less riled than earlier, confident that with Simon as my advocate, all would be well.

Word came next day that I must take all items to the museum to be inspected by a Mrs Omolayole whom Simon had spoken to and with whom he'd made an appointment on my behalf for ten o'clock Thursday.

On Thursday morning, Peter, Patrick and I, sweating profusely in the tropical heat, loaded our station wagon to the brim with the carvings, paintings and chests that we intended taking home to Australia. A few minutes before ten o'clock I fronted up to the desk and informed the clerk that I had arrived for my appointment with Mrs Omolayole.

"Mrs Omolayole is not on seat," I was told nonchalantly.

They couldn't tell me exactly when she would be back because she was travelling. I asked why, if she knew she'd be travelling today, had she made an appointment to see me. It was explained that at the time of making the appointment, she had not yet decided to travel. I was also told that there was no one else there who was authorised to issue permits. I would just have to come back on Monday when Mrs Omolayole would certainly be in. A ten o'clock appointment was made and with drooping shoulders, I asked Patrick to drive me home, where, with more huffing and puffing, we unloaded the car.

Monday arrived and we did it all again. When we arrived at the Museum, I was informed that Mrs Omolayole was not on seat and as far as they knew, she would not be in for several days. I would just have to come back another day. The last of the sentence was lost in my emphatic cry.

"No, no, no!" and I thumped the counter between the speaker and me. "I am *not* going away again. I demand to see someone in authority!"

With a shrug of resignation, the clerk led me down a corridor and into an office where a man was standing beside a large desk, his back turned.

He turned around with a deliberate swish of his robes that, I had found, often accompanied 'attitude'. He was middle-aged, thin, his face carrying the markings of his ethnic group. I could tell from the expression on his face that this was not going to be easy.

He nodded to me curtly as I introduced myself and told me that I would be dealt with shortly, when he had finalised matters with his other client. With a beckoning hand he invited forward a man whom I had not noticed in a chair behind the door. The two men sat down at the desk while I took the corner seat and watched proceedings.

As I observed the official's dealings with his Nigerian client, who intended taking goods similar to mine out of the country, I was pleasantly surprised to note that it seemed a straightforward procedure and that the tax was not exorbitant. Even allowing for a higher rate for expatriates, it would be reasonable. As the gentleman packed up his possessions and received his clearance permit, I counted eleven items. He had paid an average of N8 per item.

While I waited, Patrick had enlisted help in unloading the car and after he deposited the items around me, I asked him to attend to a chore in the city in order to save time later. He headed off and I sat waiting, Peter's blue passport and my standard issue one in my hand, because I had been told they would be necessary.

When it was my turn, the gentleman noted our passports, then asked me to provide an estimate of the cost of every item. I didn't have this information so, thinking I was being helpful, I suggested that because the goods were similar to those of the previous client, perhaps the value of much of my consignment could be calculated using that as a starting point.

My suggestion was met with a steely glance. That was not possible. I must tell him exactly what I had paid, then twenty percent would be charged. I gasped in disbelief.

"What? Twenty percent?" I couldn't believe my ears.

"The twenty percent was a mere slip of de tongue, Madame. I meant ten percent and please do not quote to me what de previous gentleman paid. Dat is nothin' to do wit' you. Just tell me what yo' paid for de items so I can calculate ten percent. And I might add," he said in an intimidating tone, "we are de experts in such matters, so we know de value of things."

"Excellent," I replied. "Please go ahead and value them for me. It should be no trouble for you to do that, because you have just completed a similar task for your last client."

Whenever I'd been able to shake off Patrick, my inexperience had cost me, so I had no desire to pay ten percent of my inflated purchase prices. Nor was I going to be forced into lies by understating the amount I had paid.

Earlier, when he had first introduced himself, the official's surname had sounded to me like 'Salmonella'. I had been self-conscious about addressing him because of the unpleasant connotations but as the minutes passed, I began to enjoy calling him by name.

Mr Salmonella fixed me with a malevolent stare. "As I said, Madame, de previous gentleman has nothin' to do with yo'. Yo' are required to tell me what yo' paid for de items. Dat is how we do business."

I bristled. "His carvings were identical to mine. Why are you trying to change the estimated value of mine?"

"Madame, are yo' being racist? Are yo' daring to tell me dat man should have paid more, just because he is black?"

The absurdity of the argument floored me. Had I not been so riled, I would have laughed. An embarrassing stalemate followed, but I am not a lion-hearted tactician and soon I was grudgingly volunteering estimates of what I had paid, my hip pocket hating me for being accurate. Where I honestly couldn't remember, I argued bitterly with him when he tried to charge me ridiculous amounts. Each time I resorted to my old argument.

"How come the other gentleman's carving like this was valued at N200, yet mine is worth N500? They are identical! I clearly heard you say to him, 'The tax on a carving like this is N10'! How come his total bill for eleven items came to N90 yet you are demanding I pay N1175 for thirty-six items? And don't mention racism to me again - they are your words, not mine." I couldn't remember being so angry.

"De man before you only had eleven items, yo' have thirty-six. Thirty-six is more dan eleven. It is therefore necessary for yo' to pay more."

Again the absurdity of the argument almost overwhelmed me. I, who had never suffered from blood pressure in my life, felt as if I could suffer a stroke at any moment.

Through clenched teeth I asked again for an explanation of how a government agency could use two completely different methods of valuing items for consecutive customers. Different *rates* I could understand, but actual *value*? This he parried with a sudden onset of deafness. I handed over the money and he wrote out a clearance permit. When he finished, he looked at me calmly and with both hands covering the permit on his desk, he spoke.

"I hope, Madame, dat yo' are appreciative of de service I have performed for yo' today?" The inference that *dash*, a tip, was required was the final straw.

"I have little reason to be appreciative," I replied tartly and I extended my hand for the permit. To my surprise he handed it over and I stalked from the room, angry and humiliated. I was sure that little of the money I had paid would ever reach government coffers.

As we drove along the dirt track on the way home, we came upon a ruckus. A man had stolen a vehicle loaded with goods from the local market. The traders had caught up with him, dragged him from the car and now had him pressed against the bonnet of the vehicle, machetes at his throat. I didn't like his chances; being in the hands of an agitated mob was not an enviable position. The last we saw of him, he was bundled into a van and driven away.

With the image of Mr Salmonella before me, I allowed myself a little fantasy. How *good* it must feel to hold a machete at the vital organs of someone who had just robbed you.

Chapter 22
TRYING TO TAP-DANCE

I raged to Peter and Patrick about my meeting with Mr Salmonella. Peter was having problems of his own, trying to finish a project against a backdrop of fuel shortages, poor communication systems and resistance from some Nigerian colleagues who had a vested interest in prolonging the programme and its funding for as long as possible. He welcomed the story of my altercation with Mr Salmonella as light relief, but from Patrick at least, I heard a few sympathetic clicks of his tongue. But his regret was so ongoing that the truth finally dawned. What our driver was upset about was not my inconvenience, but that he had missed the show. I struggled momentarily as the funny side of the saga tried to surface but I grimly knocked all amusement on the head.

I risked apoplexy all over again by recounting my tale to Maureen, but she was conditioned to such minor hiccups and merely laughed. It was not until Nancy called that I received a response that was more like my own; she even seemed to give tacit approval to my suggestion that a judiciously wielded machete would offer a wonderful release of tension.

The following week, Maureen asked me to accompany her to the children's home and as we drove through the Ibadan traffic, she told me that she and Tom had decided to shift back to the United Kingdom. It was soon to become IITA policy that the salaries of campus doctors be paid in naira. This would make it impossible to educate their sons to tertiary level in Europe. After considering several options, they had decided to settle near their boys in the United Kingdom.

After giving the children their meal, we spent time talking in English to those who understood and just playing with those who didn't. One by one we let the children know that we would be leaving in two month's time. Gbade's reaction was to fix me with a reproachful gaze as he shrugged an expressive shoulder. In recent weeks he had become a laughing, chatty little boy and I felt a special bond with him. Now I told him how much I would miss him and how I would take every opportunity between then and now to come to the home. I was rewarded with another shrug. See if I care, it said, but by now I knew Gbade and his expressive shrugs well. Saying goodbye wasn't going to be easy for either of us.

The day arrived when the carriers were due to collect our possessions for shipping. During aerobics, I peeped out regularly at our house in case they arrived early. Of course they didn't arrive at all. Late in the afternoon, Maureen phoned and I told her of my disappointment that they hadn't come. The same question was to receive the same answer for a long time.

Weeks went by and still they didn't appear, nor could I get through to Lagos by phone to find out why. By now, it was time for Akintewe's removalists to come but they didn't arrive either. Each day we'd part after aerobics, hopeful that today would be the day; the next time we'd meet, we'd commiserate over ongoing disappointment.

Then, late one afternoon, there was a knock at the kitchen door and I opened it to see two cheerful faces grinning at me.

"Afternoon, Madame. We have comm to get yo' goods for shipping to Australia." I almost dragged them inside in my relief. But first I wanted to check the details. I suggested we complete the paperwork for the insurance before they began work. My request was waved aside breezily; Madame could go to de hoffice next time she was in Lagos and sign papers. I sat down heavily onto the nearest chair.

"You mean you didn't bring the insurance papers? I'm not letting this stuff out of my sight unless it's insured."

The images of all the burnt out wrecks that littered the roadside between Ibadan and Lagos swam before my eyes.

"But Madame. We were told to pack and bring yo' things tonight because on Fridee, dey are being shipped to..." and here he consulted a crumpled note from his pocket, "...Perth, Australia."

"No, no, no!" I made a quick decision and waved the men toward the door. "You will have to go back to Lagos empty-handed. I am not letting this stuff out of my sight until this is sorted out. Not only have you forgotten the insurance papers, but Perth is as close to my home as Cairo is to here."

I ushered them, protesting, out the door and asked them to have someone in authority phone me as soon as the lines were working.

I could still hear their truck lumbering away up the street when the phone rang. Maureen had heard that a van was our place and had rung to offer congratulations.

"Congratulations?" I couldn't decide between tears, laughter, or suicide. "Getting anything done in this country is like tap-dancing in treacle!" I could hear Maureen laughing at the other end of the line and suddenly I joined in. The release of tension allowed a bright idea to pop into my head.

"I'll ring the World Bank in Washington. *I* can't get Lagos on the phone, but they can, by satellite."

As soon as Maureen and I had finished our conversation, I rang Ben, our World Bank trouble-shooter and he promised to contact Panalpina in Lagos.

I had just returned from aerobics next morning when the phone rang and over a static-laden line, I spoke to a staff member from the Lagos office of Panalpina. She introduced herself by the un-Nigerian sounding name of Mrs Peters, yet by her accent I knew she was not an expatriate. She informed me that she would be handling matters to do with our shipment from here on. As she spoke, I knew that at last we might get somewhere but the phone line deteriorated and we shouted at each other that I must get to Lagos as soon as possible to sort out the matter. It certainly sounded the easiest option.

The following week when I met Mrs Peters, I found her to be efficiency incarnate. We soon had everything organised. Together we decided against using sea-freight. With Perth being the closest that ships from Lagos come to Brisbane, I was easily convinced. The goods were to be flown home. My sanity was more valuable than dollars in the bank, I decided, but I spared a moment to wonder at Peter's reaction when he heard the cost.

The next big decision was to declare that Patrick and I would take the goods to Lagos. I was tired of waiting indefinitely for trucks that never arrived. Mrs Peters, realistic about such matters, approved wholeheartedly. In response to her question I replied dryly that yes, I did have a certificate from the National Museum allowing me to take my goods out of the country.

Leaving Mrs Peter's office, I called into the World Bank and was relating the story of last week's encounter with Mr Salmonella when Gordon 'Uzor interrupted me mid-stream.

"You certainly need a certificate stating that the items can be taken home, but you didn't have to pay the tax. You have semi-diplomatic immunity."

I turned a level gaze on the usually reliable Sunday who, with much shuffling of feet, admitted that he had thought it necessary. Gordon sent him to locate a particular document and to photocopy it. As Sunday handed me the copy, he spoke apologetically.

"Yo' will have to go buck to de Museum, Madame, an' apply for refund."

I didn't reply. I didn't need to because Gordon's wry comment said it all, "Don't hold your breath while waiting to receive it..."

It wasn't that I minded paying a tax to remove items from the country - I had gone along quite prepared for that. What irked me was that had I known of the government directive, I may have been spared Mr Salmonella's blatant attempts to extract the largest possible amount from me. Later, though, when I cooled down, I could admit that Africa's experience of exploitation didn't begin with Mr Salmonella and me. Unfortunately Africans had been receiving tuition from visiting masters for centuries.

I knew at the time of admiring the camel saddle that I should spare myself the headache that this purchase would bring, but I couldn't help myself. I had to have it. It had brass trim, hairy bits of goat's hide, and sprouting handles fore and aft. They all caught the imagination of this expectant grandmother and I envisaged a wonderful rocking horse with its Nigerian saddle atop, providing hours of enjoyment for a generation of grandchildren. All I had to do now was to get it added to the list of thirty-six items for which I already had permission to take out of the country.

As prepared as possible for such an ordeal, I loaded the saddle into the car and set out for Round Two with Mr Salmonella. When I went to lift the saddle from the car, I was too late. Patrick had no intention of missing the fun this time and the saddle was firmly in his grasp. But I had other ideas. Before I entered a surprised Mr Salmonella's office, I turned to Patrick and told him firmly to wait for me in the car. I didn't quite know how this interview was going to go and I didn't want the extra distraction of worrying about Patrick's volatility while I was handling it. Looking disappointed, he departed.

"Ah, Madame," Mr Salmonella's voice was smooth and condescending. "Yo' must have been very happy with de service I rendered yo' de other day, to come buck so soon." There were several staff members in the room and my combatant was going to show them how it was done.

I smiled sweetly. "I will be even more pleased when I receive a refund from you for the money you had no right to collect in the first place, Sir."

Mr Salmonella looked stunned by my impudence. I went on, "I also want to take this saddle from the country. Please add it to this list of things on the permit, and of course there will be no charge, seeing that what you charged me the other day was completely wrong." As I spoke, I placed on his desk a copy of the *Diplomatic Immunities and Privileges Act* of 1962. Attached was a letter to all departments, dated four months ago, dealing specifically with cases such as ours.

The man picked it up and as he read, he swallowed several

times.

"I assure yo', Madame, dat I did not know of dis instruction."

"You should have known about it, Sir. It is your job to know. I now want a refund of the money that you took wrongfully."

I knew I had no chance of seeing the money again, but this was a modified version of the machete at the throat and I was enjoying it. The man continued swallowing as if something large was caught in his throat.

"Dat is not possible. It is gone." Gradually he regained his composure. "And Madame, I cannot add de saddle to de list. That would not be correct. Also, because I am not familiar with dis sort of saddle, I am not prepared to say dat it can leave de country. Yo' must take it to Lagos."

I knew that if I was going to win this skirmish, I needed to get this slippery character back onto the ropes.

"I intend going to Lagos and I shall report that I was charged a large amount where no fee was required. Now, if you are refusing to give me a permit for this saddle, I require a letter from you saying that you do not feel competent to handle the matter. I will need that to show your superiors in Lagos."

Oh how sweet is revenge. He looked so disconcerted that I felt quite heady with power. He turned and dismissed the others who had been standing around, wide-eyed. One clerk, however, knew that skulduggery was afoot and, good public servant that he was, he tried to remonstrate with his boss.

"Sah, it is irregular to tamper with existing permits. Madame will 'ave to bring de goods buck in so we can reassess dem and make a new list, including de saddle."

He and his ethics were sent packing by a frazzled Mr Salmonella who picked up my copy of the permit and studied it.

"How can I change thirty-six items into thirty-seven without making it look very obvious, Madame?" He was putty in my hands.

"Turn it into a thirty-eight, then," I advised, "and state that the consignment also contains a large, carved wooden bowl. I shall purchase it between now and the time the goods leave."

The deed of forgery was done. As I left, I unnerved him once more by restating my intention to apply for a refund, even though I suspected that I wouldn't bother. With a curt nod of my head, I left the office, never to return, an arrangement that I'm sure suited both of us.

That evening as I was relating the story to Peter, I produced the certificate with a flourish as proof of my final victory over the obnoxious Mr Salmonella. Suddenly Peter began to laugh. I snatched it back and studied it carefully. There, for all to see, was the declaration that Mrs Cranny was leaving Nigeria with a large, carved wooden bowel.

Regardless of the discomfort that such an organ should have caused me, I felt more relaxed than I had in weeks. I was going about my housework, humming a tune, when I stepped into the lounge room to find two young boys sitting on our couch, poring over our globe. I watched as the elder of the two conducted a geography lesson. He spoke in Yoruba, but I could follow the path of his finger as it crossed the world: Brisbane, Hong Kong, London, Lagos. Reuben's son, Emmanuel, had returned with his young brother to show him not only that the world is round, but that Sah and Madame had flown here in an aeroplane from one side of the ball to the other. After my initial surprise at the informality of the visit, we had an enjoyable morning that ended with us sharing biscuits, minerals and a tub of ice-cream. The boys were like sponges, soaking up not just the refreshment offered, but any information I could share. Again, I experienced the satisfaction that must be the reward of teachers when they are dealing with willing students. As my young friends left, we made a deal: they would visit me again soon but next time, they'd knock and wait outside until I came to the door.

Peter left for a final trip to the north, his flight coinciding with the day we were to take our goods to Panalpina. By late afternoon, it was all over. The goods were safely in Panalpina's hands, insured, packed and ready to go. Common sense told me that I should stay at the Sheraton overnight, but I couldn't bear the thought of another night in Lagos. I decided that we'd brave the night-time robbers.

The traffic was incredible. It took us an hour to get to the outskirts of Lagos, by which time it was dark. When Patrick put on the headlights, they were hardly visible. We had never driven at night so were unaware of the problem. I began to regret my decision but it was too late to turn back - the thought of entering that traffic again was too much for me. I told Patrick to press on.

He could only see a few metres in front of him, yet he seemed determined to drive at a suicidal rate. He was nervous about robbers, he said.

"But why are you driving on the wrong side of the road?"

It was terrifying, hurtling along in the dark, on the incorrect side of the divided road.

"If we drive over dere, de robbers will be expectin' us. When cars comm along, dey roll out a wheel and cause a crash, den dey rob. If I drive on de wrong side dey won't be expecting us."

I listened to this crazy logic and shuddered. I didn't fancy either choice. I decided that he could choose our whereabouts on the road, but I insisted that he slow down. We arrived home at ten o'clock, far too late for safety. As I unlocked the house, the phone was ringing. It was Peter, worried when earlier attempts to find me at home or at the Sheraton had failed. Before the line went dead, we had time to reassure each other that all was well. I fell into bed and slept soundly.

Chapter 23
THE BEGINNING OF THE END

One day an English acquaintance, Clinton Hill and his wife Edida contacted us and invited us to their home on the outskirts of Ibadan. Time was running out for us but we were keen to accept the invitation because we'd had a nodding acquaintance with them for some months without ever getting to know them. They looked an interesting couple. Clinton had come to Nigeria many years ago, we'd heard, and had married here and had five children.

On the arranged day, he came to IITA to collect us and as we drove through the streets of Ibadan, he provided a running commentary on places of interest. He chuckled as we passed a police station.

"That was my address for a while..." he said cryptically, leaving the sentence unexplained.

When we arrived we saw a comfortable home which they had built themselves on a large block of land. Also on the property was an engineering workshop and a dam that held sufficient water to supply the small factory.

We were welcomed by Edida and introduced to the family. The household buzzed with life. Children played, ran, giggled and tumbled on a nearby veranda in a happy, well-behaved way that let the adults get on with conversation and pre-dinner drinks. Eventually Clinton explained what he had meant about the police station being his home for a while.

He had come to Nigeria with the qualifications to begin an innovative business and from the very start it had thrived. Edida was involved in the administrative side and the couple worked hard, remaining dedicated not only to turning out a good product, but taking pride in the fact that they were training several young men in a trade.

Pilfering had never been a major problem but suddenly valuable equipment began disappearing. They had always enjoyed the loyalty of their staff of a dozen people because they had always tried to be fair.

A few months earlier, Clinton had agreed to employ a man who had served a jail sentence for theft, in the hope that a good job would give him a fresh start. Now, Clinton heard a whisper that the new employee intended bringing two companions on a particular night for a raid on the workshop.

Clinton arranged with the local police to be there, but no villains turned up. This happened on two more occasions, until Clinton knew he'd feel foolish about asking again. When he was tipped off once more that a raid was about to happen, he decided against telling the police this time. Instead he took his rifle and went to a position between the shed and the dam, where he hoped to have a good view of what was going on.

It turned out to be the darkest night of the year and after a few hours, when Clinton heard whispers, he could see nothing. He gave the intruders time to collect items, then called on them to surrender. With shouts of panic, the thieves took to their heels. Clinton heard the sound of running feet but still couldn't see a thing. He shouted again for them to stop, saying he had a gun, and to prove it he fired several times into the dam. Edida, eight months pregnant at the time, had left to drive into town to get the police and soon two suspects, neither of them employees, were arrested in the vicinity.

The men admitted that over the past months they had come to the property several times with the new employee and each time had stolen items of value. They also said that before each raid they drank heavily to get up courage. They had no idea where their accomplice was now, but believed that he had escaped in another direction.

When work resumed at the Hill factory, the employee didn't reappear and this was taken as further proof of his involvement in the robbery attempt.

A few days later, Clinton stood watching a routine procedure as a large amount of water was pumped from the dam. The water subsided and as he watched, he saw first an extended arm then, in spine-chilling slow motion, the whole body of the missing man was revealed.

The other workers were terrified and pleaded with Clinton to allow them to take the body to a lonely spot and dump it, but he wouldn't agree. The man's family was grieving because their son was missing and they had to be told of his fate. But before going to the police, Clinton inspected the body minutely and found no evidence of a gunshot wound.

After an investigation, the police accepted that the man had slipped into the water either by accident or to hide and because of the alcohol, had passed out and drowned. One policeman, however, convinced the others that there could be money in attempting to bribe Clinton and they offered to take the matter no further if he paid them. They underestimated their man. Clinton refused to pay, was charged with murder and put in a city jail to await trial.

Edida worked tirelessly to get her husband released and in the meantime struggled to keep the business running, visiting each day for advice on business matters. With so many employees depending on the Hills for their livelihoods, there was considerable pressure on authorities not to let the business collapse. Eventually Clinton was allowed out of prison for several hours each day to supervise the manufacturing process, but he had to return behind bars each evening.

Legal processes take their time and with no proper facilities to preserve the body, each new investigation into the cause of death became more unpleasant and less productive.

Finally the charges were dropped and life for the Hills resumed some semblance of normality but the pressure placed upon Edida by the scenario must have been terrible. She had four children to care for as she battled on through the last stages of pregnancy and giving birth, the whole time doing what she could to have her husband released and to keep the business functioning. As the evening with the Hills unfolded and the couple shared stories, I found myself wishing we had got to know them earlier. In spite of their conservative appearance, they were interesting people.

Each day I was busy with preparations to pull out. A cleaning frenzy had me in its grip even though I knew that by the time Jeanette and BT returned the *harmattan* would have had its way, sneaking into the locked house and coating everything with a layer of dust. That didn't stop me - curtains came down to be washed, cupboards were cleaned out and windows were polished. I worked all day and when Reuben arrived at four o'clock in the afternoons, we'd attack two-person tasks such as replacing the furniture into the Kang configuration.

When the purge had swept the length of the house, I continued beyond the back door into the garage and laundry. In a corner I came upon five empty plastic bottles that had once held toilet cleanser, now just collecting dust and taking up space. Out they went.

"Oh no, Madame, did yo' throw out de bottles from de laundry?" It was Reuben, sounding stricken. I owned up to the deed.

"But I was saving dem until I had seven. I was going to take dem home as a surprise for my children to take to school as water bottles."

I had been here sixteen months but still the magnitude of the difference between the haves and the have-nots hit me over the head. Containers once used for a poisonous product to have a second life as drink bottles for children? I shuddered as I made a note on my shopping list.

Patrick took control of the purchase because, he assured me, he knew all about drink bottles; his children recommended a certain type. In the marketplace, he searched until he found the right ones, fossicked until he had a variety of colours, then tested each carefully before negotiating a price.

One evening while Peter was still away on his northern trip, I decided to cook some patty cakes. I could hear thunder rumbling around the night sky and soon the rain was tumbling down. As I popped a second batch of small cakes into the oven, I fancied I heard voices over the drumming of the downpour and I opened the kitchen door to find our garage floor dotted with sheltering security guards. We exchanged greetings and I returned to my baking. As I lifted the next batch from the oven, I noticed that the rain had eased and I heard the men moving out of the garage. It suddenly occurred to me that they might like a few hot cakes so I leaned across the sink to peer through the kitchen window to see if the men were still within earshot. I found myself nose-to-nose through the glass with one of four faces lined up there. The smell of baking cakes had stopped them in their tracks as they cut through our garden to the lake. There was no mistaking the hint in the row of raised eyebrows outside my window. Never was a small farewell gift received with more enthusiasm.

Each visit to the children's home was part of a countdown. One day when we arrived, Gbade was crying. Before I could ask the reason I heard Bose scold him in an exasperated but not unkind voice: "Stop crying, Gbade. It is still two weeks until Madame goes. What are you going to be like on her last day?"

I had a bad moment. Had my friendship with him caused him more pain than it was worth? I found it impossible to tell. The dilemma of how to help in any long-term, meaningful way, confronted and confused me as much as it ever had. It was not only the children who were subdued this morning.

Driving home, I looked around. I wanted to imprint everything on my mind for future memories, but today I couldn't interpret what I saw. I recalled my shock sixteen months ago and compared it with today's reaction. Not all that long ago I had been ashamed of the squalor as I showed Margaret around the city. Had much of the litter been cleared away since then? It seemed a simple enough question, but I couldn't answer it. Certainly there was still garbage lining the streets, but was it as bad as what had once shocked me so deeply? An old adage popped into my head, something about familiarity being as kind to ugliness as it is unkind to beauty. Was that behind my inability to judge?

Politically, a lot had happened in Nigeria during our time here, but the more it changed, the more it seemed to stay the same. Chief Abiola had won the 'free and fair' general election of June 1993 but he had fled the country leaving his supporters feeling abandoned. The following months had seen Babingida, Shonekan and Abacha as leaders. Now Chief Abiola had returned, declared himself President, and ended up in prison charged with treason. Throughout all these twists and turns we had watched Nigerians suffer and become poorer and although today I found it difficult to judge, reason alone told me that conditions were deteriorating.

The days rolled by, busy with visits to and from friends. Patrick was having a birthday this month so we invited Mercy and the children to IITA to celebrate but also to say goodbye. In our family, the guest of honour had always nominated their birthday meal and when I extended the offer to Patrick he asked for the same menu as I took to the children each week. Perhaps he was playing it safe; I wouldn't have known where to begin had he asked for traditional fare. At least I felt confident as I prepared dishes of meat, rice and scrambled eggs. To mark the occasion, I also made a chocolate cake and with Peter's inexpert assistance, we decorated it with candles and Patrick's name.

When the family arrived near lunchtime, we moved down to the picnic tables near our lake. I had borrowed some sporting equipment and soon Mercy and the girls were helpless with laughter as they watched Patrick and the Crannys trying to jump rope. Together we kicked soccer balls, skipped rope and threw frisbees. Later, as Patrick cut the cake to an untalented rendition of *Happy Birthday*, IITA residents probably dismissed the noise as agitation amongst the geese.

As they prepared to leave, Patrick signalled to his family and one by one they approached us, curtsied and murmured their goodbyes. I was acutely aware that I would never see them again, a strangely new experience, because I couldn't remember a parting that had this degree of finality. Farewells at home were always softened by the possibility of paths re-crossing, but this was different.

It wouldn't have been fitting that I leave Nigeria without a final joust with Mr Titoloye. With only days to go, there he was at the door again, this time with an apprentice in tow. My little sparring partner greeted me, exuding charm and cheek in equal proportions. After a mutual exchange of pleasantries, he moved to the next phase. His shoulders fell into a dramatic slump.

"Madame. I think somehow I 'ave offended yo'," he said, hanging his head and pinching his little face into prune-like contours. Obviously his young companion had been told to observe carefully how to retrieve lost customers.

"If yo' think I have sheeted yo' in some way, please name a price and I will pay yo'. Anything to have yo' custom agin."

But he didn't hold the pose quite long enough. One shrewd little eye flicked in my direction to check the effect. Satisfied, he straightened with a flourish and folded back the edges of his *agbada*, looking at me expectantly.

I was feeling magnanimous and after all, it was a time of reconciliation not ongoing battle, so I assured Mr Titoloye that no ill feelings existed. Besides, we were leaving IITA very soon. His eyebrows shot up at the news.

"Leavin'? Well, Madame, in dat case I must talk urgently to yo'. Do yo' remember how I lost de photo of us and yo' gave me de negative? Well, now I want to give it back to yo' so yo' can have a copy printed for me."

I couldn't help smiling, but I told him that the only way he'd get another photo was to pay for it. Mr Titoloye reflected for a moment. Obviously, he had to pull something out of the fire and fast. He was under the scrutiny of his young helper.

"I will be very sorry to see yo' go, Madame. Perhaps yo' would like to give me a farewell gift?"

It was my turn to think for a moment. I wanted to choose my words carefully. "Mr Titoloye," I said, as a number of responses ran through my head. In the end I chose wisely. "Goodbye, Mr Titoloye, and good luck," I said, closing the screen door between us.

A few weeks earlier, we'd heard an Englishman addressing the congregation after Mass, appealing for donations to support a project started by a Nigerian nun, Sister Stella. We listened with interest to what he had to say about her work. The nun had gained permission from her religious community to carry her ministry out into the streets of Ibadan where, quite literally, she collected sick, abandoned children in her car and took them back to her house for food and shelter. She had dreams of a large complex where such children could live, being treated with dignity and taught life skills. Her hope was to make places like the Remand Home obsolete.

About a week later an old car snorted its way into our driveway and a lady in nun's habit climbed from the car. It was Sister Stella herself and as we sat over a cup of coffee, I listened to her calm, realistic plans for her future work to be carried out under the name *Pro Labore Dei* - God's Work. As we spoke, she noticed some photos on the table between us, ones taken at the Remand Home the previous week. She went through them one by one, pausing when she came to a picture of Sunday, a delightful little boy who had been at the home for about six months. I told her about him. Bright and healthy, he'd known how to play when he had first arrived. He had not seemed particularly distressed at first and had organised Bosiyo and others into chasey and other small-boy games. But slowly the light was going out and he was forgetting how to be a child. Sister Stella was silent as she studied the photo of Sunday laughing as he leaned back against me, playing with a stocking-doll that Lisa's class had sent. She looked up.

"There will be legal problems, I am sure, but I will do everything in my power to get dat child out of dere. Yo' have my word dat I will try my hardest."

Even if one child were shifted from that place into the care of

Sister and her community, it would be a wonderful thing. I didn't know it as Sister and I spoke that day, but in the next few years Jim and Nancy were to become involved with her project. The small farm at the entrance to the Remand Home, where the boys had hoed aimlessly under the eyes of guards, was to become linked with Sister's *Pro Labore Dei* under a single farm manager, a former member of Jim's staff. The boys were taught farming techniques and whatever they produced went towards supplementing their diet. As the years passed, I heard nothing of Sunday's fate; presumably the legal obstacles were too great for Sister to gain guardianship of the little boy, or perhaps his family reclaimed him. There was reason to rejoice, though, when a joint effort by Sister Stella and the Gulleys ended in Taju being officially transferred to the nun's care.

One morning as I was packing, there was a knock at the door and there stood Doctor Sodeinde. He had come to deliver a farewell gift of a book, and to hand me a letter from Doctor Nottidge. I was touched by Doctor Sodeinde's gesture in coming and was sorry that Peter wasn't here to meet this quiet, impressive man and to hear him talk about his hopes for the hospital-based programme aimed at educating mothers about nutrition. I felt that if any team could get such a programme going, it would be one involving Doctor Sodeinde and Doctor Nottidge.

Nancy and Jim were leaving on their annual vacation before our departure date and although we had seen them at our farewell dinners, they arrived at our house late one afternoon for a final goodbye before they flew out the following day. From the start, Nancy had taken me under her wing and we'd shared good times and bad for sixteen months. She and Jim had been wonderful friends and although we knew we'd keep in touch, this parting made me sad.

The Akintewes and the Crannys weren't the only ones leaving IITA forever. Five members of the Women's Group were to be farewelled at a luncheon held at International House. As President, Juliana made a speech, singling out the departees one by one, offering kind words and good wishes for their future. When she came to 'Pum' I saw the affectionate grin I had been fortunate enough to see often during my stay, and she spoke in words as warm as her friendship.

It was important to catch the occasion on film and as we assembled in various combinations, I called to Clarice to join me because I wanted her in my farewell photo. Suddenly a camera flash lit up the room while we were still organising ourselves.

"Was dat a photo?" Clarice looked around and frowned as she spoke. "Take another one because I was not at de front. I am de senior woman. I should be at de front." Suitably assembled, with pecking order duly acknowledged another photograph was taken.

There were final visits from Reuben's family and from Beatrice, Ayo and children; photos with my friend on the supermarket steps, an articulate, friendly man who sat collecting alms, his twisted legs folded beneath him; there were phone calls to and from acquaintances around the campus. Bit by bit, the threads were being drawn up as we put the finishing touches to the tapestry of Nigerian memories.

It was the final week - time to visit the children for the last time. I cooked a smaller meal than usual because I also had made a cake and bought some minerals for my own farewell party. It was a good morning, all things considered. Staff joined in, including those from the remand section. Before I began my round of farewells, the warden stepped forward to make a speech. I may not know it, he told me, but months ago I had been given a Nigerian name that everyone called me behind my back. I too was Bose. I don't know the significance of the name, the gesture, or his purpose in telling me now - I just hoped it was not related to 'bossy'. Our differences forgotten, the warden and Matron Bose presented me with a plaque that they'd had made, all the more valuable for the work that had gone into it. The words, which were cut from timber with a fret saw and painted yellow and red, were fixed to a black background. I was asked to handle it carefully because the paint was not quite dry. Neither were my eyes as I read the words:

Thank you for
Everything
God
bless you
Mrs
Pam Cranny

Patrick and I went to each of the children to say goodbye. Some didn't know what I was saying or doing, others knew and accepted it with nonchalance because they had seen many IITA Mesdames come and go. Little Bose, Kimi, Sunday and Bosiyo gave me hugs then watched solemnly as Gbade asked if he could 'follow', come too. Knowing the answer he put his head on the table and cried. Unable to speak, I walked to the car, got in, and Patrick drove off quietly. It was a subdued departure; I turned in my seat so that I could see the children to the last.

My heart ached over the little tableau behind me. I watched until we were out of sight, knowing that these threads too had been drawn up, tied and cut.

Chapter 24
OUT OF AFRICA

Peter wished to invite to dinner as many as possible of his team but I knew I couldn't manage a large dinner party plus our departure all in a matter of days. The solution was to have International House cater for our fifteen guests at the Cappa Bar on Tuesday evening, thirty-six hours before we departed.

The matter of a meal for the drivers had to be considered, too. Peter's preference was to have an informal gathering with everyone included but he and Mr O'Keyni didn't agree on such matters and in deference to his counterpart's sensibilities, other arrangements had to be made. I talked the matter over with Patrick and we hit upon a solution. Staff from International House would deliver four servings to 20 Tropical Crescent where I'd have set our dining table ready for the drivers. Also, because Nigeria was playing Italy in the World Cup that evening, we gave Patrick a lesson earlier in the day on how to operate our television set so they could watch the game while the rest of us were over at Cappa Bar.

Even without the need to cook, it was a busy day for me. Agnes Uryio was having a final afternoon tea for those who were departing and it was late afternoon before I headed back to our house. I was not concerned about the time because our guests were not due for another hour. I had everything planned; we were to have pre-dinner drinks at our house, walk across the grass to the dinner venue, then return for coffee and chocolates after the meal. As I opened my back door on my return from Agnes' house the phone was ringing.

It was the security guards at the gate, announcing that a convoy of cars had arrived and the occupants were claiming to be Crannys' guests for the evening. I confirmed that we were expecting them and, knowing I had about three minutes, I scurried off for a shower, leaving Peter on duty lest I was late reappearing. Emerging at last, I found the lounge room full of guests. It was cruel of them, I teased, to undermine at this late stage, the *one* thing I had come to rely upon in this complex country - that Nigerians are often late but never, ever early.

When everyone was chatting and laughing with an ease that gladdens the heart of every hostess, I slipped outside to speak to the drivers. I couldn't believe my eyes. There were only four cars parked in our driveway but eight drivers greeted me with cheerful smiles. One or two of them, I had never seen before and in the midst Patrick stood beaming, extremely proud of his recruitment efforts. An urgent phone call to International House soon had extra food on its way.

Before we departed for the Cappa Bar, I stepped outside again and with Patrick, ran through his duties as host to the other drivers while I was away. He exuded confidence and told me he planned serving dinner as soon as we left so that they could give the soccer match their full attention when the telecast commenced.

When the Cappa Bar was ready for us, we strolled across in a relaxed, chatty group to where the dinner tables had been set on the covered veranda. Too late, I wondered if perhaps we should have had a main table at which Mr O'Keyni and the regional co-ordinators would have been suitably honoured. Australian style, we saw this function as an informal get-together to mark the end of Peter's involvement and had invited people to take a seat wherever they wished. We circulated between the tables, hoping our guests would make allowances for cultural differences.

In spite of my fears, it was a successful evening. The lively personalities of Simon and the delightful Andrew added to everyone's fun and we reminisced about incidents where misinterpretations of Australian and Nigerian English had led to amusing misunderstandings. Many of us were soon sympathising with Andrew's ailment of 'needing new ribs' because of laughing.

In planning the dinner I had fretted over whether to order Western or Nigerian cuisine. On the chef's advice, I'd chosen Nigerian and now I watched in satisfaction as the pounded yam and accompanying meat dishes were demolished with enthusiasm. But amid the relaxed chatter, Mr O'Keyni wagged a finger under my nose in reproof. The yam, he advised me as he sampled another portion, had been pounded by *machine,* not in the traditional manner, and the flavour betrayed the shortcut. I resolved in that instant that whenever yam was on the menu at any future dinner party in Australia, I would pound it with my very own hands.

The meal finished, we strolled back to the house, a noisy, informal group. I was surprised to see that the drivers were outside, standing quietly beside the vehicles. As Peter showed our dinner guests inside once more, I lingered behind and addressed Patrick.

"Did you decide not to watch the World Cup? Why are you all outside?"

"We were watchin' it, Marm, but we kept an eye on yo' across at dat place," he said, pointing across the grass to the clearly visible area which we'd just left. "When we saw yo' comin' back, we came outside. Mr O'Keyni would dismiss us if 'e saw us in yo' 'ouse."

I turned away, realising that this was not my argument. This society, like my own, had its own rules and would go on having them long after I left. I took wilful satisfaction, though, in taking a tray of coffee and chocolates out to the drivers before serving my lounge room guests.

As we had our coffee, Peter presented each person with a farewell gift, a book on some aspect of life in Australia. Glen had chosen and forwarded them to us, a hugely expensive exercise, but necessary because we had not remembered to bring suitable items with us. To the end, I was storing away experience in case we ever worked overseas again.

When the evening ended, we accompanied our guests to the

cars but before they drove off, Patrick appeared at my side. "Marm, did yo' notice dat we washed up our dishes?" Even in the dim light I could see the beatific expression on his face. I hadn't noticed, but I couldn't ruin the pleasure Patrick was taking in the men's gesture. I took the hint and thanked each driver, making sure Mr O'Keyni didn't overhear me.

It was late and tomorrow was spoken for twice over, but before he left, Mr O'Keyni announced that we were to be guests at a farewell luncheon at FORMECU the following day. I had to do some fast rearranging of schedules, but I was ready when Patrick called back for me at eleven o'clock the next day.

At the luncheon, conducted with more formality than our party the previous evening, we were offered an attractive spread of cold cuts and salads. Speeches filled the air and gifts were presented with much thanking of everyone and emphasis of high hopes for the future. We lined up for the inevitable photos and eventually, it was time to leave. A serious-faced Beatrice pressed a letter into my hand, asked me to read it when I got home, then she quietly departed. I later read her words which ended poignantly: "I did not speak today when they invited us because I would be shamed to cry," she wrote. The note went on, "If ever I have spare money for a stamp, I am going to write to you."

Samson and Dele, whom we hadn't seen since they were transferred from Ibadan; Alfred and John whom we'd come to know well; telephonists and clerks whose exact duties continued to baffle us; there were people everywhere. I felt like the Duchess of Kent on Wimbledon finals day, walking between lines of people, stopping to chat, moving on, stopping to chat. In the car at last, we left FORMECU amidst a sea of waving arms.

Back at IITA, Reuben was going about his household chores one last time, while I turned my attention to the final details. Items from the pantry were divided into three and offered to the men. The ultimate prize, though, was my large straw sun-hat.

"Cecelia and I will fight over dis," Reuben said, and working on the principle of possession being nine-tenths of the law, he perched it on top of his head and there it stayed.

All that week I had been setting aside things that were too heavy and therefore too expensive to carry home. Half-empty bottles of shampoo, conditioner, facecream, handcream - all lotions and potions had to go. I lined them up for Reuben's inspection and with the awe that males have of such refinements, he now held each bottle up and asked about how to use its contents. Whatever the explanation, he'd happily put it into a plastic bag, saying he would take it home to Cecelia. Finally he held up one last bottle with the usual question. I couldn't help myself.

"That, Reuben, is sun-screen lotion. If you wear that long enough, you might become the same colour as me."

His eyes crinkled in amusement as he fought back a smile. Reaching over, he carefully dropped the bottle into the rubbish bin, the only item to be rejected in two weeks. *Touche*, Reuben.

His work finished, he now stood at the kitchen door. We would be gone by the time he finished his IITA job tomorrow, so this was goodbye. He flicked an imaginary speck of dust off a nearby bench, then turned to face us. "I jest carn believe it. Tomorrow yo' will be gonn."

I didn't trust myself to speak, just stood there nodding as Peter put our thoughts into words. We shook his hand and murmured goodbye as he gathered his parcels and stepped out through the doorway. The pale straw of his new hat was the last thing to fade into the darkness.

I woke early on that last day with mixed feelings consuming me. Our sixteen months in Nigeria were over and it had been one of the most stimulating periods of my life. Peter woke too and we talked quietly as we waited for daylight to arrive. The fireflies twinkled in a final display at our window, the Muslims chanted and the bats bipped their high-pitched call. In the distance we heard an occasional honk from our friend the feisty gander. These were the sounds that had welcomed us to IITA, now they were farewelling us.

With our suitcases in the car and house keys surrendered, we were about to pull the kitchen door shut for the last time, when the phone rang. It was Reuben. He had asked permission to come to the house to see us off but it was a busy time and he wasn't allowed to leave his post. Now, with promises to keep one another in our prayers, we said one last goodbye and hung up.

Outside, David was standing near the car and the old man's eyes were moist. There weren't many words left to say - we'd said it all in the last couple of days. Peter and I shook his hand again, got into the car and moved off.

Patrick drove us around the campus one last time. Today the trees, flowers, lakes and lawns seemed particularly beautiful. Had I been going anywhere but to family and home, my heart would have been heavy indeed. We drove past Agnes' house and there she was in the front yard so we had a final word before moving on. At the security gates we were farewelled warmly by those guards who knew us, then, for the last time, Patrick swung the car south towards Lagos.

It was a quiet trip. Perhaps the others were deep in their own thoughts too. I tried to take in the sights one last time but pictures of faces kept coming to mind, pushing aside the passing parade. I had met such memorable people, been subjected to so many new experiences and had needed to confront my own attitudes so often, that I knew I'd never be the same again. And the process would go on; the tapestry wasn't finished yet. Memories, reflections; they still had work to do and I acknowledged that I had a way to go yet before the effect of this visit to Africa had finished with me.

In Lagos, all business finalised, we asked Patrick to take us to the airport. The three of us, laden with luggage, made our way inside and to the counter where we were to check in. Bookings confirmed and free of luggage, we returned to the exit with Patrick, knowing that he must get on the road before dark.

Peter and I looked back at the driver who stood there, his head on one side and a slight smile on his face. Again, there was little left to say. We exchanged words of farewell and thanks, then as I shook his hand again, I remembered something I wished to ask of him.

"Patrick, I want to hear you say our names."

But Patrick hadn't seen *Out of Africa* and the scene between Karen Blixen and Farah was not to be repeated. He smiled and fluttered his fingers in the way he always did when explaining something to us.

"Ahh, I've always called yo' Peter and Pum behind yo' backs, Marm."

With a laugh and a final handshake, we left him and walked towards the departure lounge. I stopped in the doorway and turned to wave one last time to the man who had been at my shoulder for most of my African adventures. I knew he probably couldn't hear me over the noise, but I said it anyway.

"Goodbye Patrick," I called. "Thanks for yesterday!" and I turned towards home.

Towards Australia.